P9-ELV-852

— BRING IT ON —

—BRING IT ON—

Tough Questions. Candid Answers.

Pat Robertson

W PUBLISHING GROUP™

www.wpublishinggroup.com

A Division of Thomas Nelson, Inc.
www.ThomasNelson.com

BRING IT ON
by Pat Robertson

Copyright © 2003 by Pat Robertson.
Published by W Publishing Group, a Division of Thomas Nelson, Inc.,
P. O. Box 141000, Nashville, Tennessee 37214.

All rights reserved. No portion of this book may be reproduced, stored in a retrieval
system, or transmitted in any form or by any means—electronic, mechanical,
photocopy, recording, or other—except for brief quotations in printed reviews,
without the prior written permission of the publisher.

Unless otherwise indicated, Scripture quotations used in this book are from the *New
American Standard Bible* (NASB) copyright © 1960, 1962, 1963, 1971, 1973, 1975, and
1979 by The Lockman Foundation, and are used by permission.

Scriptures marked NIV are from the *Holy Bible, New International Version,* copyright ©
1973, 1978, 1984, International Bible Society. Used by permission of
Zondervan Bible Publishers.

Scriptures marked NKJV are from the *New King James Version.* Copyright 1979, 1980,
1982 by Thomas Nelson, Inc. Used by permission. All rights reserved.

Scriptures marked KJV are from *The King James Version* of the Bible.

ISBN 0-8499-1712-3 (hardcover)
ISBN 0-8499-1801-4 (special edition)

Printed in the United States of America
03 04 05 06 07 BVG 9 8 7 6 5 4 3 2 1

— CONTENTS—

CONTENTS

— INTRODUCTION —

S HORTLY AFTER AMERICA WAS ATTACKED on September 11, 2001, a survey was taken, asking if the horrific attacks might be part of God's judgment for our sins. The overwhelming response—nearly 95 percent of those queried—was a resounding, "No! We haven't done anything wrong."

A quick glance at the moral fabric of our society will reveal the truth: Americans, even many born-again Christians, no longer believe in moral absolutes. It seems that moral relativism and situational ethics have won the hearts of the American people. We have slaughtered more than 40 million babies through abortion since 1973; millions of people are having sex outside of wedlock; several million couples are now cohabiting but are not married; approximately one out of every two marriages ends in divorce; more than 18 million children live with a single parent as a result of divorce or a pregnancy outside of marriage. Sociologists estimate that in the inner city, approximately 80 percent of births are to unwed mothers. An estimated 60,000,000 Americans have a sexually transmitted disease, some life threatening. Clearly, we are on the verge of a cataclysmic societal upheaval.

In affluent America, a casual walk through the average shopping mall will bring you face to face with floor-to-ceiling images of nearly naked men and women. Surely that couldn't be wrong, could it? Advertisements, movies, magazines, books, television programs and commercials that a few years ago would have been considered flagrantly risqué, if not obscene, now bludgeon the senses into tacit approval and acceptance of new social mores. One has to wonder if our consciences have been so seared we can no longer tell the difference between right and wrong.

Internet pornography floods cyberspace, threatening to erode what little moral fiber our country has left. One of the dirty little secrets of our nation's largest Internet providers is that their search engines are fueled largely by cash from pornography. More than 73,000 pornography-for-pay sites currently exist, with that number increasing almost daily. At least 6 percent of American males confess to being addicted to pornography. An untold number of "closet" users are addicted to computer porn. Our researchers at the Christian Broadcasting Network (CBN) have discovered that among pastors and priests, more than 50 percent report having problems overcoming pornography. In what is quite possibly a related statistic, more protestant pastors' wives than ever are leaving their marriages, as well as their mates' ministries.

Homosexuality is not only accepted by much of our society, it is rapidly becoming a legally protected and advocated lifestyle. The portrayal of homosexuality as a "normal" sexual choice is pervasive in the media and entertainment industries, not simply by Ellen DiGeneres and Rosie O'Donnell, but by the scriptwriters, producers, movie and television network executives. Meanwhile, the Catholic Church continues to reel from revelations of homosexuality and child molestation by priests. The Catholic Church has already paid more than $1 billion in damage claims to people who have brought law suits against priests and the church.

Leading the way down the path to destruction during the last decade of the twentieth century was the president of the United States, whose aberrant sexual escapades dominated national news for several years. Not surprisingly, counselors and therapists report a dramatic increase in sexual addictions in America, riddled with child molestation, oral sex among teenage high school students, sadomasochism, and unspeakable perversions of every sort. Headlines revealing new sexual scandals have become almost blasé.

In the midst of such a culture, many people honestly wonder, "Is the Bible relevant to our lives?" People have sincere questions for which they have not found answers outside the church or within. Unfortunately, in recent years, the church has not always provided clear-cut, biblically based answers. Rather than being a light in the darkness, the church has become a flickering candle struggling for survival against the winds of change.

Instead of being a counterculture within the culture, the church has so compromised and watered down its message, it is almost impossible to distinguish a true Christian anymore. It is a well established fact that the lifestyles of many Christians are almost identical to those who make no religious claims at all. Modern-day Christians passionately seek material gain, desperately watch out for number one, talk the same, look the same, imbibe in the same beverages, watch the same R-rated movies, have markedly similar value systems—including their tastes, attitudes, aptitudes, and proclivities—as their non-Christian friends.

Sadly, Christian families have experienced abortion, divorce, drug problems, homosexuality, premarital pregnancy, sexual affairs, financial stress, and other problems in the same percentages as their non-Christian counterparts. Many of these family members are crying out for answers to their earnest questions. They want to know, "What does the Bible say about my situation?"

The concept for *Bring It On* grew out of a popular segment on *The 700 Club* television program, in which I take a no-holds-barred approach to answering some of life's toughest questions as submitted by our viewers in an e-mail format. At first, we were surprised at the frankness of some of the issues I was asked to address. No doubt the anonymity of the Internet makes it easier for some people to express their candid questions and feelings more openly. Some of the questions may shock you, but let me assure you that these are real questions submitted by viewers from across the country.

Many of the questions we receive are a bit edgy, and some are almost bizarre. We get a plethora of questions on marriage, divorce, money, and everyday life issues, but we also are asked about cyber-sex, fantasy role playing, and other matters about which I never imagined people were grappling.

All of these questions are submitted against the backdrop of "Is God going to judge us for our sin?" Many people live in constant fear and anxiety, especially following the events of September 11, 2001—events that changed our world forever. Never before had the mainland of the United States of America been attacked so flagrantly without provocation. Never before had so many Americans been mercilessly killed in such a short period of time. Never before had so many people witnessed such a horrible atrocity on live television.

Our seemingly monumental problems suddenly paled in comparison to the images that filled our television screens during the day and haunted our minds throughout the night. Everywhere I turned, people were asking tough questions such as these:

"Where was God and why would He allow this to happen?"

"Is this the beginning of the end of the world as we have known it?"

"Will we ever feel safe again?"

With September 11, 2001, now indelibly impressed in our collective subconscious, this book took on a slightly different tone. While my publisher and I sought to maintain our original goal of providing practical answers to tough personal questions, we also felt compelled to face head-on the issues raised by the heinous terrorist attacks on America.

Of course, in addition to questions ripped from today's headlines about terrorism, Islam, and war, you will also find a collection of contemporary life's toughest questions about life, love, sex, marriage, divorce, miracles, pain and suffering, God's judgment, the end times, spiritual gifts, demonic oppression, generational curses and blessings, and much more. Some of these questions concern delicate matters, but we have included them not in an attempt to titillate or to be voyeuristic, but because they reflect a sincere search for genuine, practical answers, and a desire to apply the Bible to our daily lives. We can't hide our heads in the sand any longer. People want to know, "What does the Bible have to say about my problems?"

Unquestionably, life in the 21st century will be different than anything we've known previously. We are faced with unprecedented moral issues, such as genetic research and cloning. The threat of war and possible annihilation of society loom largely. In the midst of national and international tensions, many are grappling with divorce, bankruptcy, and their own end-of-the-world scenarios—at least, the end of their world as they once knew it.

Does the Bible offer direction for times such as these? I believe it does.

In compiling this book, we haven't changed our approach to handling the questions you are asking. Just as I do on our "Bring It On" segment on *The 700 Club,* I have attempted to answer these questions simply and to the point. Obviously, in this format, my answers cannot be exhaustive, so I encourage you to dig more deeply into God's Word. In John 16:13–14 Jesus promised that the Holy Spirit "will guide you into all the truth . . . He shall glorify Me; for He shall take of Mine, and shall disclose it to you." To help get you started, I offer some Scripture references for most of the questions we deal with, and I trust you will search out further what God has to say about the matters we touch on in these pages.

I must warn you: *This book is not for the timid.* Within these pages, you will find tough questions, and you will also find straight answers. Most of all, you will find hope to step boldly into the future God has for you!

CONTENTS

— CHAPTER 1 —

LOVE, MARRIAGE, AND SEX

---

*O*NE OF THE MOST oft-quoted myths about marriage must be, "They lived happily ever after." Does anybody really believe that? Even in the best of marriages, questions arise, problems occur, and conflicts happen. The real question is, "What do we do when these skirmishes threaten to escalate into all-out wars that can drive permanent wedges between marriage partners?" The answers, of course, are in God's Word.

As you will discover in this section, the questions of many modern couples tend to be quite intimate. In a society inundated by sensual imagery, where even some Christians wonder whether monogamy is a realistic long-term relationship, many of our questions in this section deal with legitimate and illegitimate sexual expressions.

Whether you are a senior citizen or a youthful newlywed, it is important to regard marriage and the sexual relationship as sacred, something that God designed to be the most intimate human relationship a man and a woman will ever know on earth, a relationship in which the couple is committed exclusively to each other for life. All sexual expressions between a man and a woman outside of a marriage relationship are sinful and wrong.

Certainly, that concept has come under vicious attack from many in our midst. But God's Word has not changed. His standards are still intact. He has written the best Book of all on marriage, and how it is to be lived out. That's not to say married love is easy to maintain. Whether you want to rekindle romance in your marriage, build a loving relationship that lasts a lifetime, conquer incompatibility, overcome past infidelity and keep your family from falling apart, or any combination of the above, it will take a great deal of effort and prayer. A good marriage doesn't just happen. It takes love, patience, time, commitment, and, yes, even *work!*

But it is possible to have a great marriage, one that will stand the test of time and reward you with exquisite joy.

BRINGING HOME THE BACON

My husband has always said that he is the head of the household because he brings home the larger paycheck. I recently accepted a job that pays more money than my husband makes. Can I now take the role as "head of the household"?

YOUR HUSBAND gave you the wrong reason he is the head of the family. His leadership role is not based on income. He's head of the household because God gave him that responsibility. In a Christian home, Christ is the head of the husband, and the husband is the head of the wife. Together, the parents have authority over the children.

The fact that you now bring home more money than he does is not a determining factor. Of course, in any marriage, if one of the partners says, "I'm making more money than you are, so I'm better than you, and you'd better do what I say," that is a relationship headed toward trouble!

Married couples are partners; they should be working together toward common goals decided upon mutually. Certainly, in our society today, with many wives employed outside the home, maintaining a balanced, mutually satisfying marriage relationship takes incredible cooperation and patience with each other. Historically, men were the protectors and the providers, and women were the nurturers in the family. Men went out and fought the battles, killed the wild animals, and brought back something to eat. The women stayed at home, taught and cared for the children, kept the house, and cooked the meals. Eventually, instead of actually killing something and dragging it home, the man started bringing home a paycheck, by which he provided for and protected the family. Meanwhile, the wife remained at home caring for their children and attending to housekeeping matters. It was not a matter of one spouse being more intelligent or talented than the other. It was simply a matter of complementary roles.

Today, many women are immersed in the workplace; some because they are extraordinarily capable, have marketable skills, and want to have a career outside the home, while others work because they feel they must to help make ends meet. Regardless, the husband is still the head of a Christian home, and he is to "love his wife as Christ loved the church and gave Himself up for her."[1] His role should not be one of a domineering spirit, but that of a servant leader, willing to lay down his life for his wife and for his family.

The Bible indicates that the concept of *family* is not simply a convenient institution created by mankind, but rather has its source in God, the heavenly Father. God is the head of Christ, and Christ is the head of the church, interceding for His "family" with the Father. On earth, the husband stands in a similar role with the family, as the head of his household and serving as a priest to the family. His primary job is to intercede with the Lord on behalf of the family and to receive directions from God for his family.

An example of this can be seen in the life of Joseph, the husband of Mary, the mother of Jesus. Joseph was not the literal father of Jesus Christ, yet God sent His angelic messenger to him as the head of the household, warning him of impending danger following the birth of Jesus, instructing them to move to Egypt for a season.[2] God later sent another message indicating it was safe to return to their homeland.[3] Interestingly, the directives were issued to Joseph, rather than to Mary. Clearly, God regarded Joseph as the "priest of the family;" he was the primary conduit through whom God sent His Word to the family. Mary was not to usurp the role of her husband, even though she had given birth to the Savior.

When a husband is truly operating as the Spirit-led priest of the family, the wife is obligated to follow his leadership. Keep in mind, though, that a husband and wife are to submit to one another.[4]

My wife, Dede, has a strong relationship with the Lord and has been walking with Him for many years. I value and appreciate her spiritual sensitivities and insights. When we have a serious decision to make, she and I sit down together to discuss it. Then we take time to pray about the matter, together and individually, asking God to speak to us. When we get back together, I'll ask, "What did the Lord tell you?" and she'll ask the same question of me. Often the Lord will give one or both of us specific scriptures relating to our prayer, and we apply those biblical insights to our decision.

As much as possible, my wife and I make our major decisions together. But

---

[1] See Ephesians 5:25–29
[2] See Matthew 2:13
[3] See Matthew 2:19–21
[4] See Ephesians 5:21

occasionally, something will come up that we can't agree on, or possibly a matter demands an immediate decision. In those cases, I will make those decisions and take the responsibility before God for them.

Because men are usually more analytical by nature, and women tend to be more sensitive and intuitive, it has often been said that the man is the head of the household and the woman is the heart. When the head and the heart are working together, the relationship can be wonderfully harmonious.

IS IT ME, OR IS IT THE VIAGRA?

My husband just began taking the drug Viagra, and now he can't seem to keep his hands off me. We've been married for thirty years and never really had that great a sex life. I can't help but think that it's not me he's attracted to, but simply the Viagra luring him into the bedroom. What are your thoughts?

VIAGRA DOES NOT CAUSE SEXUAL DESIRE; it merely enables a man to perform sexually, especially a man who has previously experienced problems with impotency or other forms of sexual dysfunction.

It is extremely difficult for a woman to understand the loss of self-esteem that accompanies erectile dysfunction. To many men, their ability to function sexually is at the core of their masculinity. When they cannot perform normally, they become embarrassed, irritated, and their self-esteem dwindles to next to nothing. All too often, a man with such a problem will begin looking for excuses to avoid sexual contact with his wife. It's not that he has ceased loving her; he knows that if he initiates certain activities or expresses affection in certain ways, his wife will anticipate sexual union, and he simply does not want to find himself in a potentially humiliating situation. His attitude is, "Why start something I cannot finish?"

This situation can be brought on by normal loss of testosterone due to aging. Sometimes excessive stress can cause erectile dysfunction, as can some medical or emotional problem. Whatever the reason, the resultant lack of sexual intimacy in a marriage can be extremely frustrating for both partners.

The good news, however, is that thanks to modern medical science, doctors can now help most men overcome this problem. Start by honestly communicating with your spouse. Then, together, without embarrassment, take the proper steps to deal with the situation.

It may well be that your husband has deeply loved you all these years and has agonized over his inability to express his love for you through sexual intimacy. The nagging self-doubt may have shown up in other areas of your relationship as well. But now that medicine is available to help your husband perform sexually, he is much more confident in lavishing his love and affection on you. He is now enjoying the relationship with you that he always hoped for but until now has not been able to consummate. Nevertheless, it is not the Viagra drawing him into the bedroom; it is his desire for you!

Obviously, your husband still enjoys you, and hopefully, you still enjoy and want to be with him physically. Rather than fretting, why not enjoy what you may have been missing over the past thirty years?

NOT ON THE SAME WAVELENGTH SPIRITUALLY

What should a Christian husband do when he and his wife are not on the same "wavelength" spiritually?

OUR RESEARCH at CBN reveals that Christian couples who pray together regu-larly rarely get divorced. By "praying together," I do not mean merely mouthing a few rote prayers before mealtime or bedtime, although those prayers are important. But couples who stay together over the years are those who take time to bring everything about their lives before the Lord in prayer—praying for each other, praying for their children, their children's future mates, their employment; for spiritual, physical, emotional, and financial needs; for the church and discovering God's heart for missions and evangelism. Couples who come before God regularly in that type of prayer eventually get on the same "wavelength."

Early in Dede's and my marriage, I was seeking more of the Lord, believing that God wanted to fill me with New Testament power. I was racing forward in my faith, attempting to drag my wife along with me. Yet we were living with little money in an extremely poor, downtrodden section of town, and Dede was concerned about how we were going to survive.

I believed that if we'd seek Him first, God would take care of us. I continued pressing in with the Lord, asking Him to fill me with His Holy Spirit. When God met me in answer to my prayer, it was as if I had punched through a spiritual sound barrier. Dede realized what God was doing in my life and, despite her misgivings, entered herself into the glorious fullness of God's blessings.

CONFESSING PAST SINS TO A POTENTIAL MATE

I want to go into my marriage (my first and hopefully last) with total honesty, but how much of my past failures and sins should I tell my fiancée?

LITTLE OR NOTHING! If you do, you'll be hearing about your past relationships for years on end. What is in the past is the past. If it's under the blood of Jesus, don't resurrect it.

If you doubt whether your past sins have been adequately dealt with, confess them to the Lord one more time, asking His cleansing and forgiveness. But if you are certain that your sins have been confessed and forgiven, it is a mistake to revisit that part of your life. Simply acknowledge, "Yes, I have sinned in the past, but I don't want to live that way anymore. I want to live with my mate in a manner that is pleasing to God. What is in the past is past." Don't keep digging up garbage; it is not useful and it is not necessary.

Now, if you sin sexually after you are married or commit some other sin that directly impacts your marriage, that failure certainly should be confessed to your partner; but what happened before you were married is over and done with.

If you lived a racy, dissolute life, you needn't provide details. Simply inform your spouse in general terms, such as, "Honey, when I was younger, I wasn't a saint. I lived a pretty bad life, and I want you to know that. But I am a different person now, because of what the Lord has done for me. I love you and am committed exclusively to you. I want God's guidance in our lives and our marriage to be grounded on His Word."

In my opinion, if the past is truly behind you, that's all the premarital confession that is necessary.

CHEATING IN MARRIAGE

I've been cheating on my wife for more than three years. Recently I repented of my sin. Should I tell my wife about my affairs?

IF YOU'VE BEEN CHEATING in your marriage, certainly you have sinned against God, but you have also sinned against your spouse. It's not good enough to say, "God has forgiven me, so that's all that is necessary." You need to seek forgiveness from the offended party.

If you are the person who was sinned against, you must handle the matter with grace and extend forgiveness to your repentant spouse. Remember, the Lord has forgiven you of your sins; you have no right to withhold forgiveness from your mate. God is on the side of redemption; He will help you to save your marriage.

Be kind but firm. Say something such as, "God forgives you, and I forgive you. But we are not going to continue to live this way; I'm not going to allow you to use me as a doormat, flagrantly violating our marriage vows. Not to mention the many sexually transmitted diseases running rampant nowadays—if you continue messing around, you are going to bring something home to me, and I do not want that to happen. Yes, I forgive you, but we are going to make some changes around here."

As the husband, even though you have fallen, if you have now repented of your sin, you are still the head of the household. Your wife is not meant to be your keeper. Neither is she your personal substitute for the Holy Spirit. You must stand up and be the man of God in your family. You must establish the new patterns in your own life and in your marriage that will enhance your relationship with the Lord and with each other.

But on this one, keep in mind that according to prevailing law, a dog is entitled to only one bite. If you continue to philander, you are not a fit spouse and your mate has every reason to leave you.

GOD'S WILL OR GROUNDS FOR DIVORCE?

I found out that my husband has been cheating on me the entire eight years of our marriage. He says he needs his freedom and wants to separate. Is this grounds for divorce? I'm struggling with how I should pray. Should I pray that God will work a miracle, save my husband, and restore my marriage, or should I let go and see this as God's will, regardless of the outcome?

IF I WERE YOU, I'd grant such a spouse his "freedom," and pray that God will bring him to his senses. If your husband continues on the course he has chosen, he will destroy himself in this life and in eternity.

Meanwhile, he has violated your marriage vows to the extent that I believe you have biblical grounds for a divorce. In filing for divorce, you should insist on receiving enough money to maintain your home, child support, and possibly alimony. Let your husband know that you love him and do not wish to harm him, but his conduct will cost him in dollars and cents now and possibly his soul in eternity. The high price of divorce may jolt him enough that he might reconsider his ways.

Is it God's will that your marriage break up? Certainly not! "'I hate divorce,' says the LORD, the God of Israel.'"[5]

In the New Testament Jesus said, "What therefore God has joined together, let no man separate."[6] He goes on to say, "Whoever divorces his wife, except for immorality, and marries another commits adultery."[7] The Greek word translated here as "immorality" is actually the word *pornea,* the root from which the word *pornography* derives. Its usual meaning is "fornication," premarital sex, although most Bible translators have rendered the word as "immorality" in this passage because of the context.

If the word were translated as "fornication," the relationship implied could be that of betrothal, or engagement, making the statement of Jesus even more stringent. If one is unfaithful before marriage, it is tantamount to adultery, and the engagement should be broken; the marriage should not even take place. Marriage is for keeps.

One does not have to be a Greek scholar to interpret the intent of these passages. God hates divorce, and marital infidelity in which the marriage vows are irreparably broken is serious enough to prevent or dissolve a marriage. Historically, the church has allowed divorce for the cause of infidelity, but Scripture makes no allowance for two sincere Christian believers to divorce because of "irreconcilable differences" or some other trumped-up excuse. An unbelieving partner or a person who chooses to disregard God's Word may tritely trample underfoot his or her marriage vows, but true believers do no such thing.

The apostle Paul goes one step further, declaring, "Yet if the unbelieving one leaves, let him leave; the brother or sister is not under bondage in such cases, but God has called us to peace."[8] This principle is often referred to as the "Pauline privilege."

Paul was not attempting to lower the bar on divorce; he was simply acknowledging that believers are not bound irrevocably to men and women who choose to leave their marriage. In 2 Corinthians 6:14, Paul further provides an important but often ignored consideration for Christians seeking lifelong partners by declaring,

---

5   Malachi 2:16
6   Matthew 19:6
7   Matthew 19:9
8   1 Corinthians 7:15

"Do not be bound together with unbelievers, for what partnership have righteousness and lawlessness . . .?"

In my years of counseling and ministry, I have expanded Paul's principle to include what I call "constructive desertion." When a spouse makes a marriage intolerable due to abuse or some other physical, emotional, or mental condition, it is impossible for the mate or children to remain in that home without being damaged. I do not believe the believing spouse is bound in such a situation.

How long should a believer remain in an untenable situation, praying that God will restore the marriage? Nobody but the Holy Spirit can set those time limits for you. Scripture encourages us to persist in prayer and not to give up too easily.

On the other hand, many believing spouses tend to be "too nice," to hang on too long, allowing a wayward spouse to make a mockery of their marriage and of God. I'm familiar with one situation in which the husband was running around on his wife, engaging in homosexual affairs. He contracted AIDS and brought the disease home to his wife, imposing a virtual death sentence on her. No woman should be subjected to that sort of conduct even for a day! Being served divorce papers may be the "wake-up call" that causes a prodigal partner to come to his or her senses, to repent, and to return to where he/she belong.

God is always on the side of forgiveness and restoration.

MY "EX" IS DOING BETTER AFTER DIVORCE

I divorced my husband a few years ago because of his numerous sexual affairs. Now he has several girlfriends, a better-paying job, and plenty of money. I continue to struggle greatly. I attend church regularly and try to be happy. Why is my ex-husband being rewarded for his heathen lifestyle, and I have to struggle while walking with the Lord?

THE PSALMIST asked a similar question: "Why do the wicked prosper?" He poured out his heart in Psalm 73, saying, "Surely God is good to Israel, to those who are pure in heart! But as for me, my feet came close to stumbling; my steps had almost slipped. For I was envious of the arrogant, as I saw the prosperity of the wicked."[9] The psalmist honestly admitted, "When I pondered to understand

---

9   Psalm 73:1–3

this, it was troublesome in my sight until I came into the sanctuary of God; then I perceived their end."[10]

If your husband pursues the lifestyle he has chosen and refuses to come to the Lord in true contrition and repentance, he will spend eternity in utter damnation in hell. He will be tormented with indescribably horrible conditions. Although he seems to be prospering right now, his pleasures will be cut off forever the moment he passes from this life.

On the other hand, even though you may be struggling now, God will reward your faithfulness to Him. Your heavenly Father has promised to provide everything you need in this lifetime—food, clothing, and a roof over your head—as well as eternity with Him in heaven. Don't fret if you miss having an abundance of material things in this life. You possess an imperishable treasure far more precious than gold.

The wicked will come to their end soon; in the meantime, pray for your former husband that he might meet Jesus as his Savior.

MENTAL AFFAIRS

> I travel a lot for business. Alone in my hotel room after a long, hard day, I'm often tempted to watch erotic movies. Usually I refuse to give in to this temptation, but sometimes I am weak. Should I confess this failure to my wife?

MOST MEN BATTLE TEMPTATIONS, not because they are warped sexually, but simply because they are males! Being married does not mean that you will cease to be tempted sexually. Quite the contrary!

While I encourage openness and honesty between married couples, I don't see the value of telling your wife that you viewed or were tempted to view a dirty movie. That should be confessed to God and allowed to remain with Him. Certainly, if your conduct is habitual or leading to worse conduct, you may want to enlist your wife's help in prayer. But if it is simply a matter of being drawn to pornography, you needn't lay that burden on your mate.

Now that you recognize your weakness, however, you should take some preventative steps to avoid temptations while on the road. Years ago, when televisions were first installed in hotel rooms, Billy Graham recognized their potential for temptation and distraction, so he requested that the hotel staff remove the television from

---

[10] Psalm 73:16–17

his room! Hotels may be reluctant to do that, nowadays, but you can safeguard your mind by either refusing to turn on the television or simply by unplugging it.

Better yet, develop positive patterns during your time away from home. Get in the habit of calling home every night to talk with your spouse and children. Use your down time to study the Scripture; read a good, spiritually uplifting book; listen to sermon tapes, Christian music, or the Bible on tape. When you are tired and lonely, don't turn on the television set in your hotel room because, as if by some unseen power, the clicker in your hand will take you slowly but surely from the news, to the documentaries, to the dramas, to the suggestive, to the pornographic. Reach for the Gideon Bible beside your bed, read it, then go to sleep.

SHOULD I TELL MY HUSBAND ABOUT MY ABORTION?

Before I married my husband of three years, I didn't feel it was necessary to tell him about my past. I had an abortion in my early twenties, and I just recently told my husband. He said that had he known this before we married, he might not have gone ahead with the wedding. Now he's considering a separation. How can I regain his trust and save our marriage?

THIS TYPIFIES ONE OF THE MOST difficult problems sincere Christian couples confront. Couples want to be totally honest with each other, and that is noble. But what you did before you came to Jesus is between you and the Lord. What is past is under the blood of Jesus, and it should not be brought up again. Yes, honesty and openness are vital in a good marriage, and I would not encourage the keeping of secrets from your spouse. But to recount your past sins is simply not wise and is usually not beneficial.

Obviously, you must inform your spouse about some things from your past, especially if those matters can impact your future. For instance, if you are HIV-positive, you must inform your future marriage partner before the marriage. That is only fair. Similarly, if you have financial obligations to another family, due to a previous marriage, that information should be shared with your future spouse. Those kinds of things have relevance to your future life together. But to provide your partner with a litany of your past sins, whether abortion, or anything else, is not necessary if those things have been forgiven. If you have repented, it is gone, buried in God's sea of forgetfulness.

Since you have already informed your partner, and he has responded negatively, the goal now is for the two of you to be reconciled. Secure the help of a wise Christian counselor who can talk with both you and your husband. Remind your husband that he, too, is a sinner who has been forgiven by Christ, and ask him to extend to you the same type of compassion that Christ has freely given to him. Jesus said, "He that is without sin among you, let him first cast a stone at her."[11] No doubt, your husband is appalled by the fact that you committed a sin that is abhorrent to him—and that is understandable—but all sin is abhorrent to God. Your husband needs to understand that if he is unwilling to forgive your sins, God will not forgive his.[12]

Remind him that he is the person that God chose for you, and you are the person God chose for him. Together you have taken marriage vows, and you fully intend to keep them. Let your husband know that you love him, and you are totally committed to the relationship. You may even ask him, "Have I broken our trust in any way since we've been married? Have I done anything since we've been married to cause you to doubt my word or my commitment to you? I'm a new person in Christ. My old life is gone forever, and I never want to return to it. I wasn't forced to tell you about my past. I did so in an attempt to be totally honest with you, and I promise to be straightforward with you for the rest of our lives."

From a biblical perspective, merely being shocked at learning of a spouse's act of sin before marriage is not sufficient grounds for divorce after a marriage has been consummated.

CONTRACEPTION IN MARRIAGE

Is there any form of birth control that is biblically acceptable? Or is taking the pill like having an abortion?

I SEE NOTHING WRONG with intelligent family planning, and that includes using contraceptives to help limit the number of children a couple feels they are prepared to adequately care for, nurture, and raise in the admonition of the Lord. Use of the pill prevents a pregnancy; it does not end a life that has been conceived.

Abortion, however, is *not* a legitimate means of birth control. Abortion is murder, and our society needs to protect unborn babies. Products such as RU-486 (commonly referred to as the day-after pill) are means of chemical abortion.

While use of contraceptives may be acceptable for married couples, it is unwise

---

[11] John 8:7 (KJV)
[12] Mark 11:25

to supply contraceptives to teenagers. Contraceptive use by unwed teenagers virtually legitimizes promiscuity. By giving high school kids condoms, we're saying, "Abstinence is okay, but just in case you can't resist temptation (or don't want to), use a condom." That is nonsense! Besides the high failure rate of condoms among sexually active teens, it's like putting a glass of water in front of a thirsty teenager and expecting him or her not to drink.

Within marriage, however, contraception is legitimate. It would be wise to discuss this matter with a doctor to determine which means of contraception is safest for you.

Some devout couples may wonder, "If children are a sign of God's blessing, is the use of birth control an attempt to override the will of God concerning whether or not we have children?"

In one sense this is certainly true. In biblical times, when the world's population was much smaller and most people lived in an agrarian society, large families were indeed considered a blessing. But in our contemporary world in which the population has exceeded six billion people, it does not seem that an all-wise God would want all of His people to procreate to the maximum. He expects us to use our common sense to determine how many children we can adequately love, care for, and educate in the things of the Lord, submitting all the while to His sovereign plan for our lives.

Granted, some people do not condone any method of birth control other than the "rhythm method," tracking a woman's days of fertility and restraining from sexual relations during the days she is most likely to be impregnated. While I respect those who hold this opinion, the evidence is overwhelming that in those countries where this form of birth control is the only method encouraged, the population is out of control. Children are regarded as throwaways, expendable nuisances; a newborn is merely another mouth to be fed. Consequently, many children are living literally in the streets, growing up in impoverished, abusive conditions with no hope for a better future. To continually reproduce irresponsibly and condemn more children to such an ignominious existence is not glorifying to God.

In Bogota, Colombia, I saw what I thought was a large pile of rags lying on the street. When I looked more closely, I saw to my horror that there were eight or ten little children huddled together in an attempt to keep warm. I later learned that when Pope John Paul II conducted a highly publicized visit to the country, the police gathered up many of these children, and sequestered them behind fences, so the pontiff would be spared the sight of them. In one area, it was reported that gasoline was poured on some children, and they were set on fire. Such atrocities are not unusual in places where children, because of their abundance, are no longer considered precious.

Yes, children are a blessing from the Lord, but God's Word also instructs us not to forsake wisdom, and wisdom for many modern couples will entail a measure of birth control.

COMPUTER PORNOGRAPHY

My Christian husband is infatuated with (addicted to?) computer pornography. He says it is harmless and educational, but I say it is ruining our sexual intimacy. Who is right and why?

THE MOST POWERFUL human instrument of sexual desire is the mind, not the genitals. To the man addicted to hard-core pornography, real physical sex with a real woman pales beside the mental eroticism found on the Internet. Your husband is comparing you, his wife, to the women he sees on the Internet. These women, like the men and women who appear in pornographic magazines or movies, are carefully chosen for their seductive bodies and glamorous faces. You are being pitted against synthetic beauty, plastic surgery, and trick photography. The women used in pornography commit unspeakable acts, not because they like to do so, but because they are pawns of some of the most evil human beings on the planet. The utter depravity being shown on the Internet is beyond belief, so don't be deceived. There is absolutely nothing educational about computer porn. That is nonsense. Your husband is kidding himself, and he needs to be set free from his addiction to pornography.

Several years ago, a survey in *Fortune* magazine estimated that approximately 6 percent of the executives in America are sex addicts. Ironically, the survey indicated that a high percentage of these addicts worked as investment bankers and watched pornography while on the job! This is a costly problem in many American corporations since so many workers are surfing the Net, obsessed with obscene materials, engaging in illicit chat-room "conversations," or passing along smutty jokes, instead of concentrating on doing their jobs. Besides the proliferation of filth and perversion, the price tag in dollars and cents for lost work hours is astronomical.

You must help your husband get some Christian counseling immediately. He needs to be delivered from the spirit of lust, which underlies his obsession with pornography, and you need to insist on it. His addiction is destroying the sexual intimacy of your marriage and will ultimately ruin your marriage completely. This is a serious situation. Our counselors report incidents of husbands who prefer pornography to their wives. The wives say, "It is either the porn or me," and the men choose the porn. They would rather have the fantasy world of cybersex than a real relationship. What a travesty of the sexual intimacy God intends married couples to enjoy!

Your husband is committing mental adultery. If he won't repent and seek professional help, you should realize that your marriage is over.

DIVORCE AS AN ESCAPE HATCH

I married my husband with the intent of divorce if it didn't work out. Now, I've accepted the Lord. I do not find my husband attractive and have a very hard time loving him. He loves Christ, tithes, and takes good care of the family, yet sometimes I can't stand to even look at him. What can I do?

You NEED TO ASK God to give you love in your heart for your husband. You married him; you went through the wedding ceremony and made some vows; you entered into a solemn relationship with him. You have established some commitments, and you should not break them! You have lived with your husband and have a family together. That cannot be ignored as though these relationships don't exist.

Besides that, you say he is a good provider, goes to church, and looks after you and the children. It may help to remind yourself of his good qualities and thank God that you have such a man.

Selfishness says, "My needs are not being met, so I'm leaving." Love says, "I will love and serve you unconditionally, no strings attached."

Often we see a transference in which one person transfers feelings of animosity or resentment to another person. She says, "I should never have gotten into this marriage. I made a mistake, so it's his fault." That's transference of blame. You have ill will in your heart, and you hate someone else for what you see in yourself. But it is not the other person who has the problem; it's you!

Perhaps the romance has disappeared in your relationship, and you need to rekindle it. Pray and ask the Lord how to do that. List your spouse's attributes, do some romantic things for him, and start acting in faith on the feelings you are asking God to give you. Soon you will be surprised at how your own attitude is changing.

Then continually shower your husband with words of affirmation and admiration. There's an old saying: "Give a dog a good name, and he'll try to live up to it."

If you start praising your husband, thinking of all his good points, letting your mind be absorbed with his best qualities, soon you will find he is no longer repulsive to you. He may, in fact, be the man of your dreams!

MY EMOTIONAL NEEDS ARE NOT BEING MET

My emotional needs are not being met in my marriage. Instead, I feel emotionally abused. I don't believe in divorce, but I'm ready to walk away. What else can I do?

THE "ME" GENERATION SAYS, "If it feels good, do it. If it doesn't feel good, forget it. Run to pleasure and avoid any pain." The concepts of commitment, sacrifice, giving without getting, marital fidelity, and parental responsibility are not preeminent in the minds of many modern marriage partners. Instead, the focus has been on pleasing ourselves.

This attitude is antithetical to everything Jesus taught and did. Jesus did not come into the world to be served, but to serve and to give His life as a ransom for many.[13] He lived to help meet the needs of others, to make others well. He gave of Himself freely, not just in the good times, but even when it hurt. Everything about His life reflected an attitude of unconditional love and service. Ironically, He who most deserved to be served became the servant of all.

Interestingly, one of the popular terms in current industry circles and the contemporary corporate business community is "servant leadership." The idea is that the best leaders are those who serve their constituency.

This attitude should be exemplified in marriage more than in any other arena of life. The goal in marriage should be to meet the needs of the other person rather than concentrating on our own. When a person says, "My needs are not being met, so I'm getting out of here," that person is operating in a spirit of blatant selfishness.

If you consistently are attempting to get something out of a relationship, if you are seeking to gratify your own needs, you will never be truly content. You will be like a bottomless bucket that can never be filled, no matter how much clean water is poured into it.

God is a giver; Jesus gave His life for us, and He promises that it is better to give than to receive. The only way we are going to find true joy is to refocus the attention on other people rather than ourselves.

---

[13]   See Mark 10:43–45

In a marriage relationship, the main question is not, "How can I get my needs met?" but, "How can I please my mate?" "How can I best serve my marriage partner?" "What can I do to help my mate?" If you are a parent, you should ask, "What can I do to help make my children better citizens? How can I best introduce them to Christ and teach them to live godly lives? How can I encourage them to be useful in society?"

The truth is, many people around you might be happy to have your "problems." I heard of a fellow who was fretting that his hair was thinning. His pastor took him along on a visit to a hospital where many patients were suffering from cancer and had lost their hair completely. The man never complained about his wide part again. Instead of complaining about what you don't have in your relationship, begin to thank and praise God for what you do have. Before long, you will be amazed at how your own attitude makes all the difference in the world!

The modern emphasis on self-fulfillment, "having my needs met," and "getting what I want out of life" is not a godly passion. Quite the contrary, the Bible says that in the last days, people will be lovers of themselves.[14] They will be absorbed with their own needs and desires rather than the kingdom of God. Moreover, the Scripture says absolutely nothing about leaving a marriage because your needs are not being met.

If your needs are not being fully met in marriage, and there honestly isn't enough in your marriage to satisfy you, look outside of it. No, I'm not encouraging you to engage in an extramarital affair! That would simply be another expression of selfishness. Instead, seek out ways to serve in your community or in your church. Become involved in a prayer group, where you can serve the kingdom of God by praying for others. The more absorbed you become with the kingdom of God, the less absorbed you will be with yourself. And as you get out of yourself and begin to serve others, you will find true love and joy.

LOVE, BUT NOT IN LOVE?

My wife just told me that she loves me, but she has never been "in love" with me. We have two children and she now wants to leave the marriage. Do I let her leave, or beg her to stay and try to make her fall in love with me?

---

[14] See 2 Timothy 3:1–5

I MAY BE DENSE, but I don't know the difference between loving your partner and being "in love" with him or her. We have built up false hopes and expectations based on fictional characters in movies, television programs, and steamy romance novels.

It sounds to me that your wife doesn't know what she's looking for and probably wouldn't know it if she found it! She loved you enough to exchange marriage vows with you, to share your bed, and to give her body to you in marital union, bringing two children into the world. Not only does she have obligations to you, but she also has obligations to your children.

True love deepens as two people grow to know and understand more of each other, appreciating each other's good points, overcoming or overlooking one another's weak points, encouraging each other, and building bonds of mutual respect.

Love is more than a feeling; it is a commitment of the will, a decision, a choice. Marriage is the uniting of two people physically, emotionally, intellectually, and spiritually. This type of love doesn't depend on transitory romance but involves shared struggles, hopes, dreams, and shared joys.

Reverend Thomas Trask tells a story about a woman who went to a marriage counselor, complaining, "I want a divorce; I hate my husband, and I want to get out of this marriage. What can I do?"

The counselor replied, "You hate your husband?"

"Yes, I want to hurt him badly."

"Mmmm, here's what I suggest you do," said the counselor. "Go home and tell your husband that you love him. Cook his meals, clean the house better than usual, and look after him like never before. Then after a month or so, just about the time he starts to really enjoy all that you are doing, tell him, 'I hate you, and I'm leaving.' That will really hurt him badly!"

The woman ecstatically embraced the counselor's idea. She went home and did exactly as the counselor had instructed. About a month later, the counselor called the woman. "When are you getting divorced?" the counselor asked.

"Oh, I don't want a divorce anymore," the woman replied. "I did just as you suggested, and I fell in love with my husband!"

Obviously, you can't make your wife love you. But if your marriage partner will begin to love you as a matter of choice, as an act of her will, the feelings will eventually follow.

HELP! I MARRIED A SLOB!

My husband was an attractive, well-manicured man on our wedding day, but since we've been married, he's allowed himself to get over-weight and lazy. I have kept myself in good shape and feel cheated. What can I do?

An ATTRACTIVE AIRLINE FLIGHT ATTENDANT asked me a similar question on a flight one day. She was a bright, articulate young Christian woman, and the man she had married had let himself go. He hadn't kept up his physical fitness regime and had grown considerably overweight. He often neglected to shave or bathe, he refused to help with any chores around the house, and spent most of his after-work hours drinking beer and watching sports on television. He rarely read a book, didn't keep up with current events, and resisted interacting with any of his wife's friends. When he consented to go to a party with her, he inevitably embarrassed her to tears in front of her peers or coworkers.

"What can I do?" the young woman asked me desperately.

My answer to her was not what she expected.

"Frankly," I said, "you married him. You have to live with him. You made your choice. He may have exhibited these slovenly characteristics before your marriage, and you may not have noticed. Or maybe you thought you could change him after you married. Regardless, now you have to live with that decision.

"The Bible says that the wife should respect her husband.[15] Your husband seems intent on destroying your love and admiration, but that doesn't rescind your responsibility to respect him." We talked further and I encouraged her to "throw a bucket of cold water in his face."

"Wake him up!" I urged her. "Hold a mirror in front of him, and allow him to see what he has become. And remind him, 'Here is what you used to be.'"

A husband and wife deserve to live with the person they married! Certainly, we all change with time; life and aging take a toll on our physical bodies, but barring some unforeseen accident or sickness, your spouse has a right to expect you to take care of yourself, and you should expect the same of him or her. Laziness, complacency, and an undisciplined, unkempt body are not complimentary to your mate or to God.

Something similar often happens intellectually. A wife and husband may begin their marriage with complementary intellectual interests and pursuits, but then

15   See Ephesians 5:33

after a while, one of them may lapse into mental laziness. He or she neglects to read, keep up with current events, or otherwise challenge himself or herself intellectually, while ingesting a steady diet of Hollywood fluff or floundering on the intellectual shores of pop novels or other tripe. Before long, they find themselves drifting apart, because they are no longer on the same intellectual course.

Marriage is not a static relationship. A husband and wife must continue to grow together, and this usually takes work. Certainly, you and your spouse may have some outside interests exclusive to one partner or the other. You needn't be intellectual or emotional clones of each other, but you should expand the horizons of your relationship together rather than allowing your individual interests to divide you as a couple.

If your spouse has become physically, mentally, or spiritually lazy, do all you can to encourage him or her, but don't be afraid to apply some pressure, as well.

I would enlist the help of your husband's friends. Have them get him on a softball team, touch football team, or basketball team. Have them take your husband to an exercise program at a local gym. If you can afford it, hire a personal trainer for both of you. Get a weight bench and some light weights. Challenge your husband to see if he can lift them. Get a couple of bicycles and take rides together. Walk together.

Since you control the food in the home, start serving high-protein meals with lots of fruit and vegetables. Get the sweets, white bread, pasta, and other fattening foods out of the house. Buy your husband some books on health and nutrition. As a joke, tack a full-length photograph of a Mr. Universe look-alike on the bathroom door and keep an accurate set of scales close-by. Health and fitness are contagious. Make it a shared, fun experience for you both.

Bring your best into your marriage!

COMMUNICATION, COMMUNICATION, COMMUNICATION!

I keep hearing that communication is one of the keys to a great marriage. How am I to communicate with a man who hardly even speaks after he gets home from work?

THIS IS A PERENNIAL PROBLEM between men and women. One of the main gifts most women want from their men is companionship. A wife wants her husband to be with her, to listen to her, and to talk with her, not simply to talk *at* her.

Unfortunately, most men don't really enjoy engaging in that type of verbal communication. After a tough day in the workplace, many men prefer to come home and relax—which by definition to most men means to simply sit down, watch television, read the newspaper, and be relatively stoic and quiet. As one man put it, "I've been talking to people all day at work. By the time I get home, I've used up all my words."

This creates a tension for a woman seeking verbal communication and a man whose needs are basically for peace and quiet. Nevertheless, if communication is a key to a happy marriage, and we know it is, both the husband and wife must find ways to bridge that gap. Allowing the husband a bit of recuperative time when he first gets home from work, time in which he can quietly recharge his verbal batteries, may be all that is necessary. Using specific, leading questions rather than the generic, "How was your day?" can also improve conversation and communication.

When you want to talk about serious matters, seek a time that is the least hectic and stressful. Ruth Graham, wife of Billy Graham, says that she never broached important matters with Billy when he was tired, hungry, or under enormous stress. For many modern-day couples, that would rule out conversation during most of their waking hours!

Nevertheless, seek to find a communication pattern that works for you and your mate. Realizing that the verbal communication needs of males and females are vastly different is a good place to start.

WOUNDING WITH WORDS

Whenever my wife and I go out in public, she has a habit of belittling me in front of other people. I've asked her to please stop doing this, but she continues, saying that I should lighten up. What should I do?

PERHAPS YOU SHOULD LIGHTEN UP!

On the other hand, your wife's belittling comments may reveal a power struggle between the two of you. She wants to exercise authority over you, and her belittling of you may be the "safest" way of doing so. She may not make such statements at home, either because she acknowledges you as head of the household, or possibly because she knows you may respond differently in private. Your wife may not truly understand how deeply her comments hurt you. She may have "inherited" this sort of talk from her parents. If asked, she might respond that her remarks are simply harmless banter, not intended to inflict damage. Regardless, her public comments are disrespectful and counterproductive in your relationship. Quite possibly, they are indicative of a much deeper problem between the two of you.

Attempt to sit down privately with your wife, and express to her how deeply her comments grieve you. Ask her if there is some reason she wants to wound you with her words. Is there something that you have said or done that has hurt your mate, and this is her way of getting back at you? Emphasize to her that you want to improve your marriage by speaking positive affirmations to each other.

The Bible says to let no corrupt word proceed out of your mouth, but what is good for necessary edification, that it may impart grace to the hearers. . . . Let all bitterness, wrath, anger, clamor, and evil speaking be put away from you, with all malice. And be kind to one another, tenderhearted, forgiving one another, even as God in Christ forgave you.[16]

NEGATIVE ATTITUDE

My husband is very negative, even vulgar at times about people in general. I've noticed our son taking on these same characteristics. I've spoken to my husband about his negative attitude and the influence he is having on our son, but he doesn't seem to care. I've considered leaving him for a while. Do you have any other suggestions?

THIS QUESTION POINTS UP THE NEED for each man and woman to be extremely careful in choosing a marriage partner. Your mate is not only going to influence your life, but the lives of your children. It's highly doubtful that your spouse suddenly acquired his negative attitude since your wedding day. His negativism was a facet of his personality that he either kept well-hidden from you or you chose to ignore or excuse. In any case, you married a spouse whose conduct and attitudes you accepted, and to whom you vowed to unite yourself. The fact that you now find his attitude, words, and conduct abhorrent does not change that commitment.

Making negative comments, using profanity, or having an overall bad attitude in front of your son is not biblical grounds for a divorce, so if you separate for a while, it should be only to get his attention. Your son is at an impressionable age, an age when many people make lifelong commitments to follow Jesus. To encourage his spiritual growth, it will be important to surround him with Christian influences.

---

16   See Ephesians 4:29, 31–32

Ideally, it would be good to have him attend a Christian youth camp program or something similar where he can experience the presence of the Lord and be influenced by positive, adult Christian men who will be role models for him. Hopefully, if your son is around men whose lives are dedicated to the Lord, whose thoughts, words, and conduct are under the control of the Holy Spirit, he will choose to follow the model of these Christian leaders. If your husband remains the only male role model that your son has, you can expect him to adopt and emulate the speech patterns, mannerisms, and attitudes he sees in his dad.

The more difficult "target" is your husband. Jesus has a wonderful way of changing foul-mouthed blasphemers into godly men. The apostle Paul is a case in point. When Saul, the persecutor of Christians, met Jesus, his life was transformed. God can change your husband's heart, too, which in turn will change his attitudes and his conversation. To help facilitate this process, it will be important to expose your husband to godly Christian influences, which hopefully will stimulate within him a desire to know the Lord and live according to His Word.

Years ago, I was invited to play golf with a prominent New York business executive. In our foursome was a wealthy retiree. After a bad shot, this gentleman would shout, "Goddamn it!" Finally, with a smile, I said, "You know, that shot wasn't God's fault." After the round was over, he told my friend, "That preacher did more to stop my cussing than anything." One afternoon in the presence of a Christian . . . seven friendly words and profanity stopped. Introduce your husband to someone who walks with the Lord and watch the change.

It may also be helpful to discover and understand the root of your husband's negativism. Was it part of his family background? Did he endure unusual humiliation in school? Has he experienced some failure on the job? Has he been passed over for a promotion? What has shaped his life that has robbed him of his own self-esteem and caused such negative thought patterns and conduct?

The Bible says that no corrupt word should come out of a Christian's mouth, this includes cursing, gossip, malicious comments, coarse jesting, and other negative comments. If someone is truly a Christian, he or she will not curse. Show your husband these scriptures and encourage him to speak positively for his own good and for the good of your family.

I ONLY HAVE EYES FOR YOU

Lately, I've noticed my husband of twenty-three years "making eyes" at his twenty-two-year-old secretary. I've called him on it several

times, but he says his attention to this young woman is harmless. What do you think?

Regrettably, the basic physiology of the aging male remains a mystery to many men and women alike. Consequently, many women misunderstand what is happening to their husbands when the previously normal, sane, dependable man with whom they have lived for years suddenly turns into something akin to the lead role in a "B-quality" teen movie.

It helps to recall that several hormones are vital for a man to function normally. Among the most important are testosterone and DHEA. At age twenty-five, these hormones, along with what is known as the human growth hormone, begin to decline. As a man moves into middle age, these hormones diminish even more rapidly. By the time he reaches senior-citizen status, these hormones are almost nonexistent in his body.

The human growth hormone helps a man's body build muscle tissue. The absence of this hormone allows the growth of fat, particularly in the stomach and abdominal areas. Testosterone is the major hormone that affects a man's sexual drive and his physical energy and vitality. Often, when a man realizes that his sexual desire has diminished and that he lacks the physical energy he once had, he panics. He doesn't understand that he is undergoing a normal hormonal change, common to nearly every man who has ever lived beyond his thirties.

Some men turn to all sorts of things in desperate attempts to regain their youth. A man may try everything from getting a toupee to having a face lift, from driving a fast, bright-colored sports car to engaging in extreme sports or wearing flashy clothes and a pile of gold chains around his neck. These things aren't necessarily wrong; they're just foolish, because they won't bring about the desired results. The aging fellow will still have a diminishing sex drive and will still lack youthful energy and stamina. As the kids would say, "He looks like an old guy still trying."

Some men attempt to bolster their sagging self-images by seeking to attract the attention of a younger woman. It's as though a man is saying to his wife, his friends, and most of all, to himself, "See, I'm still desirable. People still think I'm attractive. Look at this sweet young thing with whom I'm spending time. Do you think she'd have anything to do with someone who wasn't strong and virile?"

Sadly, if the man is wealthy or holds a position of prestige or power, he will usually be able to find some young woman who will look to him as her "conquering hero." While his flirtatious looks and comments toward her may be those of a paper tiger, her responses all too often can lead to trouble for both of them. More than a few long-standing marriages have been destroyed by this seemingly innocuous interplay.

What can be done to avoid such an unnecessary travesty? First, get an accurate understanding of the physical changes that take place in a man's body as he ages. Then, as a couple, discuss and come to grips with the fact that you are getting older and establish some realistic expectations. Working together to maintain a healthier diet and exercise program will add not only longevity to your life, but more joy in your relationship as well.

Men, see your doctor and have a complete physical checkup every year. Find a doctor who specializes in preventative medicine rather than merely treating an illness once it exists. Visit a health food store and become educated about how to replenish your testosterone, DHEA hormones, and human growth hormone.

Most of all, understand that your life is not over simply because you are aging. God has much for you to do, much for you to enjoy. He wants to bless you and make you a blessing to others. Keep your eyes on Him!

SUSPICION

Yesterday I overheard my husband on the phone with his secretary. He closed their conversation with, "I love you, too." Knowing that he is very affectionate and expresses love to everyone, is this something I should ask him to explain?

IN EVERYDAY CONVERSATION we hear phrases such as "I love you" or "Love ya!" or something of that nature. Among Christians the implication is "I love you in the Lord." In this context, these statements are usually terms of endearment, encouragement, or genuine godly affection rather than phrases filled with romantic overtones. Granted, some people tend to toss around such expressions flippantly, forgetting that every word will one day be judged. As with anything we say, without sincerity of heart even the right words can be meaningless tripe. But that should not detract from the intention of those who are sincerely expressing the love of the Lord.

On the other hand, to use such expressions with a seductive or romantic tone in your voice or an enticing look on your face can lead to misunderstanding and hurt feelings or possibly plant the seeds of full-blown adultery. When a man and woman are working in close proximity, such expressions are inappropriate and should be avoided. Many men and women have imperiled their marriages and their jobs because they allowed a relationship in the workplace to become too close.

Concerning your implied suspicion and whether you should confront your husband about this matter, asking him to explain: Before you do that, ask yourself, "Am I spying on my husband or looking for miscreant behavior as a result of something that has happened in his past or mine?"

Too often, such suspicions turn into self-fulfilling prophecies. "Overhearing" a conversation can actually be eavesdropping, listening for something that feeds your own insecurities. Jealousy is a sure way to create conflict in a relationship.

Certainly, you want to be wise, and you have every right to be protective of your husband. Perhaps you have a trusted friend within your husband's office who can give you some insight concerning the relationship he has with his secretary.

If you can warn your husband of a potentially dangerous situation, by all means do so, but be sure to bathe your words in love and prayer. Don't accuse, but in a loving, discreet manner, express your concerns to him, letting him know that you love him, and you'd prefer such terms of endearment be reserved for the two of you.

PRENUPTIAL AGREEMENTS

> I am engaged to a wealthy man whom I have dated for several years. We are talking about marriage, and he has asked me to sign a prenuptial agreement. I'm offended and hurt. Is there something in the Bible about this type of marriage contract, and should I sign it?

NOTHING IN THE BIBLE specifically deals with prenuptial agreements as we know them today. In biblical times, parents arranged their children's weddings, and dowries were often paid. Marriage was often regarded as a business relationship. But that's a different issue than we have today. Nowadays, legal agreements are often struck when one partner has a large amount of wealth and wishes to shield a portion of his or her possessions from a potential marriage partner, should anything "go wrong" in the relationship.

I frankly would advise any man or woman with wealth in excess of $500,000 who is planning to marry a younger person to have a simple prenuptial agreement spelling out clearly the financial understanding between them. There is nothing unromantic in protecting either inherited or hard-earned wealth from the emotional vagaries of a marriage. Perhaps some of the pain could be removed if in the prenuptial agreement the well-to-do spouse-to-be actually made an outright gift or a gift in trust to his beloved.

This may seem to remove romance from marriage and reduce the relationship to a business deal. To your fiancé, marriage may simply be another business contract, so he's treating you as though you were one of his acquisitions. For instance, when Aristotle Onassis wanted to marry Jackie Kennedy, Senator Ted Kennedy negotiated a $20 million payment. Apparently, the money was transferred to her account prior to the wedding. To my thinking, Onassis basically *bought* Jackie Kennedy.

While most prenuptial agreements are not so blunt, to be so concerned about the possibility of the marriage failing may appear to show a lack of trust in the other person, but it recognizes the way things are in today's world. Granted, if someone has made a lot of money, he or she doesn't want some fortune hunter coming along and marrying for the money, then divorcing, and trying to bilk him or her out of half of the net worth. That's one of the problems with marrying into someone else's money. The truth is, you didn't build this wealth together. If he chooses to share it with you, fine; if not, you need to weigh how that colors the rest of your relationship.

PROS AND CONS OF PRENUPTIAL AGREEMENTS

What are the pros and cons of Christians who are remarrying having prenuptial agreements?

It can seem cold and calculating, but for those who have a large estate, or when children are involved, a prenuptial agreement makes sense. But as I said in my previous answer, insisting on a prenuptial agreement may smack of distrust, which can destroy the love in any relationship.

This question, however, specifically deals with remarriage. If you have children by a previous marriage, it is good to spell out who gets what, should the worst-case scenario take place.

For instance, let's assume that you are a widow, and you inherited money from your husband. That money rightfully belongs to your children when you die. Yet if you remarry without a prenuptial agreement, your second husband has a legal claim to a portion of your estate, most of which may have been earned by your former husband. That is not something that your first husband would prefer, nor would his children.

If you are remarrying, it is important to enter the relationship with your eyes open. If you have a large amount of property and financial assets, you should seek godly wisdom in how to best pass on your possessions to your legal heirs. A simple last will and testament can address the disposition of your property after your death, but a will does nothing to divide property in the case of divorce. Under California law, for example, without a prenuptial agreement, each spouse is entitled to fifty percent of the total marriage estate, should the marriage be dissolved.

The most intelligent way to deal with the problem is to put the money for the children in trust with the income coming to you for your life. A charitable remainder trust can do the same thing in regard to a charity—income to you for twenty years, the remainder then to the charity. The issue is not just a prenuptial agreement, but an entire estate plan that protects you and your heirs before you are remarried.

For most people, though, the need for a prenuptial agreement usually depends on how much money is involved. If the value of the estate is relatively small, a prenuptial agreement should not be necessary.

ADULT SEX BEFORE MARRIAGE

I know that sex before marriage is wrong for teenagers for many reasons, including the possibility of premarital pregnancies, venereal diseases, and guilt. But after being happily married for fifteen years, then widowed at a young age, somehow sex outside of marriage for adults does not seem so damaging. Isn't sexual experience necessary to determine if there is a future compatibility in an adult relationship?

An illusion has been popularized that it is necessary to have sexual compatibility for a good marriage. While sexual intimacy is a wonderful part of marriage, the relationship should be built on spiritual and intellectual compatibility. Of course, physical attraction is important, but it is only one of the components of a good marriage. Great marriages require shared experiences, shared joy, shared interests, shared cultural backgrounds, and a shared faith.

I want to preface my answer to this question with this warning. A large number of single (and some married) men assume that divorcees and widows are accustomed to sexual relations and are, therefore, willing sex partners. The concept is not that she is attractive and desirable as a wife, but that she is an easy "make." Your very question reinforces that preconception. Any divorced or widowed woman who thinks as you do on this issue is going to be terribly hurt by a series of predatory males.

The fact that you have good or bad sex before your marriage reveals little about your relationship. Great sexual partners do not always make great marriage partners, but a great relationship almost always produces wonderful sexual intimacy within marriage. The issue is, do you love each other? Are you irrevocably and unconditionally committed to one another?

Researchers continually discover that living together prior to marriage is no safeguard against divorce. In fact, the percentage of divorcing couples who have lived together prior to marriage is actually higher than couples who have not lived together before marriage.[17]

That shouldn't surprise anyone. After all, a good relationship is based on unconditional love and a coupling of body, mind, and spirit. It is not, "Let's go out and have a quick fling to see if we are compatible."

In recent years, an extremely damaging sexual philosophy has been promulgated among single adults. It says, "Hey, it's the second time around; we are no longer kids; we are not virgins, so let's go for it." When you fall for this lie, you cheapen yourself.

Your age is irrelevant. Whether you are fifteen or fifty years of age, you cannot join your body to another person sexually without having serious emotional consequences. You are making a commitment to another person, but that person is not committed to you.

For a woman to offer her body to a man without the commitment of marriage is especially unwise and dangerous. Too often the man uses her sexually and then decides that marriage is out of the question. "Why should I take on the burden of supporting a wife, taking care of a household, and all the other responsibilities that come with marriage," he asks, "if I can have the sexual pleasures of marriage with none of the commitments?"

We've had nearly two generations of people who bought into the theory of premarital sexual experience. The results have been rampant venereal diseases, skyrocketing divorce rates, and emotionally devastated women, men, and children. Testing your sexual compatibility before marriage does not in any way solidify a marriage. The best mind-set for marriage is for the man to say, "I am giving myself to you, my wife, totally and exclusively, from now on." The woman should say the same. "I am giving myself exclusively to you, my husband." The two should agree, "Of all the people on earth, we have chosen one another, and we are bonded together for life."

---

[17] *Headline News,* Cable News Network, July 8, 2002.

That type of commitment produces good marriages, and it produces an unfading love. Otherwise, even sincere couples are tempted to say, "Well, we gave it a shot, and it didn't quite work. Maybe I can find somebody else who pleases my fancy."

Marriage isn't a game. Sex isn't a game. These commitments are sacred before God and important for our society. You'd be wise to keep sex where it belongs— within the confines of a loving, committed relationship of marriage.

DOES PREMARITAL SEX EQUAL MARRIAGE?

I was a teen and a non-Christian when I lost my virginity. I know that I am forgiven, but who is my real husband in God's sight: the young man to whom I first gave my virginity, or the man to whom I am now married?

YOUR TRUE HUSBAND is the man to whom you are married. Let's face it. You didn't establish a marriage between yourself and the fellow with whom you had a brief sexual relationship. You didn't commit yourselves to each other as life partners before God. With notable Old Testament exceptions for rape, the Bible does not equate your sexual liaison to marriage. Certainly, what you did was wrong, and it is good that you have sought forgiveness, but marriage is much more than sex. It is the joining of two lives to become one, not simply in a physical sense, but emotionally, spiritually, financially, and socially. Unless you and the young man somehow ratified that initial sexual experience as a lifetime commitment, I can say positively that you were never married. So get on with the life you have with the man you married and leave the teenage acts of passion behind.

ORAL SEX WHILE DATING

My girlfriend and I engage in oral sex but don't have intercourse, so we don't feel guilty. Is this considered wrong in the eyes of the Lord?

I DID NOT HAVE SEX with that woman . . ." This question is not surprising in light of recent history when the president of the United States stood trial for lying under oath. Why? Largely because of his definition of sexual relations. He had convinced himself that oral sex was not adultery and therefore was permissible. With due respect to the office of the presidency, that conclusion is wrong.

I am appalled at the rampant spread of oral sex among teenagers because of the example of this brilliant but sexually warped man.

Any nonmedical contact with the sex organs of another person is a sexual act. Any sexual intimacy, including oral sex, outside of marriage is wrong in the eyes of the Lord. Nonmarried couples play these games all too often, engaging in fondling and caressing of the erogenous areas of each other's bodies to the point of sexual gratification yet technically restraining themselves from having intercourse. This foreplay is a type of fornication, engaging in a level of intimacy designed for marriage but without the commitment of marriage. That a Christian couple can engage in such activity without feeling guilty is a matter of concern. Could it be that our consciences have become so seared that we are insensitive to that which is to be regarded as sacred and holy?

I might add, oral sex does not cause pregnancy, but it certainly causes disease. Doctors are shocked to find teenagers who complain of a sore throat, but who actually have gonorrhea. I am relatively sure that virtually any infection passed through the mucous membranes of the genitals can also be passed through the mouth.

A SEDUCTIVE COURTSHIP

I'm a single man in my late thirties and keeping myself sexually pure until I get married. I have just begun a new relationship with a woman whom I love, but who is not a virgin and is pressing me for sex in our relationship. She's pretty influencing and hard to resist. What advice can you give that will help me to remain pure in Christ?

THE BIBLE SAYS, "Flee also youthful lusts; but pursue righteousness, faith, love, peace with those who call on the Lord out of a pure heart."[18] This woman who sounds like a twenty-first century Jezebel is trying to seduce you into doing something that you know is wrong. Your conscience is telling you, "Don't have sex before marriage," but the woman with whom you are "in love," willingly wishes to ignore your desire to obey God's Word. That's a rather disconcerting sign that trouble may be lurking down the road. If there are, as the song says, "50 Ways to Leave Your Lover," find one of them and get out of this relationship fast!

The fact that your potential mate has already had sexual relationships with other men and does not respect your relationship with Christ indicates that if the two of you ever married, she will maintain that same attitude and lifestyle.

18   2 Timothy 2:22 (NKJV)

It is commendable that you have kept yourself sexually pure for more than thirty years. Clearly, you are dedicated to the Lord. You should not marry until you find a woman who shares your consecration, who regards the sexual relationship as a precious part of marriage, and with whom you can grow together in your faith.

Obviously you are looking for a mate. Believe me, there are thousands of godly women looking for a man like you. You have waited long enough. Ask the Lord for the right one to share a life with you. He will answer your prayer.

ENGAGED EXPRESSIONS OF LOVE

What physical expressions of love are appropriate for an engaged couple?

In previous generations hardly any physical expressions of affection were deemed acceptable for engaged couples. In colonial days, they had a practice known as bundling. It was so cold in the houses, both males and females had to get under the covers to stay warm, so they put a board between the young people to prevent physical contact. Those days are long gone!

Realistically, I can't see anything wrong with an engaged couple kissing and hugging. Their physical expressions of affection are commensurate with the level of commitment in the relationship. But when you start getting into what is called "heavy petting," fondling of the erogenous zones, that is a mistake. Such expressions are intended to lead to further intimacy, but sexual intercourse outside of marriage is fornication and is wrong. Furthermore, you will respect and appreciate each other more if you wait until you get married to engage in more overtly sexual activities.

The answer to "How far can you go?" depends on what stimulates you. It's like asking how close can you bring a lighted torch to a barrel of gunpowder before it explodes. For some people, even kissing and hugging before marriage may be too hot to handle. Others can express themselves legitimately without compromising their relationship with the Lord and with each other. Be careful what you allow, however, in the name of freedom. God wants you to have a great sex life; don't ruin it by starting before the commitment is sealed. If you can't wait, forget the long engagement and get married!

PREMARITAL PREGNANCY

I've been born again for about five years and began dating a Christian man about nine months ago. Unfortunately, we did not keep our relationship sexually pure, and I just found out that I am six weeks pregnant. I've asked God to forgive me for having premarital sex, and I know that I am forgiven. My boyfriend wants to marry me because he thinks it is the right thing to do, not necessarily because he loves me. Should I marry this man under these conditions? Am I spiritually bound to him for the rest of my life because of one mistake? Would God bless this baby if I choose to remain single?

YES, GOD WILL BLESS YOUR BABY! Your child is the precious person God created, and He already has a plan established for your baby. The Scripture says, "I praise you because I am fearfully and wonderfully made; your works are wonderful, I know that full well. My frame was not hidden from you when I was made in the secret place. When I was woven together in the depths of the earth, your eyes saw my unformed body. All the days ordained for me were written in your book before one of them came to be."[19] Although your child was conceived out of wedlock and as the result of premarital sex between you and your boyfriend, your child is not an accident, and God will bless this baby.

Your boyfriend wants to marry you to protect you, to give the baby a proper name, and to "do the right thing." Frankly, good and lasting marriages have been built on just such commitments if they include a true, prayerful dedication of the marriage to the Lord. Love can spring out of a shared life together if both parties are determined to make it work.

I advise a serious, thoughtful discussion between the two of you with much prayer for God's guidance. Your relationship could become lasting and rewarding.

On the other hand, you are not trapped because you made a mistake. Two wrongs don't make a right. A bad marriage with hatred and bitterness ending in a divorce can be deadly for you.

Whether you marry or not, do not allow anyone to convince you that abortion is the answer to your problem. That is a devil's lie and should be rejected immediately. The life within you is not simply a conglomeration of cells. It is a living soul, a *baby!*

---

19   Psalm 139:14–16 (NIV)

Handling the many details involved with a premarital pregnancy is never easy. You will need some help, ideally from your family or church. If such help is not forthcoming, Christian agencies such as Mercy Ministries of America, Care Net, Birthright and others are available (free of charge) to help an unmarried young woman find prenatal care, as well as arranging to have your baby adopted by a Christian family, if you should so choose.

You may decide to raise the baby yourself as a single mother. If so, pray that God will bring the right man into your life, a man who will love your child as his own and will love you unconditionally, regardless of your past mistakes. God will help you, if you will trust Him.

INTERRACIAL DATING

I'm a Caucasian female who has fallen in love with an African-American male. My parents are furious. Should I continue this relationship or go on about my business?

GOD CREATED ADAM AND EVE as the progenitors of all the races. This is evident from the beginning of the Bible to the end, where we see "a great multitude, which no one could count, people from every nation, and all tribes and peoples and tongues," standing before the throne of God and before the Lamb . . . all rejoicing and praising God, all part of His eternal family.[20] For that reason, I can see nothing biblically inappropriate about an interracial relationship between two Christians.

The problems you may face in such a relationship are not spiritual but societal. For instance, you mention that your parents are strongly opposed to your interracial relationship. If you choose to proceed, you will certainly incur their displeasure and possibly be estranged from them. Your boyfriend's African-American parents may be perturbed also. Regardless, your parents' concern over your relationship cannot be ignored. Perhaps their concern stems from racial prejudice and is unwarranted, but on the other hand, maybe they see something about you or your dating partner that causes them to be troubled. You owe it to them and to yourself to find out.

While interracial relationships are becoming more common in America, they are far from the norm. Many people, both within the church and outside the church, still harbor stigmas and stereotypes that are not easily discarded. This is not

---

20   See Revelation 7:9

to condone prejudice, but to ignore its existence would be foolish. Should you pursue an interracial relationship, you should not be surprised if the culture around you does not accept you.

The most important factor in a strong relationship is not a person's skin color, but the character of his or her heart. Ask yourself: Does this person truly know and love the Lord, and is he or she attempting to follow Him? Is his or her lifestyle consistent with Scripture? Do we have similar spiritual values? Can we serve God side by side?

The Bible does not prohibit interracial relationships, but it definitely condemns willfully entering a relationship with an unbeliever. The apostle Paul wrote, "Do not be bound together with unbelievers; for what partnership have righteousness and lawlessness, or what fellowship has light with darkness? Or what harmony has Christ with Belial, or what has a believer in common with an unbeliever?"[21] In short, to marry someone of a different race is not wrong, but to marry an unbeliever is flagrant disobedience of God's Word and is outside of His best for you.

A SEXLESS MARRIAGE

My husband and I were virgins when we married. We dated for about seven years before we tied the knot. On our wedding night we never consummated our marriage. After three years of this behavior, I sought counseling. My husband left me for a mistress. Are we married in the eyes of the Lord?

THE ANSWER TO YOUR QUESTION IS SIMPLE. Your marriage has never been consummated and you, therefore, are not married in the eyes of the Lord. Ignoring sexual intimacy in marriage was grounds for an annulment in the Catholic Church during the Middle Ages, and probably would still be today. Annulment means that the marriage is treated as if it never happened . . . null and void. You cannot live with that unhealthy situation. Since you were never truly married, you have rights to seek an annulment rather than a divorce.

Why something such as this happens is an enigma. Some men develop a "Madonna complex," in which they hold their wife in such high esteem that to have physical relations with her would be demeaning. They never allow themselves to know the intimacy that is intended for marriage.

---

21   2 Corinthians 6:14–15

Others may have a psychological problem with sex, perhaps due to past relationships. Still others may have a physical inability to function normally during intercourse. Possibly, latent guilt from past sins is involved. Regardless, all those things can be overcome if a husband and wife are committed to the relationship.

The apostle Paul wrote to the Christians at Corinth reminding them that the husband's body is not his own, but belongs as well to his wife. Likewise, the wife's body is not exclusively hers, but belongs also to her husband.[22] Paul wrote quite explicitly about the responsibilities of the husband and wife to meet each other's sexual needs. The apostle said, "Let the husband fulfill his duty to his wife, and likewise also the wife to her husband. . . . Stop depriving one another, except by agreement for a time that you may devote yourselves to prayer, and come together again lest Satan tempt you because of your lack of self-control."[23] Paul recognized that a healthy, vibrant sexual relationship is part of God's plan for married couples. He was also aware of the enormous temptations faced by men and women who did not experience sexual intimacy with their mates. The apostle who lived in a world not unlike ours that was drenched with sexual immorality must have seen the havoc Satan can cause in the lives of people who have strong sexual desires but with no legitimate means to satisfy those desires. Consequently, for a husband and wife to engage in a sort of "sexual fast" for a short season is one thing; to ignore your sexual relationship for a prolonged period of time is wrong.

Because of the intimate nature of this problem, it's difficult to say how extensive it is, but with the increasingly stressful lives many couples lead nowadays, it is not surprising to discover that by the end of the day many marriage partners are simply too exhausted to enjoy each other. Ironic, isn't it, that in one of the most sex-saturated societies in history, these couples are opting to place intimacy on the back burner?

Only God knows, however, the intimate details of their marriages, including what slights might have taken place behind closed doors. Was there some act, insult, or ridicule that created a barrier of resentment between the marriage partners? Was sexual intimacy being withheld as some sort of punishment for something else that happened in the relationship? Without an opportunity to explore the emotional, physical, psychological, and spiritual aspects of the relationship, it is difficult to speak to their situation authoritatively. That's why I highly recommend that couples seek out competent Christian counseling for such delicate problems.

---

[22]   See 1 Corinthians 7:4
[23]   1 Corinthians 7:3, 5

Although human sexuality has become the subject of all sorts of deviant, prurient, pornographic materials, we need to understand that God made each of us as sexual beings. Sex was God's idea in the first place, and He is highly in favor of it! God created the sexual relationship for the procreation of the race, and as part of the intimacy He intended to be enjoyed within marriage. To withhold your affection from your spouse or to deprive one another of this God-given gift is to open your relationship to the attacks of the enemy and to place yourself in opposition to God's plan for marriage.

SPOUSAL ABUSE / DOMESTIC VIOLENCE

My husband of seventeen years is a leader in our church, but occasionally, he loses his temper and begins hitting and kicking me, sometimes right in front of our two adolescent boys. After the beatings, he always weeps like a baby, repents to God, and begs my forgiveness. I sometimes fear for my life, but I always take him back because I think that's what God would want me to do. Is there a better way to handle this?

THERE CERTAINLY IS! Get out of that house while you still can! And take your boys with you!

I once knew a Hollywood stuntman, a tall, strong, handsome man, married to an extremely attractive wife. He was a Christian, but at times he'd fly into a violent rage, strike his wife, and hurl her literally across the room. Afterwards, like your husband, he'd repent and vow never to do such a horrible thing again. His commitment was short-lived, however, and the domestic violence continued unabated for years.

I later learned that this abusive husband had been abandoned by his father and mother and raised by an elderly woman during his preteenage years. She was unwilling or unable to discipline him, so he soon developed a rebellious spirit. Now, as an adult, he displays the same sort of temper tantrums, but his outbursts of anger frequently turn violent.

Another abusive husband grew up in a home in which the father regularly beat the mother. Not surprisingly, the boy assumed that such treatment of women was normal, acceptable conduct. When he became an adult, he perpetuated the same patterns in his home.

Domestic violence can stem from a wide variety of causes. Sometimes the cause can be neurological, sometimes it is the result of one's upbringing or childhood environment; other cases are alcohol or drug related, and sometimes domestic violence may even be demonically instigated. Whatever the cause, it should never be tolerated!

Unfortunately, many women with young children have no means of financial support except that provided by their abusive husband. They feel trapped and helpless, with no alternative but to stay in a violent home. Knowing this, an abusive spouse often threatens to throw the wife and children out, or he uses money as a weapon to control the wife and to get what he wants.

While domestic violence is perpetrated most often by men upon women, in some cases it is the wife and mother who is the perpetrator, and in rare instances domestic violence involves children abusing parents. Wherever it is found, this domineering spirit is evil and must be dealt with directly, through both legal and spiritual means—legally, by taking whatever steps are necessary to secure peace and safety in the home, and spiritually, by coming against the devilish, demonic elements of domestic violence and helping the perpetrator to be delivered by the power of Jesus Christ.

God is always on the side of marriage and family. His will is always redemptive and restorative. He wants to see families live in love and peace. Nevertheless, nowhere in the Bible does the Lord instruct a man or woman to live with a spouse who does physical violence to them. It may be necessary to separate from the abusive spouse until he or she is willing to seek help.

If you are the victim of domestic violence, pray for your mate that he or she will come to himself or herself and submit to the control of the Holy Spirit. Many men and women have overcome domestic violence and its devastating effects on their marriage and family. It's possible, and with God's help it can be done!

But don't be naive. Don't make excuses for your abusive spouse. And don't allow your mate to offer mere tears and empty promises to do better. Insist that your spouse seek appropriate spiritual counseling, medical testing, and treatment, and give him enough time to see tangible results before you risk going back into that home.

RELATIONSHIPS ON THE INTERNET

My wife carries on numerous relationships with men via the Internet. She says that she enjoys the interaction and has never been tempted to be unfaithful to me, but am I being mentally or emotionally cheated on? I must admit that with her on the computer, I am free

to lie down after work and don't feel compelled to talk when I am so tired, but it still seems wrong.

You are right. Adultery takes various forms: physical, spiritual, and intellectual. I counseled with a woman who had an Internet relationship with a man who was involved in sadomasochism. He convinced her that sadomasochism was an exciting adventure and she should try it. He did not mask his intentions of controlling her and even told her directly on the Internet, "I want your mind." As strange as it may seem, she was willing to give it to him! She decided to leave her husband and run away with her perverted Internet companion.

This was absolutely satanic. It was an addiction, but, in my opinion, it was more than that. It was a demonic hold on her life, and through prayer she was delivered from it.

While the Internet can be a wonderful tool for communications, male-female on-line relationships are rarely innocuous. You must inform your wife that this type of conduct is totally unacceptable to you and holds the potential to destroy your marriage. It is not unreasonable to ask your wife to be faithful to you, not only in her body, but in her mind and her spirit as well. The two of you are one flesh. You cannot allow her to engage in intimate "conversations" with someone else on the Internet. Too often, these "pen pals" discuss various suggestive matters, and one thing easily leads to another. Before long, either her mind or heart will leave you, or she will physically walk out of the marriage.

Perhaps she doesn't know the person with whom she is communicating. That does not lessen the danger. Increasingly, we are hearing horror stories concerning anonymous people on the Net. How any thinking person could enter a relationship with a stranger in that fashion and then begin to explore intimate matters with him or her is beyond me. But many people are doing it, and in my opinion, it is extremely foolish and absolutely wrong.

No doubt, one of the reasons this happens is because of loneliness. People are longing to be "connected," and if they cannot maintain a relationship in reality, an on-line love interest seems even more attractive. Moreover, mental fantasies tend to be more powerful and more alluring than mundane reality. People who fantasize on the Internet may imagine each other in the most glowing of terms. Yet, in fact, the person with whom he or she is communicating may be much less attractive than the person with whom they are living.

The person engaging in an on-line relationship can have intimacy on demand, whenever they want it emotionally and psychologically, without the ramifications or responsibilities of a normal relationship. A genuine, healthy relationship requires much more time and effort. It's not always easy to communicate with a spouse, learning to overcome differences and disappointments, or dealing with the minor irritations caused by living in close proximity to another human being on a daily basis. But the challenges are worth it!

Yes, on the Internet people can live in a fantasy world, similar to a daytime soap opera. But such fantasies can be very dangerous and destructive to your marriage.

DIVORCING CHRISTIANS

How can two Christians who say they love the Lord get divorced and act as if everything is okay?

Many in the church, even those who consider themselves born-again, Spirit-filled Christians, are violating the clear commandments of Jesus Christ and are adopting the ways of the world in regard to their married lives, their sex lives, and many other lifestyle issues. Concerning marriage, from the beginning of time the biblical standard has been, "'For this reason a man shall leave his father and mother and be joined to his wife, and the two shall become one flesh.' So then, they are no longer two but one flesh. Therefore what God has joined together, let not man separate."[24]

Marriage is meant to be for life. We make vows before God in a holy ceremony and declare that a man and woman are united in an irrevocable commitment that is meant to last a lifetime, not simply as long as the euphoric feelings last. But today we live in a throw-away society. If it feels good, we do it; if it is pleasant and convenient, we do it; if it involves sacrifice, extended effort, or pain, we avoid it. We shun the responsibilities of marriage or any of the unpleasant aspects of living with another person. Having some of the rough edges exposed is more than we can take, so we walk out and break the union. We act as though nothing is wrong; but in fact, we are flagrantly violating God's Word. In Malachi, God had a controversy with His people and refused to accept their weeping, groaning, or their offerings. When the people naively asked why God wasn't blessing them, the prophet spoke, "'For what reason?' Because the Lord has been a witness between you and the wife of your youth, against whom you have dealt

---

[24]   Matthew 19:5–6 (NKJV); see also Genesis 2:24

treacherously, though she is your companion and your wife by covenant. . . . 'For I hate divorce,' says the LORD, the God of Israel."[25] God looks upon a nation that is given over to divorce as a nation of sinners, and He will hold them accountable for their actions.

Can Christians divorce cavalierly and get away with it? They think they can. Often they sever the marriage ties and go on with life as though nothing significant has transpired. They regard the divorce as a disappointment or a sad failure at worst. "We'll get through this," they say, and everything seems to be all right, but they have willfully broken God's law. How are they going to reconcile that?

According to the Scripture, a believer can be free of another married partner in the case of adultery, or if the marriage partner deserts or makes living with them impossible.[26] According to the Bible, apart from that, divorce and remarriage for the Christian is not an option.

REMARRIAGE AFTER A DIVORCE

Is it wrong to remarry after a person is divorced? The Bible indicates that to marry a divorced person is to commit adultery, yet even many pastors nowadays are remarrying. Have we replaced God's laws about marriage and divorce with our society's laws? I am considering marriage to a divorced person who is a Christian but whose former wife is backslidden. They have been divorced for eight years. I wonder what would happen if someday his ex-wife gets right with God and how should it affect my marriage to her ex?

IN THIS CASE, we have a Christian woman who has backslidden. In such broken relationships, we must examine the circumstances. Did the wife walk out on the husband? In her backslidden condition did she disregard the Bible, desert her husband, and act as though she were an unbeliever? The Bible says, "But if the unbeliever departs, let him depart; a brother or a sister is not under bondage in such cases. But God has called us to peace."[27]

If she refused to honor her wedding vows, and the marriage was dissolved, then her husband is free to remarry. Don't concern yourself if she later comes back to the

---

25   Malachi 2:14, 16
26   See Matthew 19:9; 1 Corinthians 7:15
27   1 Corinthians 7:15 (NKJV)

Lord. She has made her decision, she has acted like an unbeliever, and if she repents and returns to the Lord, good for her; but it doesn't give her a claim on her husband again. She has severed that relationship by her former decisions.

DEPRESSION AND DIVORCE

I have three teenage children and my husband has been on medication for depression. He emotionally and verbally abuses our children on a daily basis. We have tried family counseling during his times of instability. I'm exhausted trying to make this marriage work. Do I have biblical grounds for divorce?

THE BIBLE WAS NOT WRITTEN by what we facetiously refer to as "Philadelphia lawyers," trying to cover every possible scenario or loophole. Generally, however, the pattern in Scripture is to uphold marriage and condemn divorce. Christians shouldn't be looking for legitimate ways to escape a marriage, but rather how we might better strengthen our marriages.

Nevertheless, in this case it's possible that your husband has some sort of neurological impairment that causes his erratic behavior and hostility. This is not uncommon. Nor are such personality changes uncommon among people who are taking strong medication for depression. Often the drugs used to combat the depression can actually cause a person to act contrary to his or her previous demeanor and personality.

You must have loved your husband when you married. How has the medication altered his behavior? Has he suffered an illness, injury, or an emotional or mental breakdown that has caused the new behavior patterns? If so, you must begin by treating physiological conditions, testing his blood-sugar level, for example, and the effects of the medication on his brain. You'll probably need to enlist the help of his doctor to encourage your husband to submit to these examinations by specialists.

If physiological and psychological help are ineffective and after much earnest prayer his condition does not improve, you cannot continue to place your children or yourself in danger. Your marriage may indeed be intolerable, and I'd regard this situation as coming under the "Pauline privilege," described in 1 Corinthians 7. In this passage the apostle Paul says, "But if the unbeliever departs, let him depart; a brother or sister is not under bondage in such cases. But God has called us to peace."[28]

---

[28]   1 Corinthians 7:15 (NKJV)

I call this "constructive desertion" because the offending spouse has made it impossible for his or her partner to continue the marriage.

STEPPARENTING CONFLICT

I recently married a wonderful man who has a different parenting style than I do. While I'm more of a listener and tend to reason with my child, he's more authoritative and unapproachable. We're having problems compromising our parenting styles in our efforts to raise my sixteen year-old daughter. Should I obey my heart or my husband?

I'M A GREAT BELIEVER in the truth in Isaiah's word, "Come now, and let us reason together, says the LORD . . ."[29]

You and your new husband must realize that, although sixteen-year-old girls can be absolute delights, they also have hormonal changes going on that make them appear to an average adult male as maddeningly irrational. You should let your husband know that he has never been a teenage girl going through puberty and beyond, and therefore he must, if possible, leave the discipline of the daughter to you. If she really gets obnoxious, the two of you should agree on what discipline is appropriate.

In a situation such as yours, a large amount of communication and understanding is imperative. Perhaps as you probe your husband's childhood, you may discover that he comes from a military family or that his parents were similarly authoritative. That doesn't solve your problem, but it does help to explain it.

I heard a story about a marine officer who was extremely strict and demanding of his children. One day, his seven-year-old son approached him, saluted, and said, "Sir, I have a request to make of the commanding officer."

"What is it, Private?" the marine replied with a twinkle in his eye.

"I request a transfer out of this chicken outfit," his boy deadpanned.

While your husband's style may not be that extreme, I'm concerned that his authoritative style with a teenage daughter that is not his own will lead to constant conflict. Your disagreement could create a deep family split or serious psychological damage to your daughter. If the two of you cannot talk this situation out and establish some reasonable boundaries, you should seek the help of a Christian family counselor who will help all three of you delineate a better plan for the conduct of each person in the family.

---

29   Isaiah 1:18

I will reiterate to you the response that I have made to many husbands and wives who have e-mailed questions concerning their marriage and sought our counsel at CBN: You made a voluntary decision to marry this person, so you must commit yourself to working through this problem.

OUR HOME LOOKS LIKE A PIGSTY!

I'm married to a wonderful, bright, hardworking woman. My only complaint is that our home always looks like a pigsty. Is there anything in the Bible about our responsibility to keep a clean house?

JOHN WESLEY, the founder of the Methodist church, said, "Cleanliness is next to godliness." While that is not a biblical rule, Wesley felt that external appearances reflected what was going on internally, in a person's heart.

In my opinion, an environment that looks like a pigsty can easily lead to thought patterns and conduct similar to that of pigs. Every successful business insists that offices, factories, or other work environments are kept clean and free of clutter. This is done for the mental attitude and emotional well-being of the employees as well as their safety. Similarly, better schools expect their students to maintain a neat desk and locker area. Why should we expect less at home?

Living in a trash-filled house weighs on the human spirit and can lead to depression. In contrast, bright, cheery, neat environments tend to lead to optimism and hope. The Medieval Church named "sloth" as one of the seven deadly sins. Failure to keep your living quarters clean and neat is an indication of sloth.

Proverbs 31 describes a woman worthy of great honor. Her husband is respected in the community. Her children rise up and call her blessed. Perhaps a reading of Proverbs 31 will open her eyes, or perhaps she has a vision problem and doesn't see the mess around her. Perhaps she was never taught housekeeping skills when she was a girl. Hire a really capable middle-aged housekeeper for a time to teach your wife and inspire her to cleanliness.

IS ONE MAN FOR ONE WOMAN REALISTIC?

Our culture has so changed today, perhaps more so in the area of marriage and relationships. How realistic is it to think that human beings can maintain monogamous relationships, for example, and remain married and faithful to the same person for life?

I DON'T KNOW about other human beings, but I have! My wife and I have been married for nearly a half-century, and we have been faithful to each other. My mother and father were married for more than fifty years; my wife's parents were also married for more than fifty years. Is it possible to remain faithful for that long? Absolutely!

When we were growing up, it was assumed that marriage was for keeps. If you wanted to date around, fine; that's your choice, but don't get married. Once you put the ring on your finger, your dating days were over. I recall that when I attended my first Democratic political convention in Chicago in 1952 where Adlai Stevenson was nominated to run for president, the principal concern about Stevenson was his divorce. Many questioned whether a divorced man could run for president of the United States, because he didn't meet the norm of American society!

Granted, public opinion has changed today, but God's standards have not. Fidelity in marriage is possible and remains God's norm. You must determine in your mind before getting married that it is a permanent relationship. Biblical safety valves exist that allow for separation in intolerable situations, but other than that, your marriage is meant to be "till death do you part."

The problem that we have created in the United States began in 1972 when state after state created legislation allowing what was called "no-fault divorce." Most states allowed couples to get divorced for almost any conceivable reason, without assessing any responsibility. Prior to that, divorces were granted only where there was clear evidence of adultery and infidelity, some horrible cruelty, or some unusual reason why the marriage should be dissolved. But now a person can get divorced on a whim, and our divorce rates have skyrocketed.

The pathology resulting from flagrant sexual infidelity and divorce and the damage in the lives of children and single moms is atrocious. For instance, single women with children comprise the fastest growing segment of the poor in America, nearly 27 percent. By our unwillingness to remain faithful to our marriage partners, we have created a monster that threatens to destroy the social fabric of our nation!

Of course it is possible to live in a monogamous relationship for life. But you'll never do so based on feelings alone; it takes a mutual commitment. One partner can destroy a marriage, but it takes two people committed to each other to make it work.

SANCTIFIED SPOUSES

What does it mean that the unbelieving partner is sanctified by the believer in an "unequally yoked" marriage?

THIS PHRASE is found in 1 Corinthians 7:14, in the apostle Paul's discussion of marriage and singleness. It's important to keep in mind that Paul was writing as a Jew, and his frame of reference was qualification to be part of the Jewish race. Paul is saying, in a similar manner, if a man or a woman who is a believer is married to an unbeliever, the children from that union will be born holy. In other words, they will be part of the family of God because of the believer's faith. They will be under the covenants of God. By virtue of the faith of one believing parent, they will have all the rights and privileges of those covenants. That is the sanctification to which Paul is referring. Paul did not mean that these children are going to be little saints, nor did he mean that they will be born again without making a personal commitment to Christ for themselves. Each one must make his or her own decision.

But they will not be given over to Satanism or paganism. One believing spouse has a spiritual claim on the children because of the believer's faith in the Lord. He will honor that and bring them into the family of God. However, each parent must continue to pray for his or her children, raise them according to the Word of God, teach them, guide them, and help them to live for God.

HOW MANY KIDS ARE ENOUGH?

My husband has approached me about having another baby. We have four children already and quite honestly, I don't think we can afford any more kids. I love our four children that God has blessed us with and feel that I'm too busy caring for our family of six. He keeps pressing me on this, saying that he's the head of the household and that I should do as he says. What are your thoughts on this matter?

GOD NEVER INTENDED for the husband to be a domineering tyrant, controlling his wife. Quite the contrary, he is to love and cherish her as his own body in the same way that Christ loved the church and gave Himself up for her.[30] It is

---

[30] See Ephesians 5:25, 28–29

anything but loving and cherishing to force a stressed-out mother of four to have another baby against her will.

In primitive societies, a man is considered virile and superior if he fathers a large number of children, and as strange as it seems in our culture, some men have fathered as many as sixty to one hundred children with multiple wives. Obviously, civilized society does not hold such reckless, indiscriminant reproduction to be a virtue.

In recent months, the case of Andrea Yates captured the attention of the world. This young mother drowned five of her children and pled temporary insanity as the cause. The jury disagreed with her and the judge sentenced her to life in prison. While few thinking people condoned the mother's atrocious acts, it became clear during her trial that her husband was also morally if not legally culpable. A domineering young man, he insisted on his wife having more children, even after her doctors warned that Andrea was not stable enough to do so.

Throughout Scripture, we are instructed to embrace wisdom and reason. Your husband's demands and your entertainment of them are no more wise or reasonable than those of that tragic young couple.

A POOR DECISION MAKER

How can you support your mate when he can't or won't make any decisions for himself? My husband does only what his parents or friends suggest. He gets defensive when I approach him about this problem.

THE TRUTH IS, you shouldn't have married him! But you did, so now you must find ways to encourage him to become the head of your family. Many times I've seen Type A women married to Type C men. The wife is energetic, entrepreneurial, and has all sorts of creativity, but the husband is a "follower," who won't accept his responsibilities to be the head of the household. There's only one way for a wife to deal with this type of situation—you must initiate circumstances that allow you to acknowledge your husband as head of the family. Although this may seem a bit deceitful, your motive is to help your husband do what is right.

Back your husband into a tough situation in which he must make a decision and take responsibility, or else the car is going to crash, the house will fall down, or some other calamity will befall you. Devise some situations in which he is forced to decide matters on his own. Most clever women—and I'm sure you are one—can maneuver and manipulate circumstances to make that happen! Then say, "My dear, it's your call. We're driving at eighty miles per hour and there's a wall down there. You can go to the left or to the right. Which way do you want to go?"

In addition, the Bible says, "For by wise counsel thou shalt make thy war: and in multitude of counselors there is safety."[31] Encourage your husband to surround himself with wise counselors who will help him make decisions. Before long he will grow more comfortable with his role as head of the household and approach the decision-making process with much more confidence.

One word of caution: It will do little good to have your husband making decisions apart from the influence of his family and friends if you second-guess his efforts. Do all you can to encourage and support him and help keep him on track. Even if he makes a bad decision occasionally, it is better than abdicating his role as the leader in your home.

CHILD CUSTODY BATTLES

I'm a single mother with full custody of my two young children. My eleven-year-old daughter wants to live with her father. I feel that my daughter is being coached by her father to request this move. My ex-husband has hired an attorney and filed for custody. I've just been laid off my job and can't afford a lawyer. What can I do to make sure she isn't taken from me and that I handle this appropriately as a Christian mother?

THE MATTER SHOULD BE HANDLED in a domestic relations court, which is not nearly as formal as many other trial procedures. It's not uncommon for a spouse or a parent to represent himself or herself in this courtroom. You may not be as skilled as a professional lawyer, but you have a legal right to state your case and question your daughter and former husband in the presence of a judge. If you have suspicions of foul play or other allegations, you can address them in court. You can also describe your relationship with your daughter and provide information regarding your treatment of her. The judge will expect you to show that you are raising your daughter in a healthy environment.

Before you engage your former spouse in court, you might ask yourself, "What's

31   Proverbs 24:6 (KJV)

happened to my relationship with my daughter? And how is her relationship with her father influencing these requests?"

Many young girls are quite attached to their fathers during their preteen years. Moreover, many divorced dads are slack on their daughters' discipline; some divorced dads—especially those who have limited visitation rights—turn into "Disney Dad," willing to do almost anything to keep their little girls happy and wanting to spend more time with them. Children pick up on this quickly, and if you are attempting to be the strict disciplinarian and your former spouse is passing out candy and ice cream, it isn't surprising that she would want to go with Dad.

But is living with her dad in the best interests of your daughter? Your daughter may be rebelling against your authority and assuming that if she can live with Daddy, she can get away with more. Obviously, an eleven-year-old girl hardly has the maturity to decide which dress to wear, let alone the wisdom to choose which parent with whom she should live. You have legal custody rights as her mother, and it would be highly unusual for a court to take your daughter away from you without just cause. By all means, explain to the judge what is going to be happening physically to your daughter—puberty, the beginning of menstruation, rapid changes in her body, selection of appropriate clothes, advice about dating, etc. These are mother/daughter issues. No father can, absent a miracle, deal adequately with your daughter's nurturing requirements at this stage in her life. You have the inside track. Don't give it up!

If possible, sit down with your daughter and explain the facts of your situation. Emphasize that you love her and want the best for her. It might also be helpful to seek the assistance of a godly pastor who can talk with her and listen to your daughter's side of the story. Simply having the opportunity to vent what's going on in her heart and mind may diffuse the situation.

Most importantly, be much in prayer that God will give you wisdom and grace in this situation; pray that God will give you favor with the judge or arbitrator who will hear your case.

OVERBEARING MOTHER

I am a mother of eight and married many years. I have an overbearing mother who constantly tells me how to raise my children and run my life. When I tell her how she frustrates me and hurts my feelings, she says I'm being disrespectful. We are continually fighting. What can I do to help her understand that I don't need her daily advice?

I HAD AN OVERBEARING mother-in-law (who is obviously no longer with us!) with whom I found myself embroiled in numerous arguments early in Dede's and my marriage. She'd often say things that I considered outrageous. At first I made the mistake of arguing with her.

Then one day, the Lord spoke to my heart and mind, and said, "Keep your mouth shut. No matter how outrageous her statements are, hold your tongue, smile, and say, 'Well, thank you for that.'"

My mother-in-law continued to make her presence known, but it was absolutely amazing what a peace and calm came about in our home, as I learned to hold my tongue.

Similarly, you must honor your mother, regardless of your age. At the same time, the Bible makes it clear that when we marry, we leave our father and mother, cleave to our spouse, and the two marriage partners become one flesh.[32] Your first priority now is your commitment to your husband. You are no longer under the control or dominion of your parents. Certainly, the duty to honor and respect your parents remains, but the way you and your husband handle the details of your family life is out from the purview of your mother or father. You have created a new, distinct family unit. You are to submit to your husband, and your husband is to love and cherish you as Christ loved the church.[33] Any meddling by parents or in-laws is unbiblical and wrong.

Recognize, however, that unless the Lord changes your mother's heart, you will not change her mind. Your best tact is to pray for her and leave her in the hands of the Lord.

In the meantime, listen politely to what she says, smile kindly, and then do whatever you and your husband think is best. Avoid any temptation to engage her in argumentative conversations. You will only aggravate the situation. The Scripture says, "A soft answer turns away wrath."[34]

KIDS FACING DIVORCE

I am fourteen years old and I'm pretty sure my parents are headed for a divorce. I constantly hear them fighting about money and other things. I'm scared about what my mom will do without my dad. I

---

[32] See Genesis 2:18
[33] See Ephesians 5
[34] Proverbs 15:1

know she loves him very much, but Dad never seems to be home anymore. Sometimes I feel like I'm the only reason they are staying together. Should I tell my parents that I'm afraid?

THIS IS A PAINFUL THING, and it is being experienced by more and more teenagers. Parents refuse to understand how divorce impacts their children negatively. Either that, or they consciously choose to ignore the facts. They are convinced they must seek their own happiness first, regardless of the impact their actions have on their children. We aired the results of a survey on CBN revealing that 75 percent of the fathers and mothers contemplating divorce said they understood the harm that divorce could do to their children, but that was not their primary consideration. They were determined to get divorced anyhow! This reflects an attitude of unmitigated selfishness on the part of these parents.

I think a teenager who knows his or her parents are considering divorce *should* express his or her heartfelt concerns to his or her parents. Try to arrange a family meeting attended by both parents, but if that's not possible speak to them individually. Regardless, tell them, "This is really affecting me. I'm very scared. I love you both, and I want you to work something out." Because they love you, they might decide to patch things up in their marriage.

Be sure to spend time in prayer prior to your conversation with them, asking God to soften their hearts and make them receptive to what you have to say.

ONCE A MOLESTER, ALWAYS A MOLESTER?

My husband molested my daughter. Since then he has given his life to the Lord. We have been advised to be careful with whom we share this information, because society is extremely unforgiving of this crime. My husband accepts the consequences involved and is careful not to be alone with children. Should we share this with family members and friends in the event that they might unwittingly leave him with a child?

DO NOT SHARE THIS SECRET WITH ANYONE. It is between you, your husband, and your daughter—and of course, it is between each of you and God.

Information such as this circulates broadly and would brand your husband permanently. In my opinion, the best thing you can do is to let it go and move on with your lives. Moreover, if his life has borne a consistent witness of the spiritual change within, I don't agree that you must keep him from having any contact with children. Has he attempted to molest other children, or has he exhibited other tendencies toward pedophilia since committing his life to Christ? If so, then of course you must take appropriate precautions. If your husband has ongoing, strong urges toward pedophilia, you should indeed help him to avoid the temptation by restricting his contact with children. If not, then you should consider him as a new man.

Society assumes "once an alcoholic, always an alcoholic"; similarly, a sex offender will always be a sex offender. This attitude does not take into account the saving and redeeming grace of Jesus Christ. It disregards the supernatural transformation that takes place when a person meets Jesus and doesn't allow for the fact that God can change a person's heart.

Writing to the Corinthians, the apostle Paul reminded them, "Do you not know that the unrighteous will not inherit the kingdom of God? Do not be deceived. Neither fornicators, nor idolaters, nor adulterers, nor homosexuals, nor sodomites, nor thieves, nor covetous, nor drunkards, nor revilers, nor extortioners will inherit the kingdom of God. And such were some of you. But you were washed, but you were sanctified, but you were justified in the name of the Lord Jesus and by the Spirit of our God."[35]

Paul readily admits that some of these people perpetrated heinous sins, but he states emphatically that they have been delivered from their sin by the redeeming grace of Christ. Notice they have not only been forgiven, they have been set free from sin's power in their lives. Paul says, they were washed, sanctified, and justified in the name of the Lord Jesus and by the Holy Spirit.

Admittedly, government programs can't do that for a person; hospitals and rehabilitation programs are only marginally helpful in curing someone of compulsive behaviors. But the blood of Jesus Christ cleanses us from all sin![36] Deep sin, dark sins, things that we don't even like to think about or discuss in polite company, are all washed away when a person repents and asks for God's supernatural help to live right.

Can a child molester be forgiven, cleansed, and changed? Absolutely!

If your husband has been accepted by God, and changed by His power, he ought to be able to enjoy normal fellowship with family and friends, confident that the Lord Jesus Christ has set him free from his past problem.

---

35   1 Corinthians 6:9–11 (NKJV)
36   1 John 1:7

CONTENTS

— CHAPTER 2 —

KIDS AND PARENTS

Scripture says that parents are to bring up our children in "the training and admonition of the Lord."[1] More than anything, this means that parents should teach and model the love of God to our children. Your children don't need you to be their friend, buddy, or playmate; others can fill those roles in their lives. Your children need you to be a mother or a father. Only you can be your child's parent.

More than ever before, kids need the time and attention of Mom and Dad. "I can't spend a large quantity of time with my child, but I spend *quality* time with him," is the misguided rationale many absentee parents use to convince themselves that they are not sacrificing their children at the altars of materialism, career, or pleasure. In fact, kids still spell love: T-I-M-E.

Your children are facing a raft of issues we never had to deal with growing up. Promiscuity among teenagers is rampant; premarital pregnancies are common; many public high schools now have day-care facilities in the school so children can bring their babies to school with them! Morality issues have always been with us, but today it is the teenager who chooses abstinence who is considered "weird" and in the minority rather than the other way around. The college student who has never been drunk or high on drugs is increasingly rare.

---

[1] Ephesians 6:4 (NKJV)

Violence and death are very real threats in many modern-day high schools. The shadow of Columbine haunts every classroom and library. How can we best prepare our children not simply to withstand the pressures of the secular world around them, but to be "salt and light" in it, to make a difference for God in future generations?

We can start by facing some tough questions ourselves. Some of these questions may make us uncomfortable, but if we are going to raise our children in the admonition of the Lord, we must address them and come to biblically based answers.

VIOLENCE IN SCHOOLS

It appears that violence in public schools will continue as long as morals, values, and respect for life are not taught. What can parents and students do to protect themselves? (We cannot afford private school, and I'm not convinced that is the answer anyway.)

WE MUST TRAIN OUR CHILDREN concerning the sanctity of life, yet it is very hard to do that in a culture where many of them may have had brothers or sisters who were aborted. These children know that a baby is a human being, and yet their mother has been able to kill their brother and sister—and they know it! By cheapening the value of life for the unborn, we have cheapened life for everyone. We must foster a culture of reverence for all human life.

We also must insist on discipline. Kids need discipline. Educational theories that purport that man is a noble savage and all you have to do is turn him loose and he will grow up in the right direction are just so much hogwash! They simply aren't true.

The Bible says, "Foolishness is bound up in the heart of a child; the rod of correction will drive it far from him."[2] We need discipline. We need to punish conduct that is wrong, and we need to restrain conduct that is harmful to others. Certainly, we must have searches for knives and guns to keep people from bringing dangerous weapons to school and from harming their fellow students. Moreover, we must insist that students treat each other with respect and not stigmatize those who are less popular than others. Some of the worst school shootings have been wrought by young people who felt that they had been ostracized by their classmates. As a way of fighting back, they went on a killing spree.

---

2   Proverbs 22:15 (NKJV)

A great deal needs to be done. Our PTAs should put pressure on our school boards to have an influence on teachers. The public school system is a very difficult thing to tame. In my opinion, we need legitimate competition, and a voucher system for those who are not satisfied with the job their local school is doing. This could raise some standards outside the public school system that public schools can emulate.

DAUGHTER WITH THE WRONG CROWD

I'm a single mom who works an eight-to-five job, and my daughter hangs around other teens who are not good for her. I have taken away privileges, grounded her, and tried every sort of punishment short of tying her to her bed! But I am not home after school, and she has lots of opportunity to get involved with the wrong crowd. What can I do?

GRIEVE FOR SINGLE MOTHERS. We don't know all the details here, but this story points up the terrible problem of divorce, of single motherhood outside of wedlock, and of those single parents who are forced by economic circumstances to work outside the home. In the process, they attempt to parent latchkey kids, children who come home after school to an empty house, unsupervised from the time school ends until the workday is over. The possibility for temptation is horrendous.

Perhaps your daughter is rebelling against the fact that she doesn't have a father at home. She somehow resents it and may feel that in some way you are responsible for her father's leaving.

The best thing you can do for this child is to talk with her frequently about her feelings, to love her unconditionally, and to pray with her often. If she won't hear you, then get her to a counselor who is skilled in dealing with matters of this nature. She may resent the fact that you are not home and that in many ways she has been deprived of both Mom and Dad's time, and this is the way that she shows it. She wants your love and attention. She also wants a father, but she doesn't have one, and she doesn't know what to do about it. She may be blaming God, blaming you, or blaming someone else, but the results are self-destructive behavior, and you must do something about it.

There are jobs that can be performed from home by working on-line or on the telephone. There are other jobs that begin at seven and end at three or three-thirty. Some companies have "flex" time to accommodate workers' schedules. Some allow a four-day workweek. Surely as important as your daughter is to you, you can find some work that says to her, "I'm here for you when you need me."

IN-LAWS AND OUTCASTS

My in-laws will not forgive one of my teenage sons for something he did years ago. I feel it is because he is a stepgrandchild. They've asked that I not bring my son around during holidays or other family get-togethers. Should I abide by their requests?

IT IS ALWAYS SAD when supposedly mature adults act like jerks. And that is precisely what your in-laws are doing! There is no excuse for treating a teenage boy as an outcast because of some remark he may have made, or some act he may have done when he was much younger.

First, pray that God will show your in-laws the error of their ways, and give them love for your son. Second, your husband must become involved in this dispute. His parents are acting foolishly, and as head of your household, he has an obligation to confront them and say, "Mom and Dad, you are offending my family and me by this attitude. Either you can change your tune, or kiss my family and me good-bye. We'll not be attending future family functions as long as you continue to harbor a grudge against my wife's son."

If your husband's parents insist on excluding one member of your family, you should all stay home for the holidays.

ADOPTIONS BY HOMOSEXUALS

A friend of mine who is a homosexual is considering adopting a child who has been physically abused. My friend feels that he can at least give this child a loving home, and he has asked my advice. I've been trying to lead my friend to Christ, so I want to be cautious with my answer. What do you suggest?

FOR ANY SINGLE MAN to assume that he can adopt a child and provide the nurture and love that a child needs is either extremely naive, uninformed, or foolish. Most single men must go to work, so that creates further childcare issues, all of which are difficult enough for single, working parents to juggle with their own children. But to take that responsibility for someone else's child while appearing noble on the surface is even more difficult.

Homosexuals, especially single homosexual men, should not be adopting children. To expose a youngster to a homosexual environment, particularly one in which a man welcomes his male lover or lovers, is not as emotionally healthy as having a child in a normal mother-father adoptive situation, despite surveys purporting that children raised in homosexual environments are "better adapted." Those same surveys admit that children raised in homosexual environments also have a much higher tendency toward becoming homosexuals themselves. Children should not be subjected to that type of influence.

Emphasize to your friend that you are concerned for him spiritually. Say something such as, "Look, Jesus loves you, and right now, we ought to concentrate on establishing your relationship with Him, before you take responsibility for a child."

If you know for sure that the child is currently in a physically abusive home, you should contact the appropriate local authorities. If you don't know how to go about it or where to start, contact the Salvation Army or your church leadership for assistance.

POSSIBLE CHILD ABUSE

I know someone who is being physically abused by a father. Should I report the situation to the police, knowing that the child will probably be taken from the home or the father prosecuted, thereby destroying the family?

How serious is the situation? Is the child simply being spanked? Is he a strong-willed child who needs extra doses of discipline? Or is he really being abused, beaten, or hurt? If he is being sexually abused or beaten, the child should be taken from the family. The mother should have interceded for him long before this point.

To report such circumstances to the authorities is not wrong. However, be careful that you are not overreacting. I know of an instance in which a good mother was reported for child abuse when she left her child asleep in a car seat in the driveway while she unloaded the groceries and took them into the kitchen. That's nonsense! There was an instance reported in the press of a little kid who slammed the door of the family car on his sibling's hand, and the father smacked him on the bottom a few times. The incident occurred in Canada, and the American father was arrested for child abuse. Such overreactions are ridiculous! Parents have a responsibility to discipline their children, and a certain amount of judicious corporal punishment is appropriate.

Be careful that what you report is something that is truly abusive and not simply normal parental discipline. If it is abuse, as I said, this must be reported to the proper authorities.

DANGERS OF INTERNET DATING

My eighteen-year-old sister met a man over the Internet and now wants to meet him for coffee. I offered to go with her, but she refused. I know she's an adult, but should I tell my parents of her plans so they can try to prevent this meeting?

Yes! Under no circumstances should a young woman go out for a private meeting with someone she meets on the Internet. You have no idea who you are dealing with. It may be a criminal with a long arrest record; it could be a sexual predator, or even someone with a history of mental illness. It is simply foolish to risk such a meeting. The whole idea of anonymous romances is risky and potentially dangerous.

Concerning whether to tell your parents: Yes, this is a matter of trust between you and your sister, but it is also a matter of her safety. Don't try to hide what you are doing, just tell your parents. Then tell your sister, "Look, I love you too much to sit by and watch you get hurt, so I've told Mom and Dad about this." Make sure she knows that you are breaking a confidence out of love for her, not an attempt to ruin her fun or for any other reason. Love covers.

ALCOHOLIC PARENTS

I'm a Christian teenager whose parents are both alcoholics. Because of the way they act at home, I don't like having friends over. I'm having trouble maintaining the few friendships I do have, because I don't want anyone to know about this situation. I feel lonely and ashamed about this. Can you offer any help?

This question breaks my heart every time I hear of this type of shame and embarrassment on the part of teenagers.

Despite their bravado and bombast, most teenagers embarrass quite easily.

They have a tough enough time dealing with their changing bodies, school, and social issues. It's appalling when the people to whom they should be able to look for wisdom and support are themselves in need of a major renovation in their lives.

A teenager tends to think that the problems that exist in his or her home are unique, that "our family" is the only one grappling with these issues. Consequently, they are ashamed to discuss their home life with anyone, especially their close friends.

We read in the Bible that Jesus made a show of the truth openly. Don't be afraid of the truth. Usually the best thing you can do in an embarrassing situation is to confront it head-on, bringing the truth out in the open, being willing to discuss it and deal with it. You might tell your friends, "I'm embarrassed about it, and I hate to admit it, but I think my parents have a serious drinking problem. I love my parents, but I'm worried about them."

You may be surprised to discover some of your friends have similar concerns about their parents. Not only will you find a source of comfort for yourself, but you may be an encouragement to your friends.

If you have Christian friends, enlist their help. Discreetly share the problem with them, and ask your friends to meet with you regularly to pray for your parents. If your friends are strong Christians, you might even bring them home to meet your mom and dad. Warn your friends in advance, however, about the sort of situation they may be walking into, and pray together ahead of time that God might open an opportunity for your friends to have a positive impact on your parents.

Many people have been set free from the bondage of alcohol, and they go on to enjoy vibrant, happy lives. Your faith and witness and that of your friends may be instrumental in influencing your parents in this direction.

Moreover, you needn't carry this burden by yourself. You didn't cause this problem, and you don't have to be ashamed of it. Enlist the help of your friends, and you may be surprised at their love and concern for you and your parents.

HAUNTING MEMORIES OF INCEST

As a young girl, I was a victim of incest. Although I've moved on in my life and now have a family of my own, I've never been able to shake the terrible memories or thoughts that somehow I was at fault. How can I find permanent freedom from my pain and self-blame?

INCEST IS FORBIDDEN in nearly every civilized culture. It is such a heinous sin, the Scripture says of those who practice it, "The land will vomit them out."[3]

A defenseless child is not guilty of the parent's actions. In my opinion, no young child is ever to blame for being the victim of incest or any sort of child molestation. It is not your fault that your father or brother molested you when you were too young to know better or to do anything about it.

The guilt feelings that plague you as an adult may emanate from the seething caldron of emotions, filled with a strange, mixed brew of feelings you endured as a child—feelings of happiness, perhaps, about the attention you received from the adult, yet feelings of horror at the way the attention was expressed. Maybe your abuser told you that he loved you or that you were special, or perhaps you interpreted his actions in that light. Now, guilt feelings resurface anytime your memory flashes back to some incestuous incident.

I recommend that you find a quiet place by yourself where you can read again those passages in the Bible that emphasize God's forgiveness. Remind yourself that your sins are forgiven, that your sins have been paid for by the blood of Jesus, and that they have been removed as far as the east is from the west. Sit before the Lord, and allow Him to cleanse your conscience and remind you that you are precious to Him. Let the love of God permeate your being and let Him take down the pictures in your mind that haunt you. From then on, anytime those thoughts return, take them immediately to the cross of Jesus. Leave that burden at the foot of the cross and walk away in freedom, thanking God for His forgiveness and His goodness. It is not God's plan for you to be continually weighed down by past sins, yours or those of your elders.

MUSIC MAYHEM

My parents won't let me listen to alternative music anymore. They like country music, much of which has the same subject matter as what they don't want me to hear. I don't think it's fair. What's the difference?

I'M A BIT PREJUDICED HERE, since I'm a Nashville kind of guy and enjoy a good bit of country music. But there's no accounting for musical tastes! Different styles and beats appeal to different people. Regardless of the style or the beat of a song, however, obscene music should not be listened to by anyone.

---

3   See Leviticus 18:28

Most parents are concerned about the increasing number of songs that glorify premarital sex, suicide, drugs, violence, rebellion, and other mayhem. Their concerns are justified. But it's not the style of music so much as the lyrical content that we need to be on our guard about. We don't need to fill our minds with smut and garbage.

Ask your parents to listen to some of the "alternative music" with you and seek the reasons for their dislike of it. You might persuade them, they might persuade you, or at a minimum you may begin to understand each other.

TEENAGE MUSIC MADNESS

My teenager's music is offensive to me. I know our music was not what my mom and dad liked, and I turned out okay, but modern music themes seem so destructive. Should I risk alienating my teen by demanding different music in our home, or just pray that this too will pass?

As an informed parent you should sit down with your teen and discuss the lyrics in the music your teen is listening to. Just because it is blasting at 120 decibels or is loud, clanging, banging, and raucous shouting, that is not necessarily reason to be upset. But if the lyrics are filled with various sexual innuendos, suggestions that your teenager use drugs, advice on how to commit suicide, or to murder his or her parents or to go burn down a town, or to shoot a policeman, or some other violent, inappropriate, or offensive actions, you must forbid your child to listen to that sort of material.

But listen to the music and hear what is being said. Don't just say, "I can't stand that garbage! Turn it off; if I hear that again in this house, I am going to throw you out!"

That is not the way to go. Engage your teenager in a reasonable conversation about the content of the music. Ask him or her, "What are they saying here? Does this glorify the Lord? Do you think this is something that Jesus is pleased with?"

Look for better alternatives and help your teenager discover them. It's better to light one candle than to curse the darkness. Find some Christian rock music with positive messages. A plethora of such music exists nowadays, performed by sincere Christian artists and skilled musicians who desire to glorify God and encourage kids with their music.

Keep in mind that music is a language of acceptance among teenagers, today as much as ever. The question is not always over the music so much as what the music represents to your teenager. But offer some creative alternatives and keep the lines of communication open. Ask his or her opinion concerning new artists or albums and use the music as a point of discussion to bring you closer together rather than drive you apart.

FILTHY LANGUAGE

My nephew and his ten-year-old son recently visited in our home. The ten-year-old used awful language while playing with our children and told them of his having sex with his "girlfriend." How should I approach my nephew about this terrible conduct of his son?

I'M HARDLY A PRUDE, but I confess to being astounded at the idea of a ten-year-old having sex, let alone using filthy language.

You must talk to your nephew and inform him of this situation. If he doesn't soon get control of his boy, he will one day be visiting him in prison. It is neither confrontational nor judgmental on your part to say that it is entirely inappropriate for a ten-year-old to be using filthy language and bragging about having sex with a little girl!

Perhaps your nephew is unaware of his son's language and conduct. Also, you must consider that little children often brag about things they haven't really experienced and sometimes use language they have heard adults using to make themselves sound older or more "worldly-wise."

Approach your nephew out of earshot of the children and say, "I have a problem and maybe you can help me with it. We're trying to set certain standards for our children. We love your son, but are you aware of the influence he is having on our kids? Here's what happened." Then tell the story and ask for your nephew's help. If he does not see the need to intervene in his son's conduct, you may have to suggest a moratorium on visits.

You should also emphasize to your children that such language and conduct is unacceptable in your family. Just because someone else chooses to wallow in dirt does not mean your family must lower your standards.

SHOULD I GIVE MY DAUGHTER THE PILL?

I'm a single parent of two teenage daughters. Some of their friends are experimenting with sex and are on birth control pills. I've tried to explain the consequences of premarital sex to my daughters, but I don't think they are "hearing." Should I go ahead and put them on the pill in the event that they are having sex, or should I take my chances that they will use good judgment?

YOU SHOULD NOT put your daughter on the pill for several reasons. First of all, birth control pills are not totally failsafe. A small percentage of women on the pill get pregnant despite using the contraceptive. Furthermore, the pill does not prevent any venereal diseases, which are rampant. With the looming threat of AIDS, herpes, and other incurable diseases contracted through sexual contact, it is biologically foolish to encourage sex outside marriage in any way.

More importantly, for you to give birth control pills to your daughter is tantamount to saying, "I know you are going to go against everything we believe, and that you will have sex outside of marriage. But to avoid pregnancy, I'll provide you with birth control pills." This is an insult to your daughter's intelligence and integrity.

It is both possible and preferable for teenagers to abstain from sex until marriage. Hundreds of thousands of teenagers have subscribed to a program sponsored by the Southern Baptists, known as True Love Waits. These young people make a firm commitment to abstain from all forms of sexual activity until marriage. Other churches have similar covenant ring ceremonies in which children who have made a commitment to sexual purity are given a special ring to be worn until marriage. Interestingly, incidences of premarital pregnancy among these groups have decreased markedly.

If you love your daughter, explain to her the beauty of love, sex, and procreation according to God's plan, and that sex outside of marriage is fornication and is condemned by God. Emphasize to her that her body is the temple of the Holy Spirit, and for her own good and for God's glory, she should care for it appropriately. Part of that care involves avoiding the physical, emotional, and spiritual dangers of premarital sex.

PORN UNDER THE MATTRESS

I'm a single mother of three boys and one girl. Recently, while making the bed of one of my teenage sons, I found a pornographic magazine under his mattress. I threw it out immediately, but I didn't confront him. How should I handle this situation?

CONFRONT HIM. Frankness is a good thing in communication, and you need to let him know right away that pornography is unacceptable in your home and that it is unhealthy in his life. Let your son know, "Look, God created sex as a beautiful part of a marriage relationship, but this is cheap and demeaning, it's tawdry, and it will hurt your relationships with women in the future, so you don't want this stuff in your mind."

The impact of pornography on teenage boys is devastating. Pornographic images lodge in the minds of young boys, warping their attitudes toward women and distorting their ideas about sexuality sometimes for a lifetime. Rather than seeing a woman as a potential wife, mother, and lifelong partner, pornography portrays a woman to a teenager as an object to be obsessed over, used carnally and brutally, and made a fetish for masturbation. The concepts of commitment, sharing, and the beauty of love and respect in male-female relations are ignored in pornography. Sexuality and only sexuality is the focus.

The best thing a parent can do to help prevent pornography's influence in your family is to talk about a biblical attitude toward sexuality. Talk about true love, commitment, and intimacy in marriage and let your children know that God has a better plan for them. Do not be embarrassed to discuss sex with your children when they are old enough to understand. Make sure your discussions are appropriate for your child's maturity level, and keep the information simple, straight-forward, and honest. Better to err on the side of giving too much information than too little.

DANCING WITH ADDICTION

I'm a teenager, and my mother doesn't know that I have been smoking and drinking with my friends after school, and she'd be very disappointed. I'm a Christian, and I'm sure this is just a phase I'm going through. I'm not addicted, but I feel a need to experience these things. Should I talk to my mother about this or just let it slide?

YOU NEED TO TALK to the Lord, not your mother! You are sinning against the Lord. You say you are a Christian, so surely you are aware that your body is the temple of the Holy Spirit. The Scripture says, "Do you not know that you are the temple of God and that the Spirit of God dwells in you? If anyone defiles the temple of God, God will destroy him. For the temple of God is holy, which temple you are."[4]

I ask you, as a Christian teenager, would you take a bucket of bright orange paint into your church sanctuary and splash it all over the walls?

No doubt, you'd respond, "Of course not! That would be vandalism and a sin against the Lord."

And you'd be right.

Yet your body is the temple of the Holy Spirit and is much more precious than a church building! And you are polluting the house of the Lord by smoking and drinking. Cigarettes cause lung cancer, emphysema, and other debilitating diseases. Similarly, alcohol destroys brain cells with every drink. You needn't experience these things or other destructive substances to know that they are not good for you.

Although you say you are not currently addicted, the potential for addiction increases with use. You never know when the last drink or the last puff will take a permanent hold on you and subsequently destroy your life.

Understand, you are not sinning against your mother. You are sinning against the Lord. You should repent and seek His forgiveness, asking Him for His power to live free of these habits. If you choose to share this with your mother or enlist her support in your struggle to overcome the effects of these substances or the pressure exerted by your peers to become involved in destructive activities, that's up to you. Your body is the temple of the Lord, and it's time you start taking better care of His property!

BIRTH MOTHER OR ADOPTION?

Is it better for an unwed mother to raise her child herself (with help from her parents, friends, or church) or to give the child up for adoption to a Christian couple?

THIS DEPENDS on the mother herself. She might be brokenhearted to give up her baby. But is she prepared to raise the child? Many babies are born to unwed teenage mothers. The mothers are not emotionally capable of raising children. They don't have the financial support. They are mortgaging their future by taking on a child at that early age without the support of a husband. In that situation, it

---

4   1 Corinthians 3:16–17 (NKJV)

would be far better to let a mature, Christian couple raise the child and let the mother get on with life and maybe be joined in a marriage in which she can have other children with the husband she loves.

QUESTIONS CHILDREN ASK

In addition to many hundreds of questions that we have received from adults, I have received some fascinating questions over the months from children . . . some as young as eight or nine years old . . . some in their teens. I am going to dedicate this section to some representative questions from this group with relatively brief answers. It is amazing how perceptive children are and the questions that they ask. These young people understand about God, and they understand about the Bible with a great deal more maturity than most adults give them credit.

WHAT HAPPENED TO ADAM AND EVE?

Patrick, age nine, inquires . . . **Where were Adam and Eve buried? Do they have tombstones? Did they go to heaven?**

I FRANKLY DON'T KNOW where Adam and Eve were buried or whether they were buried. There is a possibility that, because of their intimate relation with God Almighty, they were taken to be with Him in heaven. They were still alive, according to my calculation, when Noah came on the scene. So whatever burial place they may have had was undoubtedly covered by the great flood that took place at the time of Noah.

COMMUNING WITH GOD, MAKING MIRACLES

Lindsey, age nine, writes . . . **Can you talk to the Lord besides in prayer? I also want to know how you and God combined make a miracle. Thank you! I love** *The 700 Club.*

I BELIEVE that it is possible to talk to the Lord from our heart. That, of course, is really a prayer, but our heart and our spirit can be in communion with the Lord all day long without making a formal prayer. In other words, it's not necessary to sit or to stand or to lie down and recite certain words or to say certain words. The Bible says that "deep calls unto deep,"[5] and so the depths of our spirit can commune with God.

It is amazing, though, that God allows people like you and me to participate with Him in "making a miracle." We have been allowed to be His representatives and His agents on earth. He can do miracles without any of our help, but somehow, in His great wisdom, He has allowed human beings just like us to participate with Him in miraculous things.

NO LOVE INTEREST . . . I JUST WANT TO BE FRIENDS

I am only ten years old. I'm having a hard time with my friend's brother. You see, I told him I thought he was cute and had a great personality, and I think he's taking it too seriously. He's sitting next to me in class, and every once in a while he will try to scoot closer to me. I'm starting to regret I ever told him I liked him. He's making me feel uncomfortable. What should I do?

WELL, MY FEELING IS THAT, at your age, you shouldn't be getting serious with any boy. I am sure that if that friend's brother has any sense and he's ten years old as well, he will realize that you just wanted to be friends. You are both much too young to be doing anything more serious, and I think the sooner that you could stop any serious activity, the better.

You might just tell him that although you want to be friends with him as you are with his sister, nevertheless you never intended anything serious. At your age, this shouldn't hurt his feelings, and if it does, he'll have to get used to the fact that this isn't the last time that he will experience rejection from a member of the opposite sex until such time as he finds the one who is right for him.

Be frank. Don't try to hide things. But tell him how you feel, honestly and openly, and I believe that at his age he will receive it.

EARTH TO HEAVEN . . . WHY BOTHER? WHY NOT STAY HERE?

I am fourteen years old and I heard Jack Van Impe say that after Jesus comes again and a thousand years have passed, there will be a new and perfect earth. My question is, if there will be a new and perfect

---

5   Psalm 42:7 (NKJV)

earth, then why take everyone to heaven when we could stay here on earth?

THAT'S A VERY GOOD QUESTION. What we have to understand is that we are not going to have a perfect earth. We will have an earth that is at peace under the rule of Jesus. But in that earth, human beings will still be human and people will still grow old and die. There will still be some of the suffering and pain that we have in this present earth. It's only after we become spiritual beings and spend eternity with God as spiritual beings that we will know the full bliss of heaven.

The thousand years is merely a transition period from the meanness and the hatred and the suffering and the death of this particular age until we come to the time when we are citizens of heaven and the former things have passed away and God has made everything new. You see, God intends to create a new heaven and a new earth where there will only be righteousness. The devil will not be there. The demons will not be there. And people who hate, kill, and destroy will not be there. This is the kind of thing that we long for.

The thousand-year period which is called "the millennium," which means a thousand years, will only be a transition. So we don't want to live in the transition . . . we want to live in the final destination.

HOW CAN I SHOUT IT FROM THE HOUSETOPS?

I am eleven years old and I am in fifth grade. I like to tell others about Jesus Christ, but in my school we're not allowed to talk about Christianity. How can I tell others about Jesus Christ without getting in trouble?

I WANT TO TELL YOU that whether it's the fifth grade, the seventh grade, the tenth grade, or any other grade in school, you do not lose your rights of citizenship merely because you're attending classes. An organization that I helped found some years ago, The National Legal Foundation, brought a lawsuit in Omaha, Nebraska, to insist that students had a right to have Bible study and Bible clubs in the school premises after school hours. That case, which was called *Mergens vs. West Side School District*, was ultimately argued at the Supreme

Court by Jay Sekulow, who is the General Counsel of a new organization I started called The American Center for Law and Justice. Jay won that case. In a seven-to-two decision, the Supreme Court said that students have a constitutional right to discuss their faith and to evangelize among their fellow students while they are at school. If your school is not permitting you to do that, it is violating a decision of the Supreme Court. I dare say that the American Center for Law and Justice would be delighted to send a demand letter to your school with threat of a lawsuit to make sure that your school obeys the ruling of the Supreme Court.

CAN SOLDIERS BE FORGIVEN FOR KILLING?

My name is Alec. I am thirteen, and I want to know if you can be forgiven for killing another human being? I ask this question because I have wanted to be a U.S. Marine since I was eight years old. Since the terrorist attacks on this great nation, it made me think about it more.

WELL, ALEC, I was a lieutenant in the marines and I served in Korea. The Bible says that "he that wields the sword does not do so in vain, but he is a minister of God to execute judgment on evildoers."[6] I don't like war any more than any other thinking person. But the time does come when free people must defend their freedom and rescue those who are oppressed from wicked men who would enslave them and destroy them.

All countries have a right of self-defense. If they are attacked, it is perfectly appropriate to go to war against the attacker. The marines have played a very valiant role in many significant battles in which the United States has been involved. I would tell you that you do not have to feel ashamed if you wish to join the marines; nor, if you go into battle in a just war, of the fact that you may have to wound or even kill another human being who happens to be an enemy soldier coming against you.

---

[6] Romans 13:4

IS SATAN THE ONLY ONE WHO PUNISHES ME?

I am twelve years old and I would like to know whether God punishes us or not, or is it always Satan?

THE ANSWER IS VERY SIMPLY that God indeed punishes people for doing wrong. He brings about things in their lives that they don't like, and the ultimate punishment is to be separated from Him forever in a place that is known as hell, which I've discussed at length in another chapter in this book. Satan is not allowed to punish us, but he certainly does attempt to hurt us in various ways. That is not what you would call punishment, but an attack of a vicious enemy. God is like a loving Father, and the Bible says that everyone has an earthly father who disciplines his children.[7] The Bible also says that if we do not have discipline from God, then we aren't legitimate children but are illegitimate.[8] So everyone who is loved by God will be disciplined by Him so that he or she can learn a much more righteous, holy life and will be prepared by God to spend eternity with Him in heaven. If God loves you, He will discipline you. It's only those who have no part in heaven who perhaps are left alone by God.

It is important to realize that some of God's laws carry with them their own punishment. For example, there is a physical law called the law of gravity. If a person decides to jump from a ten-story building, he will have violated the law of gravity and he will crash to the ground, either killing or maiming himself. God has laws about sexual purity. We are seeing an epidemic today of sexually transmitted diseases. God is not punishing people for committing immoral acts. He has built into the universe the punishment for that conduct. In America, at least 60 million people are feeling the consequences of that built-in law.

The reverse is probably true: Those who are loved by God will be attacked by Satan, and those who have given themselves to Satan may at least for a time be left alone until such time as they are ultimately taken to hell.

FAMILY STRESS

I'm an eighteen-year-old teen who is about to go off to college. I haven't always done the right thing in my life, but I would appreciate your advice. Stress from family-related problems have been a burden in

---

7   Hebrews 12:9
8   Hebrews 12:8

my life for a few years. Everything about my father gives me stress and problems with my wrist. I love my father, but he can't maintain a job and support the family. My mother works at night, six days a week, nine hours a day. Please pray or give me advice about what to do.

AT THIS STAGE IN YOUR LIFE, there is not a great deal that I can tell you. You owe your mother and your father the honor that is to be accorded your parents. You only have one father on earth, and you only have one mother on earth. Therefore, you owe them honor.

If being around your father causes you stress, then perhaps the wise thing would be to stay out of his way when he is feeling out of sorts, and do what you can to make life easier for him and to pray for him.

Being eighteen, you are almost at the age when you can be emancipated from the family responsibilities that you have. You are speaking of going off to college. Who is going to pay the bills to send you to college? If you are able to pay the bills yourself, then college might be a welcome relief from the pressures of your family.

I would examine your own heart to see if there is something that you are doing that is contributing to the stress. You don't have to be a burden to your parents, but look back and ask yourself what you may have done. Did you get in trouble in school? Have you been in trouble with the law? Have you been experimenting with alcohol and drugs? Have you had some sexual relation that has caused your parents grief? In short, it may be you that is causing your father stress instead of him causing you stress.

Frankly, I don't have enough details from your situation to give you a more comprehensive answer.

VALUING A RELATIONSHIP WITH GOD VERSUS FAMILY

My parents are divorced and my father was remarried. I am ten years old and my dad and my sister and brother aren't Christians. They don't go to church, and the music they listen to is just gross. I tried to tell them about God, but they just don't want to listen. What should I do?

I THINK THAT YOU ARE VERY WISE and mature for your years. Somewhere along the way, someone, perhaps your mother, has introduced you to Jesus Christ, and there is something growing in your life which is very precious.

As I read back in the Bible, I see the story of two brothers. One was named Jacob. The other was named Esau. Although Jacob had a deceitful spirit in some of the things that he did, nevertheless he valued the relationship with God very highly. His brother, Esau, on the other hand, was concerned about his immediate physical needs. He was willing to trade his birthright for a bowl of stew. In your case, it seems that you are valuing the things of God highly, and your dad, brother, and sister are willing to settle for a bowl of not-too-good stew. You have chosen the better part. This means that you should pray for your dad and your brother and sister, but you need to get on with your life. You know the truth, so don't let their conduct pull you down. God has a special calling on your life. The good news is that at ten years old, you've heard it! Don't walk away from it, but learn more of Him and let your heavenly Father take the place more and more of your earthly father who has apparently abandoned his true responsibilities for you.

MY FRIEND IS SUICIDAL

I am thirteen years old and I have a question. My friend Rachel is suicidal and has tried to overdose herself multiple times. I've tried to be compassionate to her, but she seems to push me away and she refuses to tell me why she tries to do such a thing. I have prayed and prayed and prayed for her, and she said once she felt a little better. What should I do next?

IN MY OPINION, the care of a suicidal teenager is frankly beyond the skill set of another thirteen-year-old teenager. Your friend Rachel obviously needs professional help.

Why is she suicidal? There must have been something in her background that brought this on. There's a chapter in this book about depression and suicide to which I would refer you.

But what is causing the problem for this girl? Is it something medical? Is it something that is in her genes? Is it something related to abuse at home? Was she sexually molested by her father or perhaps a brother, uncle, or some other male relative? Has she been beaten? Has something happened in her life where she hates herself because of the way she lived? To probe these things is the job of a skilled psychiatrist, and I believe it's important that Rachel's parents understand what she is going through if they will listen to you. If not, there may well be a compassionate guidance counselor in the school where you go, and that counselor could put his or her arm around Rachel and try to help her through this problem. It is obvious that she is not willing to confide in you and to tell you the real depths of what she is feeling. But clearly she needs medical help, and she needs skilled psychiatric help.

Indeed, continue to pray for her. God will answer your prayer. He may do it supernaturally, or He may send along some skilled practitioner of medicine to be the answer to your prayer.

WITNESSING TO MY FRIEND . . . A JEHOVAH'S WITNESS

I am twelve years and a born-again Christian since I was seven years old. My best friend, Allie, is a Jehovah's Witness, and when I talk to her about Christianity she tells me, "Well, I am a Christian." How should I respond and reach her in a way that the Lord expects me to?

REGRETTABLY, the Jehovah's Witnesses are a cult. They do not believe that Jesus Christ is the Son of God but say that He is "a God." They were told to preach the kingdom and their work was supposed to bring in the end of the world at a particular time in history. When that time came and the end of the world did not take place, they then shifted their theology to something else and said what they were really talking about was an event that took place in heaven. The Jehovah's Witnesses are under a strong delusion.

If you want to talk to her about her faith, you must get her to explain to you what the Bible says. Don't let her use "proof-texts" that are taken out of context. The best way to deal with a Jehovah's Witness is to use the verses before and after their so-called proof-text to show them that what they believe and hold as truth is not supported by the Bible. If you are twelve years old, I am not sure that you have the Bible skills to carry this off.

Above anything, your radiant faith and your love for your friend and your desire to see her come to Jesus will have more of an impact than any amount of theological discussion that you could enter into. More important than anything else is to continually remind her that you love her, that Jesus loves her, and that Jesus is the Son of God . . . that He is the unique Son of God, and He died for her and rose again from the dead. If she will receive Him, He will enter into her life.

Beyond that, I think those who hold to cultish beliefs are under satanic delusion. You need, in your own prayer, to bind Satan and command him to loose your friend Allie, from the hold he has on her. Continue to pray and continue to expect her to come to full faith in the Lord Jesus Christ.

CHURCH ATTENDANCE VERSUS OBEYING MY PARENTS

I'm fifteen years old and I have been a Christian for a few years now. My parents aren't Christians. They don't agree with me getting into Christianity. I really want to go to church, but if I do, I will be going against my parents' wishes. Should I go to church and go against my parents, or just not go at all? Thanks.

THIS IS AN EXTREMELY DIFFICULT PROBLEM for a fifteen-year-old. You obviously don't want to defy your parents, but at the same time you don't want to defy the Lord who commands you "not to forsake the assembling of yourselves together."[9]

It could be that there are youth groups in your church or Bible studies that take place outside your church or meetings of Christian people at your school. If you are attending, for example, a Young Life meeting, your parents might not be aware exactly of what you are doing and might not be able to stop you. On the other hand, I find it very hard to believe that any parent in the United States of America would actually forbid his or her child from going to church on Sunday.

The Lord will show you how to proceed and to give you wisdom. The most important thing is don't give up your faith. It is hard to be a Christian in today's world, and it's much harder when your parents are trying to keep you from doing what you know is right and which is what God wants you to do.

I would say this: Parents are entitled to honor. However, if parents try to force their children to do something against what the children know is right in God's sight, then, in that instance, the parents have given up the rights and privileges that they enjoy as parents. I don't believe, therefore, you are violating the law of God if you do not accept what your parents say in regard to seeking the Lord Jesus and living for Him. However, if you pray, or if you read the Bible, or if you worship God in your own heart by yourself or with a few of your Christian friends, then you will be strengthening yourself and growing in the Spirit. You can also attend church by watching services on television. You can listen to radio broadcasts. You can avail yourself of video recordings, DVDs, audiocassettes, etc., so that you can get Christian instruction and fellowship without attending a formal church, if that leads to a major confrontation with your parents, which you probably want to avoid.

---

[9]   See Hebrews 10:25

MY FRIEND BAD-MOUTHED ME

I am twelve years old. There's a girl at my church and we used to be friends, but we aren't anymore because she said some awful things about me. I've given her the cold shoulder when she's tried to talk to me and I know it's wrong. Should I confront her and tell her why I haven't talked to her, or should I leave it alone?

JESUS SAID, "When you stand praying, if you have aught against any, forgive that your heavenly Father might forgive you."[10] If you want to walk in miracle power and in the forgiveness of God, it is vitally important that you do not hold any grudges against someone else.

Teenagers can be very, very cruel. They can say things that hurt and cut and wound, and yet later they're either sorry that they said these things or they dismiss them as not being important. I think the best procedure that you can follow in this case is to go to the individual who has hurt you or said terrible things about you, and tell her the problem. Tell her that you're a Christian and that you forgive her and hope you can love each other in the Lord.

I believe that if she indeed is trying to be a Christian, the two of you may find this is a way of overcoming a barrier. Instead of being enemies, you will wind up being closer friends than you've ever been. Whatever you do, you shouldn't "leave it alone." That bitterness will hurt you and wound her. This is not the way that we want to live with each other as teenagers or with each other when we become adults.

OVERWEIGHT AND NOT WANTING TO GO TO SCHOOL

I'm sixteen years old, and for some reason I'm scared to go to school. No one is bothering me. I think it's because of my weight. I'm overweight and insecure. I just need courage to go to school.

THERE IS A SO-CALLED PHOBIA or fear that is called agoraphobia, which is a fear of going out among people. You don't have agoraphobia now, but if you continue the conduct in which you're engaging, it will soon grip your life to such a degree that you will be afraid to go out of the house.

I think first of all you need to go to school because that's the road to your future.

---

10 See Mark 11:25 (KJV)

It probably is also a matter of obeying the law. I would recommend strongly that you get a book such as Bill Phillips's *Body for Life* and start the exercise-diet program that he lays out in the book. Get to a gym, and begin working out. If you can't afford or find a gym, start working out at home and walking and running. If you do sit-ups, push-ups, and some kind of running or fast walking, before long you will find that you are better adapted to the world around you, that your muscles are growing instead of flab, and that you feel more confident about yourself.

It may be that you need to knock off a lot of weight, fifty or sixty pounds, and that's going to take discipline. But every time you step on the scales and find that your weight has dropped, and you look at what used to be pockets of fat and what has now become muscle, you will begin to feel good about yourself and won't be afraid to go out to join the other kids. You want courage. The Lord will give you courage. However, in this case, action is going to be the foundation for your courage.

I'M THE PUNCHING BAG FOR MY MOTHER AND BIG BROTHER

I've been the "punching bag" of my mother and my big brother since I was a kid. It's only now that I'm eighteen years old that I've come to realize the negative effects of that tragedy. I feel nothing more for them than hatred. I feel I'm not capable of loving anyone because of this. How can I forgive them? I feel I can't move on. Every time they beat me up, I curse them. I always tell myself that they will receive their "karma." Please, I really need peace of mind and heart.

THIS IS A TRAGEDY, and it's hard for me to conceive of a mother who would join with an older brother to punch and beat up a younger boy. I've heard of abusive fathers, but seldom a mother who would do this to her own child. There must be something more in this story than that of which I'm aware. Since you've asked for peace of mind, here's the suggestion.

First of all, as much as you hate it, you must forgive them so that God will forgive you and work in your life. The second thing you must do is to ask God to bless them. Now you feel hatred, but your prayer must be for their blessing. The Bible says to "bless those who spitefully use you and persecute you."[11] It certainly is easy

---

[11] Matthew 5:44 (NKJV)

enough to be nice to those who are nice to us, but it takes the supernatural love of Jesus Christ to pay back evil with good.

The Bible says, "Don't return evil for evil, but return evil with good."[12] If somebody does something to you and hits you on one cheek, then you are to turn the other cheek. Love will overcome whatever it is that is going on in your mother and brother's life. If you curse them and wish them to receive some horrible tragedy in another life, you are actually damaging yourself. You have got to let this go, however difficult the treatment you have received. If you truly love them and begin to pray for them, you may notice a dramatic change in their attitude toward you.

The good news is that you have now reached eighteen years old and, in the eyes of the law, you are considered an adult. You can leave home if it's intolerable. You can go out and set up a household all by yourself if that's what you want to do. But whatever you do, remember that this woman is your mother, and you are to "honor your mother and father that your days might be long on this earth."[13]

Finally, it's clear from what you have written that you have never received Jesus Christ in your life. If you want peace of mind and of heart, you start by surrendering the old you . . . the you that has been hurt, the you that has been abused, the you that is full of hatred, the you that is full of sin. Surrender it to the Lord and ask Him to be your Savior and the Lord of your life. Out of that surrender will come great peace. When people begin to despitefully use you, remember that they beat up Jesus to such a degree that He didn't even look human. Having beaten Him to a virtual pulp, they then hung Him on a cross and killed Him. When someone is doing something to you, identify with Jesus and then allow Jesus to receive the pain that is being aimed at you. Instead of giving back pain, suffering, and curses, give back blessing and praise to God. If you have this new attitude, you suddenly become superior spiritually to your mother and your big brother. You will not be the "little brother;" you will be the one who is in charge, because you will now have spiritual power that they can't touch. In the process, they may well be asking you, "Where did your change come from, and how can we get what you've got?"

PANIC ATTACKS AND FEAR

I will be fifteen years old October 27. I have a panic disorder which means I have really bad panic attacks. I'm currently not in school

---

12 See 1 Thessalonians 5:15
13 See Exodus 20:12

because of them. They control my life. I've finally found out that they don't have to . . . God can. I read the "Knowing God's Will, Freedom from Fear" that you have on this Web site and started crying because I know there is hope. I've been a Christian all of my life. My dad used to be a pastor, but I didn't get saved until a couple of years ago. I want you pray for me so that I will have freedom from fear. I want to be free from this, and I know with God anything is possible.

THERE IS A DISCUSSION of a spirit of fear in another chapter in this book. You need to do several things that are very important. First of all, you are to take your fears and spell them out in great detail. Describe them and what they do to you, and then take them to the cross of Jesus Christ. Tell Him that you are bringing those fears and that you're laying them at His feet. The next thing you do is to ask Him to come into your life, be your Savior, and be the Lord of your life. Ask Jesus to fill you with His love to such a degree that fear will have no hold over you. The Bible says, "Perfect love casts out fear because fear has torment."[14] So as the love of Jesus fills your life, that love will crowd out the fear.

Beyond that, you need to address the fears. Most fears that you are experiencing are irrational. They don't have any basis in fact. No one is really trying to "get" you, but you are imagining it. Therefore, you need to rebuke this spirit of fear that has come upon you. Recognize that it comes from Satan, tell it that you will not allow it to have any part of your life again, and command it to leave you from this moment on. Then ask Jesus to cover you with His blood, with His sacrifice, with His atoning death, and from that moment on you will be free. Don't receive fear again, but let the love of Christ fill you to such a degree that there is no room for fear any longer.

OLD ENOUGH TO DATE?

Is it okay for a thirteen-year-old boy to date? My mom says that I can't. What do you think?

I DO NOT HAVE ANY TROUBLE with a thirteen-year-old dating; however, age thirteen is just too young to begin any kind of serious romantic involvement. I

---

[14] 1 John 4:18

also think for young people age thirteen to begin to pair off is an invitation to more serious action because their hormones might get the best of them and lead to sexual problems that they don't need.

The best solution for someone thirteen, fourteen, or fifteen is to begin going out in a group. If you want to call it "dating," that's fine, but it should be dates with three or four couples so that you are all out having a good time together and not put in a position where there has to be ever more intimate romance in order to allow the date to be a success.

UNEQUALLY YOKED

I was seeing a guy from my school, and I realized it wasn't right because he wasn't a Christian. I told him it was over, but he wants to know why I don't like him anymore, and I'm not sure what to say because he doesn't understand anything about Christians or how I believe. What should I tell him?

I THINK YOU SHOULD REFER to 2 Corinthians 6:15, which asks, "What fellowship has Christ with Belial?" as well as the previous verse which directs us, "Do not be unequally yoked together with unbelievers." Take this to him and tell him that you have given your heart to Jesus Christ, you are a born-again Christian, and, as such, you don't think it's appropriate to get involved romantically with someone who is not a Christian.

At that point, this young man may very well ask you what it means to be born again. With this opportunity, you could take him to the Bible to the place referred to as the Roman Road and show him how "all have sinned and fall short of the glory of God."[15] Show him how Jesus has been offered as the sacrifice for sin and that except a person be born again, he can't enter the kingdom of heaven. Jesus died on the cross to pay the price for our sins, and if anyone will receive Him, he can have everlasting life. Ask this young man if he would like to pray with you to receive Jesus, and it may be that he would. At that time, lead him in the sinner's prayer. Pray him through to meet the Lord, and you have introduced him to Jesus. Begin to help him understand the Bible. Pray about him and encourage him to walk in the Christian life.

After that, it's not a question of Christian/non-Christian, but a question of a

---

[15] Romans 3:23

young Christian man and a young Christian woman. What do you want to do beyond that? If you're not attracted to him as a potential boyfriend, then tell him, "I like you in the Lord, but I'm not ready for any type of romantic involvement with you." I think frankness is a very important thing. You run the risk of hurting somebody's feelings, but you run a worse risk if you lead them on into someplace where you are not prepared to go.

I believe that in a case like this, frankness is important, and it provides you a great opportunity to see a soul won to the kingdom of God.

TWINS ON OPPOSITE SIDES OF THE CROSS

My twin brother and I have never been very close. We were raised in a good home but were not very religious, though we were baptized. Then our father died when we were sixteen. At eighteen I moved out. My brother is now being abusive to my mother and friends, and I know he's dealing with abandonment and maturity issues that I dealt with two years ago. I've recognized Jesus Christ as my Savior. How do I reach out and heal my brother?

I THINK THE MOST IMPORTANT THING you could do for your brother is to introduce him to Jesus so that he will get to know the Lord. He is dealing with his mother, his friends, the abandonment, and other issues in a totally secular fashion. He has been hurt and he doesn't know how to deal with what has been done to him. Only when he understands and accepts the love of Jesus Christ in his life will he be able to have a mature understanding of what has happened so far and what will be happening in the future.

The greatest help you can give him is to tell him how to find the Lord. Show him that we are all sinners. Show him that Jesus died for sinners. Show him that Jesus is standing at the door of his heart and knocking and wants to be let in. And then ask him if he would like to invite Jesus into his heart. If he says yes, pray the sinner's prayer with him right then. When you are both finished, you put your hand on his shoulder or head and pray for him that he might be filled with God's power and set free from all of those things that have hurt him in the past. Beyond that, help him read the Bible and understand how much God loves him. That's how you can heal him.

I DON'T LIKE MY BODY

I am thirteen and feel so bad about my body. I know I shouldn't, and I know God made me perfect, but I can't help feel this way. My dad left us, and my mom is struggling so much just to keep the apartment we have. My dad came to me. Now he expects me to feel so tight with him, even though he was never there for me. I'm involved in my church, but I still feel lonely because everyone I know is never there. I know God is always here, but again I can't help but feel this way. Help!

My HEART GOES OUT TO TEENAGERS who are going through a very difficult period in their life. They are entering into puberty. Their bodies are changing. In the case of young women, they are developing what are called secondary sex characteristics which are essentially preparing them for motherhood. This means they are beginning menstruation, they are beginning to develop breasts, and experiencing other major changes in their bodies.

As in this case, this young girl verbalizes it as "I feel sooooo bad about my body." What is happening to you is not something you should feel badly about, but praise God about. It's going to prepare you one day to be a wife and a mother.

However, coupled with the normal confusion that comes upon a teenager as to his or her identity, you are faced with a problem because your father walked out on you. Interestingly enough, it is fathers who seem to play the most important role in the social development of daughters. Without the father being there, there is no way that a young lady can totally adapt to the situation around her. She feels lonely and as if no one is ever there for her. God is there for you. Jesus Christ is there for you. He will be the Father of the fatherless, and He will be the Husband of the widow. God will come and make Himself real in your life, and you will know somebody who loves you and cares about you. You have received Jesus as your Savior, and I want you to know that He is your protector. Talk to Him . . . talk to Him every day. Tell Him the deep longings of your heart. He knows everything you think anyhow, so why not let Him know your problems. Share with Him what's going on inside you, and let Him reach out to you in comfort and love.

Beyond that, get together with Christian people in your church, your school, and other associations available to you, and let them talk to you, help you, and encourage you. Find someone you can trust and confide in. Perhaps it's another woman, an older girl, or someone who knows the Lord to whom you can go and just talk. There are people who will love you and bless you and encourage you.

My prayer is that you will know the answer to the cry of your heart.

These questions are merely a small example of the e-mails that we receive from young people and teenagers. You can be thrilled with their maturity, but you can also sense the anguish of their hearts in dealing with life's problems, many of which are caused by abusive, indifferent, or hostile parents. As I read these questions, I am terrifically encouraged at what is happening in the next generation. We certainly cannot term them the "lost generation." As a matter of fact, they may be on more solid spiritual ground than their parents.

CONTENTS

— CHAPTER 3 —

MONEY AND
HOW TO USE IT

$\mathcal{M}$ONEY TALKS, but what is it saying *to* us and *about* us? Maybe one of the reasons money speaks so loudly is that for most of us, money means power. The person who controls the purse strings calls the shots. For some people, money equals security. For others, it is a means of control. Sometimes it signifies independence; often it is viewed as an indicator of status or self-esteem. You may be reluctant to admit it, but your money is you! How you obtain and spend your money indicates a great deal about your priorities, principles, and commitments.

When you realize how important money is to people, it's no wonder we have so many questions about how to get it, how to keep it, how to use it, and how to invest it. The Bible clearly says that money is never the problem; the "love of money is a root of all kinds of evil."[1] Money matters, and it matters a lot. It's vital that you get a grip on money before it gets a stranglehold on you.

Remember the words of Jesus, "What is highly prized among men is an abomination in the sight of God."[2] "Seek first," he told us, "the kingdom of God and his righteousness, and all these other things will be added unto you..."[3] "It is more blessed to give than to receive."[4]

---

[1] 1 Timothy 6:10 (NKJV)
[2] See Luke 16:15
[3] See Matthew 6:33
[4] Acts 20:35

HOW CAN I GET MY HUSBAND TO TITHE?

I understand what the Bible says about the husband being the head of the household. However, my husband does not tithe, and I do. I have dreams of getting out of debt in the next year. What can I do as the wife, without overstepping my bounds?

Serve god wholeheartedly yourself, obey His commands, and do what you know to be right in regard to paying your tithes. To avoid usurping your husband's authority you can approach him with the questions, "What do you think is appropriate for us to give to the Lord? What do you think God wants us to do in this situation?" By doing so, you are honoring him as the leader of your household and asking for his spiritual insight and wisdom on an important matter. It also indicates that you are not acting unilaterally, making your own decisions despite what he thinks. In a subtle way, you are encouraging him to take his God-given leadership responsibilities.

In turn, your husband may get the correct impression: "Wow! Maybe I am supposed to make some decisions about how we handle money, and my wife is helping me to sort them out."

One caution: No woman should ever do anything her husband or anyone else tells her if it is contrary to a biblical mandate or principle. If a husband misuses his authority, or if he encourages actions, attitudes, or words that contradict what the Bible says, a wife is under no obligation to submit to his leadership. At that point, his headship role has been abrogated; he has forfeited the right to speak to that situation until he aligns himself with Scripture.

I NEED TO BORROW TUITION MONEY

I've read in the Bible that we are to lend money, not borrow it. Yet I see many ministries borrowing money to build humongous churches. I'm about to begin medical school, and I need to borrow my tuition money. Is borrowing okay for this sort of purpose?

The bible says, "Owe nothing to anyone except to love one another,"[5] and "The borrower is the servant to the lender."[6] Borrowing and debt often turn into curses rather than blessings.

5　Romans 13:8
6　1 Timothy 6:17

On the other hand, if you are an astute businessperson and have a productive enterprise that you are fairly certain will earn adequate money to pay down the debt quickly, the risk may be worth it. Especially in times of financial growth, such ventures can be quite successful. During inflation and boom, debt multiplies earnings, but in times of deflation, a debt burden becomes a hellish prison. From 1999 to 2002, just such a reversal occurred and people and businesses in debt are beginning great financial suffering.

The average individual or family is being buried by debt, borrowing money for normal living expenses, borrowing on credit cards, home equity loans, and other personal loans. Then they are living at the bank (or the banker is living in their living room!), and they plunge further into debt. It is a vicious, downward spiral, and it's a terrible trap.

In considering whether to borrow for medical school, or for any sort of education, you must analyze the debt incurred against your potential earnings upon completion of your schooling. Will you make enough money over the early years of your career to make such borrowing pay off for you? Or will you be signing your life away, nailing the lid on your own coffin by willingly taking on so much debt? Millions of students are caught in a debt trap. They leave college owing anywhere from $60,000 to $100,000 or more, and they have no conceivable way of repaying that enormous amount. Many college graduates are defaulting on loans, filing bankruptcy, and ruining their credit for years to come because of the debt they incurred while in school.

This is extremely foolish, especially when there are so many scholarship opportunities available for people of almost every academic major and financial status. The best plan is to do as the Bible says and ask God to provide the money you need to get your education. "He will bless you to such a degree that you can lend money to many nations, but you won't have to borrow."[7]

CREDIT CARD HELL

I started using credit cards as a freshman in college and have been getting further and further in debt every year. It seems there is no end to the downward spiral. What should I do?

I AM SHOCKED when I read statistics showing that the credit card debt burden of most Americans is in excess of $6,000. Worse yet, for many families in credit

---

7   See Deuteronomy 15:6

card debt, the amount can skyrocket to $50,000, $100,000, to more than $150,000. The stress caused by this enormous load has led some people to lose hope, to give up believing that they can ever get ahead. In some cases, over-whelming credit card debt has led to suicide. I've heard of college students mired deeply in a debt from which they could not extricate themselves; the only way out, they thought, was to kill themselves.

Too often, once a person accumulates several thousand dollars in credit card debt, the tendency is to pay only the minimum payment or slightly more. With interest rates on many cards exceeding 15 to 18 percent and higher, it will take nearly thirty years to pay off this debt! The amount of interest paid will be two or three times as much as the original debt!

Credit card companies continually devise new methods of luring customers into their snare, making it extremely easy for the gullible to plunge into a quagmire of debt. Once a person is entrapped, the formerly friendly credit card companies turn up the heat, often charging as much as 28 percent interest on delinquent accounts. At that point, the debt trap grows alarmingly deeper and deeper and many people lose hope of ever pulling out of the downward slide. Currently, the total amount of consumer credit debt in America exceeds one trillion dollars and is skyrocketing exponentially!

Although a credit card can be a convenient tool for a person with adequate financial resources to pay it off monthly, it can also be a temptation to spend more than necessary. It is a proven fact that people who use credit cards for purchases spend more than they would have had they paid cash. If you cannot use credit cards carefully, it would be wise for you to have "plastic surgery." Cut up your cards so you can no longer use them. Determine the smallest debt you owe, and work to pay off any remaining balance. After paying it off, close the account. Then move up to the next debt and pay it off, using the extra money you now have available from paying off the previous debt and adding it to your normal payment. Continue this process until you have eliminated all credit card balances and have closed the accounts.

One of my associates began working toward financial freedom a few years ago. It took him nearly three years to do it, but when he paid off the last debt, he said, "It's like getting a $430-a-month raise!"

If you want to avoid bankruptcy, get out of debt, or stay out of debt, start by writing out a specific, accurate budget of income and expenses. Be sure that at least 10 percent of your income goes to the Lord. Some portion of your after-tax income should also be designated for monthly savings. If you don't plan to save, you probably won't.

Don't forget to plan for medical expenses, birthday gifts, Christmas, auto repairs, and recreation. Food, clothing, housing, and transportation costs should also be planned ahead of time on paper. It's much easier to avoid devastating financial potholes if you know the path you want to travel. Beyond that, think how peaceful your life will be when your money is compounding interest in your account rather than in the accounts of your creditors!

DONATIONS ON CREDIT CARDS

All major Christian organizations, including CBN, ask and receive donations using credit cards. At the same time, they advise people to get out of credit card debt. Isn't that a double standard?

THAT'S A VERY EMBARRASSING QUESTION! You're absolutely right.

Understand, it is not intrinsically wrong to use credit cards. I use them myself and pay off the balance almost every month, so I avoid paying the horrendously high interest rates most cards carry. In a sense, I am getting a free loan of the credit card company's money for twenty-five to twenty-eight days.

If you use credit cards, you should pay off all balances every month. Do not merely pay the minimum payment required. On even a few thousand dollars' worth of charges, it will take literally years to pay off your debt if all you pay each month is the minimum required payment. In the meantime, you are tempted to use the card again, incurring further charges and taking even longer to pay. This allows credit card debt to build up, and before you know it, you will be wallowing in debt. Don't allow that to happen.

If you want to make a donation by means of credit card, fine. But if it means you must carry that balance and pay interest, I would not advise you to use credit to make that donation to CBN or any other ministry. Pay off your balance completely every month, or don't use credit cards at all.

SHOULD A CHRISTIAN FILE BANKRUPTCY?

When, if ever, is it permissible for a Christian to file bankruptcy?

THE OLD TESTAMENT designated that there should be periods of jubilee. Every seven years certain debts were cancelled, and every fifty years all debts were cancelled. During these times of jubilee, slaves were set free, any personal land that had been obligated by a debt was restored to the families from which it came, and the economy began afresh. This radical approach to finances provided that the perpetual compounding of interest on debt would be stopped so that families would not live forever in bondage to debt.

While we look askance at such a system today, compound interest threatens to bankrupt millions of lives, either through stress and worry or literal financial bankruptcy. A member of the Rothschild family once referred to compound interest as the eighth wonder of the world. Indeed it is, when it is working for you, but when it is working against you, it can be devastating. Someone estimated that if the thirty pieces of silver given to Judas Iscariot for betraying Jesus had been put into an interest-bearing account, compounded annually tax free at 4 percent, the account would now include enough money to give every man, woman, and child on earth more than $300,000. Similarly, compound interest can become overwhelming when you are in debt and it is dragging you down toward bankruptcy.

Recently, Bono, the spokesman for the popular Irish band U2, publicly encouraged his peers to take up the cause of the poor nations of the world. I vigorously supported the singer's efforts. Moreover, I was delighted when the U.S. government took the lead in forgiving certain debts of Third World nations that have no wherewithal to repay.

Bankruptcy laws were established in the U.S. to grant a similar release from debts to individuals or businesses that for various reasons have gotten themselves into a financial mess from which there is no realistic hope of emerging. Bankruptcy relief comes in several forms. Some bankruptcies allow an individual or business to "reorganize," to temporarily cease from servicing debts until they can get back on their financial feet. Other bankruptcies bring about the total liquidation of a family's or business's assets, which are sold and the money is divided between the debtor's creditors. It seems legitimate for Christians to make use of these provisions to help get a second start in their business or personal finances. It is not morally appropriate, however, to transfer assets and run up big debts in anticipation of bankruptcy for the express purpose of defrauding creditors.

Some Christians feel a moral responsibility to pay back debts after bankruptcy, even though they are no longer legally liable for them. This is noble, but not always advisable.

In business, a certain amount of "bad debts" is factored in as a cost of doing business. Usually, these debts are often written off the business's taxes. Consequently, the creditor is already receiving some reimbursement on the bad debt, so it is not necessary for the debtor to feel obligated.

Sometimes people feel obligated to pay back only certain creditors after a bankruptcy. Again, this can create more problems for the person who filed. By designating one creditor over another, it is possible that the entire bankruptcy can be vitiated, thus reinstating all the debts as though the bankruptcy never occurred. I'd advise anyone pursuing this route to be sure you have very good legal counsel.

MY MONEY SUPPORTS MOM'S ALCOHOL

My mother is a recent widow. One of my brothers pays her mortgage, another brother maintains her car and yard, and a third brother is handicapped and lives with her full time. My mom has a drinking problem and smoking addiction, therefore I do not support her. She continually complains about her financial problems. Should I pitch in with her finances?

THIS IS A TOUGH ISSUE. If someone is going to take your money and use it to buy alcohol or cigarettes, draining their resources, the most merciful thing you can do may be to withhold funds until the person shapes up. But it's very difficult to say that when the person in question is your mother! Sometimes the love of a child who helps out in such a situation will win the person to the Lord. At other times, withholding help may bring her to her senses, and ultimately to the Lord. You must pray for the Lord's specific direction for your situation.

Obviously, smoking cigarettes can cause cancer, heart disease, emphysema, and a host of other health problems for your mother. If her drinking is limited to a glass of wine with dinner, or some similar limited usage, she probably will not impair her health and might even prolong her days. But addiction to hard liquor will only complicate any other health issues she may have. You and your siblings should discuss these issues and determine a plan to keep your mother from hurting herself.

In the meantime, try to find a way to help support your mother by paying specific bills directly to the store or person where the services are received. For example, rather than giving her money for food, purchase the groceries and take them to your mother. This isn't a cure, since she is obviously taking advantage of your brothers' kindness, receiving the benefits of their money while using her own to buy alcohol and cigarettes. But at least you will be showing your mother that you care, and it may help to relieve some of the burden from your brothers.

SHOULD WE BE WEALTHY BELIEVERS?

I read in the Bible about Job, Abraham, Isaac, and others who were wealthy by their society's standards. Should I expect that God will bless me financially in similar ways today?

I DO NOT BELIEVE IT IS REALISTIC or biblical for every Christian to expect to be as wealthy as the Old Testament saints. The Bible tells us that "if we have food and covering, with these we shall be content."[8] Even those who are rich materially are instructed not to trust in material gain. The apostle Paul wrote, "Instruct those who are rich in this present world not to be conceited or to fix their hope on the uncertainty of riches, but on God, who richly supplies us with all things to enjoy."[9] Furthermore, Paul implied that those who were wealthy should "be rich in good works, to be generous and ready to share."[10] The rich should be willing to contribute to help others in need.

God has a purpose and a plan for each of us. He ordinarily does not simply drop money from the sky; instead, He grants wisdom, ability, opportunity, and creativity to His people who then prosper financially. The purpose, though, is to use God's blessings not simply for ourselves, but to do His work in the world. If He has given you gifts and talents to make money, by all means make it! God uses businessmen and women who have money. He places people in His church body that have the means to pay for the work. He used some wealthy women to help finance the earthly ministry of Jesus. Clearly, God could have bestowed enormous wealth on His Son, but He didn't. Instead, He chose to use men and women who had a heart for His work. Having money is never the problem if it is used for God's glory; it is the love of money that gets us in trouble.

Some people are gifted in business, others in art; some are gifted in the pastoral ministry, and some are gifted in prayer. The Bible says that somebody who goes to warfare should not engage in business; he should be out fighting.[11] The issue for each of us is: What is our calling? What gifts and talents has God given to me to use for His glory and my good?

Indeed, in the Old Testament, the blessing of God was clearly on Abraham, Isaac, and Jacob, all of whom became very wealthy and had considerable posses-

---

8   1 Timothy 6:8
9   1 Timothy 6:17
10   1 Timothy 6:18
11   See Numbers 32

sions. Joseph was the leader of the greatest power on earth during his lifetime. Daniel was the third most powerful ruler in Babylon. Job, too, had great wealth. Many of Old Testament saints were well to do. In the New Testament, Joseph of Arimathea, the man who provided a tomb for Jesus, was a wealthy individual.

Having wealth is not wrong. On the other hand, we should not covet what God gives to others but does not give to us. The real question is: What is God's calling for me? To make money, teach, minister, sing, perform, paint, write books—what is your calling? Discover what God wants you to do, then do it with all your heart!

A TITHER LACKS MONEY

We have been tithing for some time, yet our financial situation continues to get worse. We have one crisis after another, forcing us to pay for basic needs with a credit card instead of cash. Sometimes, we have only twenty to thirty dollars a week to feed a family of six. We keep holding on to the faith that God will provide for our needs, but we are discouraged. How do we escape this stressful situation?

FIRST, HAVE SOME FRIENDS from your church come to your home and pray for you, perhaps a Bible study group, or whatever spiritual fellowship group you are a part of. It sounds as though you have been set upon by some devilish spirit of poverty, and that spirit needs to be rebuked and broken. The way to do that is through prayer. Take authority over the devil by speaking aloud something such as, "Satan, in the name of Jesus, I break the hold of this spirit of poverty on me. I bind this thing. I will not receive it, and my life is going to be better because my faith is in Jesus Christ."

Begin to confess good things. Scripture says in Proverbs that "a man shall eat good by the fruit of his lips."[12] You need to confess that blessing. Now this is not hocus-pocus; it is agreeing with what God has already declared to be true. It is taking authority over the physical world by the power of the Holy Spirit.

Certainly, this is an excellent time to take a hard look at your life and your relationships. Is there some unconfessed sin in your life that the devil could be using against you? Confess it, repent, and get clean. Is there disharmony in your home? A family needs to be on the same page spiritually speaking if you expect God to bless you. Are your children in obedience, respecting your instructions, and honoring

---

12   Proverbs 13:2

God? Are you really working together as a family to get out of debt and to move forward financially? The Bible says, "Again I say to you that if two of you agree on earth concerning anything that they ask, it will be done for them by My Father in heaven. For where two or three are gathered together in My name, I am there in the midst of them."[13] Husband, wife, and children need to be in agreement as you pray, "In the name of Jesus, we are going to declare victory."

Continually speak good things, to yourselves, to others, and to the situation. It's all too easy to lapse into negative talk, gloom and despair, and to start talking about all the tough times. "Oh, no! Here's another medical bill!" or whatever the case. Keep speaking words of faith and encouragement to each other.

God's Word is true. If you have been tithing, you can count on Him to provide for you. God says, "Prove me with your tithes and offerings to see if I won't open the windows of heaven and pour you out such a blessing you can't contain it."[14] But that doesn't mean you should just sit back and do nothing. You need to be making wise choices, working as hard as you can to eliminate your current debts and to avoid future debts. It sounds as though a second job is needed for a while, until you clean up the mess and start getting your feet on solid financial ground.

It would also be wise to sit down with someone who is good in finances and who can help you work out a realistic budget—one that actually shows how much money is coming in, and where you plan to spend it. Do this before you get your paycheck! Many people merely keep track of what they are spending. That is not a budget. That's simply bookkeeping. A budget is a plan—any plan you choose—but it is a plan that you decide upon in advance of spending your money. Many people don't even realize that they are spending more than they are taking in, due to credit cards, loans, and other recurring obligations. No wonder they are always running low on funds! Get your financial house in order, and God will bless your efforts to honor Him with your money.

WHY ARE CHRISTIANS POOR?

Why are so many Christians materially poor?

MANY CHRISTIANS have been taught that poverty and godliness are the same thing. How could they get that impression? Easily. The Bible says that it is an error to think that gain is godliness. In other words, don't think just because you

---

13   Matthew 18:19–20 (NKJV)
14   See Malachi 3:10

are wealthy that it is a proof that God is pleased with your life. The fact that you are rich does not make you godly.[15]

On the other hand, being poor does not necessarily make you godly, either. The presence or absence of money is immaterial to our character, although Scripture warns that the rich are especially susceptible to various snares and temptations. The Bible says, "But those who want to get rich fall into temptation and a snare and many foolish and harmful desires which plunge men into ruin and destruction. For the love of money is a root of all sorts of evil, and some by longing for it have wandered away from the faith, and pierce themselves with many a pang."[16] Notice, however, the apostle Paul says it is not the money that is evil; it is the *love* of money that is the cause of all sorts of evil, and those who are lusting after wealth create a lot of problems for themselves. Consequently, some Christians have deduced that having an abundance of money is a problem.

While misuse of money can indeed lead to misery, let me hasten to add that I do not believe it is God's will for anyone to be trapped in the grinding poverty I have seen in so many nations of our world. Millions of people live in squalor, on the verge of starvation. This is not God's plan.

In almost every society where the gospel of Jesus Christ has been received by the people, the life expectancy and the standard of living of that society have gone up. Where the gospel is lived out and the people love God and love each other, when they keep His commands, where they give generously to those less fortunate than themselves, when they do not waste their money on harmful, destructive substances, when they live in holy matrimony with the husband and wife working together to create a better life for their family, invariably there is a sociological uplift, which pulls people out of poverty into the middle class and above.

The psalmist said, "I have been young, and now I am old; yet I have not seen the righteous forsaken, or his descendants begging bread."[17] I believe that God will look after His people, if they will live by His principles. It doesn't necessarily mean they will be rich, but they will not wallow in poverty, either. God has promised "to supply all your needs according to His riches in glory in Christ Jesus."[18]

Granted, the poor seem to have a special place in God's heart; perhaps God has given more grace to the poor to receive His bounty of spiritual wealth than He has to the rich. Jesus said, "It is harder for a rich man to come into the kingdom of God

---

15   See Mark 8:36
16   1 Timothy 6:9–10
17   Psalm 37:25
18   1 Philippians 4:19

than it is for a camel to go through the eye of a needle."[19] Rich people are often proud, arrogant, or overly self-confident to the point that they feel they don't need help from God. The poor sense their need and reach out to God for help. As they do, they find spiritual, heavenly riches that can never be taken away.

PLAYING STOCKS ON A CREDIT CARD

My husband insists on borrowing money from credit cards to invest in the stock market. We're broke, but he insists God is saying to do this. Is this gambling?

Yes, it is gambling, and it is obvious that your husband doesn't know much about the stock market, and maybe even less about hearing the voice of God! Scripture says to "owe no one anything except to love one another."[20] You can be sure that God will not contradict His Word by telling your husband to go into credit card debt to play the stock market.

Only surplus funds should be invested in stocks, money that you don't need to live on. This is especially important since stocks vacillate—sometimes they go quite high, and sometimes they plunge through the floor. If you are investing well, over time you will usually profit between 9 and 12 percent annually. But you can't pay 18 percent interest on a credit card to make 10 percent in stocks and hope to ever get ahead!

Clearly, your husband is not making wise financial decisions, and the two of you need to work together in this area. Read some books on budgeting, or attend a financial seminar by a reputable Christian authority on the subject. Then sit down and do it! Lay out your budget for each month before the month begins and spend only where you have allocated your money.

STOCK MARKET DAY TRADING

Is day trading on the stock market investing or gambling?

Day trading is done by individual investors using computers moving money into and out of various stocks, according to the hour by hour, up and down ticks of the market. Then, sometimes in a matter of minutes or hours, they sell or buy

---

19   See Mark 10:23–27
20   Romans 13:8 (NKJV)

and move their investment dollars to something else. Granted, a great deal of money can be made if you consistently make the right calls by guessing which stocks will go up and which will lose value, but it is also easy to lose money just as rapidly.

Day trading is essentially gambling, tossing your money into the stock market and hoping you'll be able to scoop up a quick return. It is extremely unwise because there is no investment philosophy to it; it has nothing to do with logical, systematic analysis of the macroeconomic trends that affect modern companies. Many day traders pop in and out of the market, with hardly a clue about the stocks they are throwing their money into. Yes, some people will make a lot of money quickly, but many more will lose their shirts in no time at all.

Investing is for long-term growth, with intelligence, not luck. Do the research necessary to find the history, organization, and complete financial data of the companies in which you'd like to invest. Warren Buffett's advice is sound: Only buy the stocks of companies that you would like to own if you could.

LOTTERY TICKETS AND GAMBLING

I have tried to explain to my family that gambling is against God. They continually purchase lottery tickets. They say that gambling will not keep them out of heaven. What is the biblical position on gambling?

I'M HESITANT TO SAY that gambling will keep someone out of heaven, or if a person buys a lottery ticket, that person is going to hell. The Bible does not specifically condemn or condone gambling. Yes, gambling is mentioned in a negative context when the soldiers gambled at the foot of the cross to see who would win Jesus' garments.[21]

On the other hand, the apostles cast "sacred lots," a practice similar to rolling dice, to help them decide which man should be the replacement for Judas, following his betrayal of Jesus. After they had prayed, "they cast their lots, and the lot fell on Matthias. And he was numbered with the eleven apostles."[22] Moreover, Scripture says, "The lot is thrown into the lap, but the outcome is from the Lord."[23] Casting lots to determine choices or direction has long biblical tradition.

---

21   See Mark 15:24
22   Acts 1:26 (NKJV)
23   Proverbs 16:33

Gambling is wrong when it runs contrary to the scripture that says, "Thou shalt not tempt the LORD your God."[24] As a Christian, you belong to God, and everything you have belongs to God, including all of your possessions, money, and financial resources. You are a steward of His resources. To gamble is taking what belongs to God and laying it out at risk, whether determined by the throw of a dice, the turn of a card, or the bounce of some lottery balls. This is tempting (or testing) the Lord, because you are "testing" Him to see if He will cause things to go your way, trying to make God cause the dice come your way, to make the ball stop on your number, or bring you the card to fill your inside straight.

Beyond that, gambling has a much more pernicious effect in many people's lives. It becomes addictive, compulsive behavior. This type of gambler receives a tremendous "rush" by risking his resources, a feeling similar to that experienced by a person on a giant roller coaster, going up and suddenly rushing downward. The excitement and exhilaration is there, win or lose.

This thrill often leads from an innocent pastime, to compulsive behavior, in which the gambler ceases to view his or her actions rationally, and will do almost anything—risking life savings, retirement money, mortgage payments, or even food money for his or her children—simply to make another bet. In that sense, gambling is just as wrong as any other addiction that harms our bodies or takes money or resources from the family.

Most importantly, God wants us to trust Him as our Source, not a deck of cards, a slot machine, or a lottery number. He is more than willing to provide for us as we seek Him first in our lives.

IS IT OKAY TO PRAY FOR MONEY?

Is it a sin to pray for money? If I really need it desperately, is it okay to pray that God will prosper me, and not feel bad about it?

YOU'D BETTER BELIEVE IT! It's more than okay to pray for money; it is often *vital* that we pray for our financial needs to be met, that our loved ones prosper, and that God's work in the world will be financed sufficiently. The real question is, what are you going to do with what God provides?

In some cultures, basic items can be obtained through bartering or trading services. While that isn't out of the question for us, most people in Western culture

---

24   See Matthew 4:7

use money to pay for basic needs such as food, clothing, shelter, and transportation. Is God interested in providing these things? Yes, He is! Does He always do so by providing more money? Not necessarily. Sometimes He chooses to change us rather than to simply change our financial circumstances. In other situations, God provides the money and we become stewards, managers, of His resources. We will, of course, give an account one day regarding what we have done with what God has given to us.

Certainly, God isn't some big slot machine in the sky, where you pull a lever or punch in the right data and out comes a jackpot. Nor is He a Santa Claus who provides all the toys on His children's wish lists.

But God does give to His children. Jesus said, "Whatsoever ye shall ask the Father in my name, he will give it to you. Hitherto, have ye asked nothing in my name: ask, and ye shall receive, that your joy may be full."[25] Isn't that amazing? God wants us to ask! And God wants to give to us!

Some years ago, my income was so low that I was living very close to the financial edge. Nevertheless, I believed that I should give a significant amount to the Lord's work, so I did. Several weeks later as I was driving my car, God spoke to me, and said, "Ask Me for something."

I said, "Lord, I think I have everything I need right now."

He said again, "Ask Me for something."

"Okay, Lord. Please provide me with one thousand dollars." I wasn't sure why I mentioned that figure, but it popped into my mind, so I spoke it in my prayer.

Within days, I had received an extra thousand dollars out of the blue. Shortly after that, Dede and I discovered that our daughter needed some orthodontic work done immediately. The cost? One thousand dollars! God had provided for the need even before we knew that we needed it. He asked me to ask for it, and He was ready and willing to supply the amount needed.

Your heavenly Father wants you to know that He is there, that He cares, that He is Jehovah-Jireh, the Lord, your provider. Ask and you shall receive.

One caution: James reminds us, "Ye have not, because ye ask not. Ye ask, and receive not, because ye ask amiss, that ye may consume it upon your lusts."[26] To ask for God's blessings only to satisfy our selfish lusts is to invite condemnation. But to ask your heavenly Father to provide for you, and through you for others, is to be blessed indeed.

---

25   John 16:23–24 (KJV)
26   James 4:2–3 (KJV)

WILL NOT TITHING SEND YOU TO HELL?

If a Christian doesn't tithe, will he or she go to hell?

THERE'D BE A WHOLE LOT of Christians in hell if that were the case! The percentage of church members who tithe is woefully small.

No, a lack of tithing will not send you to hell, nor will tithing keep you out of hell. Tithing is an act of obedience, since the first 10 percent of our wealth belongs to the Lord. God spoke through the prophet Malachi and posed a series of pointed questions and answers: "Will a man rob God? Yet you are robbing Me! But you say, 'How have we robbed Thee?' In tithes and contributions. You are cursed with a curse, for you are robbing Me, the whole nation of you."[27] In the Old Testament, the rule was to give the first 10 percent of your income or produce to the Lord.

Tithing isn't mentioned in that context in the New Testament, but Jesus didn't lower the standard; He raised it. He demanded to be Lord of all, the other 90 percent as well as the first 10 percent of your resources.

Tithing is an act of love on the part of a Christian. If you love the Lord, you will want to give back to Him (via your church or other ministries), because it is the path to blessing. God says, "Prove me now, with your tithes and offerings. I will open the windows of heaven and pour out such a blessing that you are unable to contain it."[28] God does not say, "If you refuse to tithe, I will send you to hell." He says, "Give, and it will be given unto you . . . in the same measure that you give, it will be given back to you."[29] God says, "Because you give, I'm going to give you a great blessing, and I will rebuke the devourer, who tries to destroy your effectiveness."[30]

I'm convinced that the biblical standard is not 10 percent, but may be closer to 25 to 30 percent of our income. The tithe is not always given to churches or other ministries; it may be given directly to the poor and needy. Regardless, God promises, "He who sows sparingly shall also reap sparingly; and he who sows bountifully shall also reap bountifully."[31] If we sow liberally into meeting the needs of others, we will reap a prosperous harvest. It's as though the money that is given to the poor becomes seed out of which will grow a new harvest.

---

[27] Malachi 3:8–9
[28] See Malachi 3:8–12
[29] See Luke 6:38
[30] See Malachi 3:11
[31] 2 Corinthians 9:6

TITHE THOUGH LAID OFF WORK?

After working for twenty years for the same company, my father has just been laid off. I heard him tell my mother that to save money, they'd stop tithing. How do I explain my misgivings about that?

THE BIBLE clearly describes a way to prosper and a way to want. Scripture says, "There are some who withhold more than is right, and leads only to poverty."[32] Again, let me remind you that the only place in the Bible where we are commanded to test the Lord is in the realm of our tithes and offerings.[33] God challenges us to prove Him at the point of our finances, to see if He will not provide more than we need. We must give expectantly, looking for God to keep His Word.

At the same time, God does not demand that we give what we do not have. If a person is laid off and has no pay coming in, he has no income on which to tithe. He or she is merely giving offerings from the resources available. But this money given is truly seed for future miraculous income opportunities from the Lord.

Encourage your father to look for income-producing activities that he can pursue outside of the usual "work-for-wages" approach to making a living. It is not wrong to work for wages; it's just extremely difficult to get ahead financially when you are laboring for someone else's increase. Seek opportunities to provide services that people need, which will provide supplemental income, or even an entirely new career. Your father has been obedient over the years and can certainly stand in faith expecting a righteous God to keep His word to provide.

Whether it is a lawn-care business, telemarketing from your home, or some other opportunity, get creative and find some way to work for yourself. It takes courage, creativity, and innovation, but it also takes a sense that God is with you, leading you, caring for you, and supplying for you.

Too often, we seek other things first, but the Lord has promised, if we will seek His kingdom and His righteousness first, He will provide all the other things we need.[34]

He is powerful and He is able to supply our needs "exceeding abundantly beyond all that we ask or think."[35]

---

[32] Proverbs 11:24 (NKJV)
[33] See Malachi 3:10
[34] See Matthew 6:24–34
[35] Ephesians 3:20

USING TITHE MONEY TO BUY A BIGGER HOUSE

My wife and I are homeschooling our five children, and we've run out of room. We'd like to buy a larger home, but that will leave us strapped for cash. Would it be against God's will to use some of our tithe money to pay for a larger home?

THE LORD HAS SAID, "Prove me with your tithes and offerings, and see if I won't open the windows of heaven and pour you out such a blessing you cannot contain."[36] Buying a bigger home isn't really the most important issue. The real issue is a matter of priorities. What holds first place in your life? Are you honoring the Lord *first*, or are you giving Him the leftovers? You can't expect the abundant blessings of God to flow in your direction if you are spending so much on a house payment that you are financially strapped. You may be borrowing your way into slavery—slavery to your mortgage payment and to your bank. Scripture says, "The rich rules over the poor, and the borrower is servant to the lender."[37]

Robert T. Kiyosaki, author of the bestselling book *Rich Dad, Poor Dad,* was an intriguing guest on *The 700 Club.* Kiyosaki pointed out that, contrary to popular belief, a house is not an investment; it is a liability. If you want to think like a rich person, you must recognize that the taxes, maintenance, insurance, repairs, utility bills, and all sorts of other expenses incurred in the purchase and upkeep of your home are drains on your income. They do not produce income, until you sell your home. Hopefully, by then, your home will have gone up in value, but even then, you may not earn back the huge sum of money you have poured into your home over the years.

Certainly, homeschooling your children is a noble effort and worth the sacrifice, but you don't want to rob God to do it. Moreover, you will be better off if you honor the Lord first with your finances and allow Him to provide what you need for the larger home. He knows what you need, not simply what you want. Pray, "God, I'm going to give the tithes and offerings to You, and I ask and believe that somehow You will provide a way to acquire this property if it is Your will for us." That is much more honoring to God than to say, "I'm going to steal part of the tithes and offerings from You, Lord, but since it is for a good cause, I know You'll understand." He will understand! He'll understand that you are seeking your own

---

36   See Malachi 3:10
37   Proverbs 22:7 (NKJV)

desires, rather than seeking Him first, and trusting Him to provide for your needs.

NOT ENOUGH MONEY FOR A STAY-AT-HOME MOM

My wife and I want her to stay home to raise our two children, but the financial reality is that we need two incomes just to make it. We tithe on our income, don't live extravagantly, and try to make wise decisions, but we still can't make it without me working two jobs or extended overtime. That, of course, defeats our purpose, since it keeps me from my family for most of the day. Where's God in all this? If He's so pro-family, why won't He help me make ends meet? I want to do right by my wife and children, yet we can't seem to get ahead.

THIS IS THE HEART CRY of many people in America. To gain financial freedom, start by saying, "What are my necessities and what are my desires?" Often the reason that we require all these extra jobs is because of the lifestyle we've picked for ourselves. We must have a new car, and we must have an upscale house. We have to have this, that, and the other. Once the wants become payments, then they become necessities. We transfer the optional into the essential.

But many things in our lives are not essential. Seek to simplify your lifestyle by getting your spending down to where your lifestyle and your income are equal. In other words, don't spend money you don't have by using credit or going into debt! In today's low-interest environment, look to save by refinancing your mortgage. Perhaps selling your home while prices are high and either downsizing or renting might be an option.

Opportunities abound to make money. I mentioned previously, Robert T. Kiyosaki, author of *Rich Dad, Poor Dad.* Robert's father was a Ph.D. and a distinguished educator who was broke. His friend's dad was rich and taught him the secret of being rich: Work for yourself, not somebody else, and invest and allow your money to work for you.

So where is God as you are trying to get ahead financially? God has what you need; you just need to ask Him. If you think like a wage slave, then you will be a wage slave; but if you think like an entrepreneur, you can begin to move into a whole new realm. What skill do you have, what is the need in your community, what service could you provide? What training do you need to get started? Being an entrepreneur takes courage. It takes bravery and you have to be willing to go without a paycheck sometimes, as you build your business. You must be willing to sacrifice, but the rewards are great at the end of the road.

Ask God to show you new ways and other avenues whereby you can get money working for you. That is the secret: Have money working for you, have property working for you, have somebody else working for you, and have something besides your own sweat and toil providing the only paycheck coming in. God wants you to be financially free; He wants you to keep your family first, after Him. You can pray confidently, and believe that He will help you find the way to do it.

CHOOSING BETWEEN JOBS

I have three equally attractive job opportunities, all paying about the same amount of money. How can I determine God's will concerning which job is right for me?

OVER THE YEARS, I have employed hundreds of people. I've noticed one essential truth in regard to those who succeed and do well in their work, and those who don't. Simply stated, those who work doing what God created them to do are happy and productive. If we seek employment in the area that fulfills the desires of our heart, we will not only do a good job, but we will be happy and satisfied in our work.

Too often, we think that doing the will of God means that we must be miserable, that we must force ourselves to do something that is distasteful, something that we otherwise would not have chosen. This attitude is antithetical to the God who created you as you are. Success is understanding who you are and then fulfilling the plan that God has for you in union with Him.[38]

In sorting out your job opportunities, determine first what truly makes you happy. One test is to think back to when you were eight or nine years old. What in your life caused you to feel the happiest at the time? If you can extrapolate those feelings as an adult, you may discover where you will be the most satisfied in your career. Did you enjoy creating things as a child? Perhaps you should consider art or engineering. Did you enjoy sorting and organizing items? Maybe you have a natural affinity toward accounting. Did you enjoy advising or leading your playmates? Maybe you should be a counselor or in some type of management position. Certainly, these are broad-brush generalizations, but if you can ascertain what

---

[38]   See Jeremiah 29:11–14

makes you the happiest, you will have a much easier time sorting through your job options.

Beyond that, the Bible says that if you will trust the Lord and commit your way to Him, He will give you the desires of your heart.[39] Moreover, ask God to close the doors and give you a check in your spirit concerning those opportunities that are less than best for you. Allow the peace of God to be an umpire in your heart and mind. Look for this rule of peace—a calm assurance that this step is pleasing to God—when you are trying to make up your mind about a particular course of action.

Should you feel a sense of disquiet in your spirit concerning a particular career move, draw back and wait. Don't plunge into something without a sense of God's peace in your heart. The Bible says, "Trust in the Lord with all your heart and do not lean on your own understanding. In all your ways acknowledge Him, and He will direct your path."[40] God has promised to direct your path. As you allow this process to take place, you will sense one or the other of the options rising to the forefront. If you don't receive positive leading from the Holy Spirit, then perhaps you should allow all the opportunities to pass. The Bible says that we can hear a voice in our ear when we turn to the right or the left saying, "This is the way, walk in it!"

Regardless, do not allow money to play a major role in your decision. Most people who work simply for the money are miserable in their careers. The old adage is true: "Do what you love and the money will follow." God can provide the money you need. Look for His peace and your satisfaction as you make your decision.

TAXATION WITHOUT REPRESENTATION

I just paid my federal taxes for this year. When I think of how much the government gets of my hard-earned wages and the poor representation I get in return, I wonder, would Jesus pay taxes?

Yes, WE ALL PAY TAXES and so did Jesus Christ. I recently filed my final 2001 taxes, and was interested to see that our benevolent uncle gave me the privilege of paying enough to cover the salaries of two cabinet secretaries and their secretarial staff. So in the words of our former President Bill Clinton, "I feel your pain." When Jesus was asked whether He and His disciples were going to pay

---

39   See Psalm 37:4–5
40   Proverbs 3:5–6

taxes to the Roman government, He turned the question around and asked, "Do the kings of the earth collect taxes from their subjects or from their own children?" The implication was that the children of God are free from paying taxes. Nevertheless, to avoid causing an offense, Jesus instructed the disciples to go catch a fish, find a coin inside the fish's mouth, and use that coin to pay the taxes.

Although it's highly unlikely that you or I will receive the same specific instructions and provisions for paying our taxes that the disciples did, the principle of not giving an offense is still valid for us. To avoid creating an offense, God's people do indeed pay taxes.

On another occasion, the Pharisees and Herodians attempted to trap Jesus into saying something for which they could bring a charge against Him. They posed the tricky question of whether it was right to pay taxes to the Roman government that ruled the Jewish nation. Jesus asked to see a coin. "Whose image is on this coin?" He asked.

"Caesar's," He was told.

"Then render to Caesar the things that are Caesar's, and to God the things that are God's," Jesus replied.[41]

Regarding the government's role in our lives and our need to be good citizens, the apostle Paul said, "Therefore you must be subject, not only because of wrath but also for conscience' sake. For because of this you also pay taxes. . . . Render therefore to all their due: taxes to whom taxes are due, customs to whom customs, fear to whom fear, honor to whom honor."[42]

Ostensibly, in a free, democratic form of government, "we the people" are Caesar. As such, one of the most important services we can render to "Caesar" is intelligent citizenship, which includes being aware of the issues and electing wise, honest, capable representatives to carry on the business of government, men and women who will handle the money collected through taxation as a sacred trust. We need to vote into office men and women who are best suited to the task and whose policies align with the Bible. If we exercise our duties properly, our representatives should not place unnecessary, excessive, or unfair tax burdens on us.

Taxes are a necessary element in a country such as ours. In the United States, it costs an enormous amount of money to provide roads, public schools, community water and sewage services, police and fire protection, a justice system with its various courts, a standing military, and other services. It is legitimate for governments to tax people to help pay for those services that we could not afford as private indi-

---

41   See Matthew 22:15–21
42   Romans 13:5–7 (NKJV)

viduals. As good citizens, Christians should pay our fair share of taxes without grumbling or complaining.

But it is also imperative that citizens demand fiscal responsibility from our leaders, and a more equitable, understandable tax code. Former President Jimmy Carter described the American tax code as a "disgrace to the human race!" It's become even more so since President Carter was in office. The waste of taxpayer money by the federal government is frankly unconscionable. The tax code has more words than the Holy Bible. It is incomprehensible, even to many professional tax lawyers. Corporate income is taxed two or even three times. If people are going to comply voluntarily, the tax code must be radically overhauled toward simplicity and fairness.

HOW TO BUILD WEALTH

Now that the Lord has helped me to get out of debt, what is my next step to start building financial security?

THE INITIAL REACTION a person feels after getting free from debt is a sense of elation, verging on sheer giddiness. Combined with that is an intense desire to go out and spend the extra money you are noticing in your bank account each month. You must reject that temptation! Otherwise, your splurging will quickly exhaust your potential savings.

Now that you are debt-free, keep your spending level consistent to what it was before, and take the surplus money you formerly applied to paying off debts, and begin using that money to build your savings and investments. The object is to have your money working for you, rather than you working for money.

As soon as possible, establish an "emergency fund," some readily available money that you can get your hands on in a hurry in case something disrupts your employment, or some sort of medical emergency occurs. Most financial advisers suggest a cash reserve of about six months' worth of living expenses. This money can be kept in a "liquid" account, such as a money-market fund, a bank certificate of deposit, or better yet, short-term U.S. Treasury bills. While you are saving your emergency fund, lay aside a small amount to be used for "everyday" emergencies, such as auto repairs, broken windows, medical bills or deductibles not covered by insurance, and other miscellaneous expenses. When accidents happen or the unexpected occurs, you can draw from this fund rather than dipping back into debt. Afterwards, replace the funds you have spent so your emergency fund remains fully funded. Only then are you ready to begin investing.

You can invest for all sorts of reasons—to save for your retirement, to pay for your children's college education, or simply to make more money so you can give more.

For most individuals, the best places to invest are those for which the government will give you tax credit or tax shelters, such as an Individual Retirement Account (IRA), which enables you to deduct the amount deposited currently ($2,000 per year) while sheltering the total savings from tax liability until retirement. Many employers provide a 401 (k) plan, many of which have a matching funds feature, by which the employer will match and sometimes even double the amount that the employee deposits in the plan.

For self-employed workers, or those who get much of their income from sales or royalties, such as authors and songwriters, keogh plans are good investment vehicles. Do all that you can to build your savings tax free until retirement. By doing so, you automatically will be earning a 20 to 30 percent return on the amount invested simply because you can put off paying the taxes on it.

One of the best ways to increase your net worth is to pay down your home mortgage. This will give you equity in your home, while reducing the amount you owe the bank. If you have a thirty-year home mortgage, do all you can to renegotiate it down to a fifteen-year mortgage. The savings in interest alone will be astronomical! If you can't arrange a fifteen-year mortgage, try to make one extra payment on the principal of your house loan each year. This will usually save you thousands of dollars in interest over the lifetime of your loan.

A wide variety of investments are available nowadays. Wise investment counselors encourage diversity when it comes to where you will save and invest. Rather than investing in individual stocks, unless you are quite savvy financially, it is usually safer to invest in mutual funds. Mutual funds, as the name implies, are stocks that are invested in "mutually" by a large number of people. They are usually comprised of a group of reputable companies rather than one business.

If you don't know which mutual funds are best for you, *Morningstar* reports rate the various funds and chart their progress simply enough that even someone who is not a financial expert can easily understand. These reports can be obtained inexpensively over the Internet and are usually a good guide to follow.

You should purchase "no-load" mutual funds with low annual expense ratios, because your money will grow faster. In past years, Treasury bonds have been fabulous investments. Right now, the attention of professionals is toward corporate bond funds, especially high-yield funds.

Obtain as much knowledge as possible about the funds in which you want to invest. If you don't understand investments, find a trustworthy financial counselor who does, and who will teach you what you need to know to make wise investments. I have always been a "value" investor. This means that the stocks in which I invest normally have a price-earnings ratio of around eight to twelve, rather than some of the more risky technology stocks with stratospheric price-earnings which can bring a quick return, but can also crash overnight. Today the emphasis is on stocks that earn real cash and pay real dividends. It is easy to find the dividend history of stocks and the percentage of earnings that is paid to dividends. In a low-interest-rate environment, yearly dividends of 3, 4, or 5 percent look very good. Normally over time, assuming no catastrophic shock to the U.S. economy, stocks with compounding dividends should yield annual returns of 6 to 8 percent. Over thirty or forty years, this type of compounding can be very rewarding.

IS INSURANCE AN INVESTMENT?

What kind of insurance should I invest in?

I DON'T BELIEVE THAT INSURANCE IS A GOOD INVESTMENT. It's wise to purchase enough life insurance to adequately support your family in the event of death, but even in that, we must use good judgment.

One of the worst insurance products ever foisted upon the American public is the type of policy known as "whole life." Ostensibly, this sort of policy combines a savings program wrapped in a life insurance policy. The loads are enormous and the sales commissions "earned" by the sales representatives are much larger than necessary. Often, the attractive feature of a whole life policy is that after paying premiums for about seven to ten years, the policy "begins paying for itself." True, it does. Out of your interest earned! Worse yet, when a person with a whole life policy dies, the insurance company simply pays the death benefit, then keeps the savings feature for itself.

A better insurance vehicle is the "term life" policy. This policy is simply a specific amount of money paid upon the death of the policy owner. No savings plan is involved. Term life policies are much less expensive than whole life policies, since you are paying for insurance only, and the amount of death benefit is predetermined. Couple the term policy with a regular purchase of mutual funds so that you are creating your own "whole life" policy where all of the money is yours.

The best insurance plan is to increase your own savings and to pursue making wise financial investments. That way, your money is under your control, and you basically become self-insured. As your children leave home, you can gradually decrease the level of insurance coverage and increase your level of savings until there is enough savings to care for a remaining loved one.

Regardless how wealthy you become, a major medical health insurance policy designed to cover the expenses of a catastrophic illness or accident is a wise policy to maintain. Most counselors suggest the purchase of health insurance with a high deductible, usually in the range of $500 to $1,000. The cost of this sort of policy is dramatically lower than those without high deductibles. In the event of some devastating, major calamity, you will have coverage, but for everyday problems, you can afford to pay the deductible from your savings.

Another insurance vehicle you may wish to consider, depending on your age, is a long-term health care policy, designed to cover extended stays in a nursing home or other facility. Normal insurance policies don't cover stays in nursing homes, and many families have been wiped out economically in their attempts to finance an aging relative's stay in such a facility. The price of this type of insurance is relatively modest as compared to the cost of long-term care.

LOANS TO FRIENDS

A friend borrowed $2,000 a year ago and has made no attempt to pay it back. Unfortunately, we didn't have a written agreement about the loan, nor did we agree to a certain time frame. I have asked him time and time again, "When should I expect to receive my money?" He says, "Next month." That was six months ago. What should I do as a Christian, take him to court or just wait for him to pay me when he can?

TREAT THE MONEY AS A GIFT and forget about it. Write it off, and where permissible take a tax deduction for the loss.

Otherwise you will tear yourself up emotionally and spiritually. It simply is not worth it. I've learned this lesson the hard way myself. I've made loans of much larger amounts to individuals and have had them run off without paying the money back.

For my own spiritual and financial well-being, I have written these loans off my mind and off my financial books. I suggest you do the same. Don't allow a few thousand dollars to be a stumbling block or to otherwise impair your spiritual life. Although you have a right to take your friend to court, I would not do that. The Bible says it's better to be defrauded yourself.

God can repay the $2,000 to you many times over. I know He has given back to me much more than the amount of money my "friends" absconded with. The Scripture teaches that if someone comes to you and asks, loan freely, without regard to being paid back.

On the other hand, I've had to learn that I am not a bank and neither are you! We are not in the business of lending money, nor do we have the legal clout to collect on collateral when a borrower defaults.

Moreover, one sure way to separate friends or even family members is to loan money to them. The relationship suddenly changes. No matter how compassionate you may be, or how determined to pay you back that the borrower may be, you have entered into a slave-master relationship. The borrower is slave to the lender.

If you want to help someone financially, it would be better to simply give the person the money with no strings attached.

COSIGNING A NOTE

When is it okay for a Christian to cosign on a loan note?

UNDER NO CIRCUMSTANCES should you *ever* cosign somebody else's loan. The Bible tells us that if you have signed somebody's note, you are like a bird caught in a snare. Do not let sleep come to your eyes until you get off that obligation. Why should your bed be taken away from you to pay somebody else's debt?[43] This is absolute folly.

During the Civil War, many people in the South cosigned notes for family members and friends. They eventually lost almost everything they owned. One of my relatives lost a plantation that later became a part of Birmingham, Alabama, because she cosigned the notes of friends.

When my children were very young, I gathered them together and said, "Children, I want you swear an oath to me."

"Okay, Dad," they said. "What is it?"

"I want you to swear an oath to me that you will never cosign on somebody else's loan."

They weren't fully aware of what I was asking, but they agreed in principle anyhow. In the future, though, they could always say to anyone who asked, "Well, I

---

43   See Proverbs 22:27

promised my father under solemn oath that I'd never cosign on a loan, and I cannot break my vow!"

COMPOUND INTEREST, EXPONENTIAL CURVE, AND THE RULE OF 72

What are compound interest, the exponential curve, and the rule of 72?

INDIVIDUALS, CORPORATIONS, AND NATIONS forget the law of compound interest at their peril. Money compounds when interest is added to principal and then interest is charged on the new principal and the new interest which is, in turn, added again. The results begin as nothing, then become staggering. For simplicity, imagine a loan of $100 at compound interest of 100 percent. For a few years, the loan or the investment grows very slowly, then suddenly the amount, if drawn on a graph, seems to shoot for the sky. This is the exponential curve. At ten years of compounding, the $100 debt (or investment) has reached $51,000. At the end of twenty years, the lowly $100 compounded at 100 percent each year is now $50,000,000. The rule of 72 says that money compounded will double in the number of years that result from dividing the interest rate into 72. For example, a loan at 10 percent compounded will double in 7.2 years and then will double again in another 7.2 years.

In 1982, U.S. government long-term zero coupon bonds were yielding 12.5 percent interest compounded. I urged our partners to load up with them for their tax-deferred accounts. In just twenty years, their risk-free investment had grown between 500 to 600 percent.

Space does not permit a full discussion of every aspect concerning financial matters,
so I strongly suggest you make yourself aware of materials by authors such as
Terri Savage, Ron Blue, Larry Burkett, Dave Ramsey, and others
who approach financial matters from a biblical perspective.

CONTENTS

— CHAPTER 4 —

CHRISTIANS AND 21ST CENTURY PROBLEMS

---

*T*HE CHURCH—those true believers in Jesus Christ from every denomination, social status, every country, and race—is to be "salt and light" in the world. When nonbelievers look at us, something about our lives should make them thirsty for God. Our lives should light the way, pointing them to the Lord. In a real sense, Christians are called to represent, to *re-present*, Jesus Christ to the world.

The apostle Paul most frequently compared the community of believers to a body, giving the church anthropomorphic characteristics such as hands, feet, eyes and ears. Clearly, Paul intended to imply that believers are figuratively the hands, feet, sight, and sound of Jesus in our world.

It's important to remember that Jesus Christ is the head of the church.[1] And we are to be His body in this present world. The purpose of the body is to fulfill the desires and commands of the Head, so as Christians, our priorities ought to be the same as our Lord's. Christ's church should demonstrate Christ's love in such a way that the world can once again see the character, power, and personality of Jesus Christ manifested in and through us!

How we are to do the work of God in our world, and how we can best reach out to hurting humanity without compromising our own integrity raises many interesting questions.

---

[1] 1 Colossians 1:18

REPUBLICANS WITH CLOSET SKELETONS

Please realize that many Christians are not Republicans. You always cut down Democrats. Are there no gay Republicans, or those who have had abortions? Don't Republican politicians have skeletons in their closets, too?

Yes, UNFORTUNATELY, some Republicans have closets loaded with skeletons, too. And yes, God loves Democrats as much as He loves Republicans! Many Democrats will be in heaven right along with their Republican brothers and sisters, because we are not saved by our political affiliations. We are saved by trusting in Jesus.

When it comes to politics, we must decide who we will vote for based on the policies they support. Ironically, Abraham Lincoln himself lamented,

> All but three ministers in my hometown are opposed to my presidency because I am opposed to slavery. Do they not see that this is an abomination to God? How can they read the New Testament and say that we should hold other human beings in bondage? And how can they oppose somebody who wants to set men and women free?

Lincoln had previously been a Democrat but became the leader of what is now known as the Republican Party when the Democratic Party lost popularity over the states' rights–abolition of slavery debates during the years before and immediately after the Civil War.

Similarly, today we have moral issues that Christians must vote on in the public political arena. Abortion on demand, as well as partial-birth abortion, and euthanasia are abominations to God. Driving God out of our schools has proven to be counterproductive in the quality of education, as well as the safety and security of our students and teachers. This is an abomination. The anti-God decisions of the U.S. Supreme Court have been detestable before a holy God. Attempts to legitimize the homosexual lifestyle, which is clearly prohibited in Scripture, are simply wrong. These issues are not private matters; they affect all of us.

If a political party endorses those positions, whether the candidates are Republican or Democrat, they are willfully placing themselves in opposition to the Bible, and Christians should not support them. On the other hand, if a candidate stands for biblical ethics and morality, Christians should support that person regardless of party affiliation. For instance, Governor Casey of Pennsylvania was a Democrat who embraced biblical positions, and Christians supported him wholeheartedly. Their support wasn't based on politics or party affiliation, but on principle.

I was a Democrat for more than five decades. My father was a Democrat, as was his father. My dad was a United States senator who ran as a Democrat. But my concern is about issues. If a party or a candidate supports anti-God, nonbiblical policies, I cannot in good conscience support them. And neither should you!

AREN'T ALL POLITICAL PARTIES GOOD?

Instead of endorsing one political party, why not pray for all the parties, and that the party leaders' hearts would be turned toward God?

ALL CHRISTIANS SHOULD PRAY FOR OUR POLITICAL LEADERS; moreover, we are instructed to respect those who have authority over us.[2] But we must also be wise in deciding who we will support in the political arena. Do you favor abortion on demand? Do you think that unrestricted drug use is a good thing? Do you think people should be able to engage in infanticide or euthanasia? Would you like to see laws that support homosexual teachers in schools or homosexual behavior being taught to our children as a normal lifestyle?

Most Christians hold strong opinions on those issues not simply for political reasons, but on biblical grounds. Therefore, we should support candidates whose political positions best align themselves with biblical principles. That doesn't mean that Christians should cease to be kind, considerate, and civil when discussing these issues. We don't need to agree with members of a political party to act in a Christlike manner toward them. We need not be vindictive, mean, or spiteful toward people of another political party. But neither must we support them in their error. We have a responsibility to support political parties or candidates on the basis of moral principles; that is not a divisive "party spirit."

Party spirit in the church, however, where people are purposely set at odds against each other, is divisive, destructive, negative, fleshly behavior and should be condemned.

While acknowledging that we are citizens of another kingdom—the kingdom of God—and that prayer is our greatest means of bringing about positive change, Christians have a responsibility to participate in the political process of the nation.

---

2   See Romans 13:1–8

Edmund Burke said it well: "All that is necessary for evil to triumph is for good men to do nothing." If you don't participate in the political process, somebody who disagrees with you probably will. If we sit back in our complacency and do nothing, we will one day have to answer to our children and grandchildren.

WHY DISTURB PEOPLE CONTENT WITHOUT JESUS?

Most people I know are content without Jesus. Why should I try to make them do anything different?

IF YOU TRULY LOVE SOMEONE, you want to help them. If you had a friend who was enjoying life, but you happened to notice a cancerous tumor growing on that individual's face or leg, wouldn't you interfere with their harmony long enough to get them to an oncologist before he or she died? If you really love someone, you will disquiet that person about a problem that can potentially destroy him or her. If someone is driving a car blissfully down a road, getting ready to run over a cliff, wouldn't you try to get that person's attention and warn him or her of the impending danger? Likewise, if you see someone leading a destructive lifestyle, and you really care for that person, you are compelled to say something such as, "If you keep this up, you are going to kill yourself!"

That is what sharing the gospel is all about. Some people actually have grown accustomed to living in darkness, ignorant of or oblivious to the joys of living in the light. Many people prefer to live in spiritual darkness. But if you care about your friends or family members who don't know Jesus, pray for an opening in their hearts and minds, and then do all you can to bring them to the knowledge of the Lord.

Don't be fooled by appearances. You might be amazed at how few people are truly content. Many people are searching, looking for something better than the temporary happiness they have found. They know there must be more to life than simply waiting to die! Their hearts are hungry to really know God. St. Augustine said, "Our hearts are restless till they find their rest in Thee." In every strata of society, at every income and educational level, people are hungry for genuine spiritual reality. They may not show it. They may look as happy as they can be, but inside, they have a deep, unsettled feeling that something is not right.

God loves them and He can disquiet them so they will sense their need. The Holy Spirit convicts of sin, righteousness, and judgment.[3] That's why before you

---

[3]   See John 16:8–11

start talking to people about their relationships with God, the most important thing you can do is to pray. Pray that God will reveal to them their need, that they will sense it and want to find the Answer.

Years ago, I was working at a small church in Mount Vernon, New York, and my friend Harald Bredesen and I decided to visit people in the housing projects that were close to the church. The population of that part of town was primarily African-American. We were right on the edge of the Bronx, a pretty tough part of the city of New York. We went to an apartment building, but we didn't know anyone who lived there, or even which door to knock on where we might find someone wanting to know God. We asked the Lord to lead us, and then I took my finger and literally went down the roster of names on the little bulletin board listing the people in the building.

My finger pointed to one name and it felt as if something had hit me in the stomach. I knew this was the one, so Harald and I stepped into the elevator. We went up to the apartment and rang the doorbell. A black woman in her late thirties answered the door and stared back at us.

We said, "We are from the First Reformed Church in Mount Vernon, and we just came by to talk with you about the Lord."

"Come in," she offered. I talked to her for about five minutes and recognized that she was in a desperate condition. Finally, I simply blurted, "Would you like to know the Lord?"

"Oh, yes!" she said.

"Let's just kneel down right here, and the three of us will ask the Lord to do something," I said. "You pray with me, and we will ask God to touch you."

I began to pray and she repeated my words after me. When I said, "And Jesus, I ask you to come into my heart . . ." the woman suddenly called out, "Oh, yes, Jesus! I've got to have You; oh, Jesus, please come into my heart right now!" When we left, she was a new person, her sins were forgiven, and she was rejoicing in God.

That is why we need to see every person who doesn't know Jesus as lost; that's why we need to boldly present the gospel, trusting God to give us the right opportunity. You don't have to have all the answers; Jesus is the Answer! God is already preparing the hearts of people who want to know Him. We don't force anything, nor should we ever try. All we have to do is follow God's directions, find them, and tell them the good news!

---

3   See John 16:8–11

MY CHURCH SPLIT LEFT ME DISILLUSIONED

> I'm a Christian who has not been in church since 1994. At that time,
> I was a church member and attended every Sunday. Our church had
> a split, our pastor was asked to leave, and now I can't bring myself
> to set foot in any church for fear of losing another church family.
> What should I do?

YOU HAVE BEEN HURT because of the loss of dear friends, but you must overcome your fear. It does not come from God. Your fear does not comport with the
reality of who church people really are. Christians aren't perfect . . . they are just
forgiven. Therefore no church is perfect. In any group of human beings,
Christian or not, there will be occasional problems, squabbles, disagreements,
and even choices to part company. Paul and Barnabas had their differences over
John Mark, and the two great missionaries went separate directions. We shouldn't
be surprised when we have similar differences in the church today.

But don't allow disagreements to keep you from fellowship. The Scripture says
to keep on, "endeavoring to keep the unity of the Spirit in the bonds of peace,"[4] till
we come into a perfect man unto the knowledge of God. We haven't attained doctrinal unity yet, but we can have the unity of the Spirit in the body of Christ.

Find a church that you enjoy, get acquainted with the people, and see how
things fit. Do they believe the Bible and live out its teachings? You may have to visit
several congregations before you find one with whom you feel you can worship
freely and with whom you can serve the Lord with vigor and enthusiasm. Refuse to
allow past failures to keep you from future fellowship. Step out in faith. Remember
perfect love casts our fear, so try love. It will be worth the effort!

MY BROTHER HAS TURNED OFF THE CHURCH

> My brother has been a Christian all his life, yet in his mid-fifties, he
> has become so disillusioned and disappointed with Christians. He
> still believes in Jesus, but he refuses to become involved in any
> church. What can I do to help him?

EXPLAIN TO HIM that the sun may shine on a dirty mud puddle, but that
doesn't in any way diminish the sun. It just means that there is a dirty mud

---

4   Ephesians 4:3 (KJV)

puddle. Clean pools and clean water exist. In nature there are ugly plants and pretty plants, weeds and flowers; some smell fragrantly and some have an awful stench. We should not resent God for the reprehensible actions or attitudes of people who claim to know Him well, but may not.

Remind your brother that Jesus cleansed the temple, saying to them, "My Father's house will be a place of prayer, but you have turned it into a den of thieves."[5] These were all so-called religious people, but they were blocking the entrance to God's house. Jesus said, "Woe to you, scribes and Pharisees . . . for you do not enter in yourselves, nor do you allow those who are entering to go in."[6]

We must understand that only Jesus Christ is perfect, and even people who claim to know Him well are not perfect. John and Peter were apostles of great note, but there was also Judas Iscariot, who betrayed Christ.

Encourage your brother to see his disillusionment as an excuse to avoid religious commitment by blaming it on "those hypocrites" in the church. That is nonsense. It is a judgmental attitude that needs to be dealt with, either by reason or perhaps simply by confronting him with honesty and love. I also would encourage you to take your brother to a nonchurch meeting of Christians—a home meeting, a rally, a breakfast, a luncheon, or a dinner. Let him enjoy for a time the company of real joyous Christians. Perhaps his attitude will change.

HOW CAN WE DO GREATER THINGS THAN JESUS?

Jesus said that we (believers in Him) would do even greater things than what He did. What does this mean, and why aren't we?

IN SOME MEASURE, we *are* doing greater things in this world than Jesus did. Remember that He traveled on foot in a tiny area called Palestine, or Israel. He spent most of His ministry speaking to small crowds in small synagogues in small towns.

Today, we can board a jet and go around the world in a matter of hours. We can broadcast the message of Jesus by satellite and reach out to the world. We can broadcast the gospel in English and have it translated into fifty or sixty different languages. We can see simply millions of people come to the Lord in a few days or weeks. In terms of the scope of outreach of those such as Billy Graham, Bill Bright,

---

5   Luke 19:46 (NLT)
6   Matthew 23:13

or CBN, it is a much larger ministry than what Jesus had. In that sense, just as Jesus said, we are doing greater works.

Unquestionably, Jesus was looking ahead to the Holy Spirit's work in and through our lives when He said, "He who believes in Me, the works that I do shall he do also; and greater works than these shall he do; because I go to the Father."[7] The Holy Spirit working through the lives of millions of believers surely has more of a widespread impact than Christ's localized, earthly ministry.

Now, are we as pure and holy as Jesus? Not a chance. Do we see the kind of miracles that He did when He walked on water, raised the dead, stilled the storm, restored the eyes of the blind? Collectively in the church, we are seeing some of these things, but to my knowledge, none of us have attained the works Jesus did, and we certainly haven't exceeded them. In terms of quantity of miracles? Yes. Consistent quality? Not yet.

Nevertheless, potential exists for those of us who serve Him to indeed do even greater miracles than Jesus did. But we haven't seen them yet, so perhaps our best days lie ahead.

WHAT IS GOD'S PURPOSE FOR ME?

How do I know if I am accomplishing God's purpose for me? I constantly feel that I am not doing enough. I wonder if that thought comes from Satan. Do I wait for a word from God, or do I go find things to do to help other people?

THE CROWDS CAME TO JESUS with this same question. What must we be doing to do the works of God? His answer was simple: The work of God is to believe in him whom God sent.[8] The greatest work we can do is to believe in Jesus Christ and to trust Him. After that, the most important service any Christian can perform is to love one another as He loves us. Beyond that, we can enter into the ministry of intercession for the world, for our nation and our leaders, for people to be brought into the kingdom of God, and for your fellow believers.

Before you worry about what you should be doing—"I need to visit the senior citizens in the nursing home," or, "I ought to be cooking meals for the hungry and homeless," or, "I feel awful that I haven't told that person at work about Jesus yet"—

---

7 John 14:12
8 John 5:26–29

spend time with the Lord yourself. Grow in your relationship with Him. Out of your relationship with God, you may begin to sense Him leading you to become involved in some particular service, ministry, or activity. But allow the Holy Spirit to guide you. Don't get involved in some activity simply because of guilt. God does not heap guilt upon us. He does not desire our work so much as our fellowship. He wants to draw you into intimacy with Himself.

Some of the great men of God spent five or six hours in prayer for every hour of service. We try to spend twelve hours of service with twelve minutes of prayer. Remember Jesus said, "Without me, you can do nothing."[9]

PROBLEMS AT HOME . . . WHY EVANGELIZE THE WORLD?

Why should we spend so much effort trying to evangelize the world when we have so many problems in our own country?

BECAUSE THERE ARE PEOPLE IN THE WORLD WHO NEED JESUS, and Jesus commanded us, "Go therefore and make disciples of all the nations, baptizing them in the name of the Father and the Son and the Holy Spirit, teaching them to observe all that I commanded you; and lo, I am with you always, even to the end of the age."[10] The great commission didn't say, Stay in your own community and keep taking more water to the ocean. America has been evangelized in so many ways and so many times, it hurts. We have so many churches, so many evangelical organizations, so much Christian literature, so many Bibles. In many homes, we have three or more Bibles, and we rarely read one! Yet around the world, hundreds of millions of people have never even seen a Bible and never had a chance to learn about Jesus. That is why we need to go into the world—because God told us to, and because people are out there waiting to receive the gospel with open arms.

Ironically, in America those who have heard the gospel but not received it are often the most hostile to it. They decided to be their own gods. We should never give up trying to reach them; we should pray for them and ask God for wisdom as to how to approach them in a fresh way. But at the same time, Jesus told us not to cast pearls before swine.[11] If somebody doesn't want to hear the gospel, shake the

---

9   John 15:5
10   Matthew 28:19–20
11   See Matthew 7:6

dust off your feet and go somewhere else. Multitudes of people have never heard the message of God's love and forgiveness even one time. Why spend most of our time, energy, and resources trying to convince people who have rejected God over and over? Others deserve a chance to know Him, and He's given us the responsibility to tell them about Jesus.

NATURE STEWARDS OR TREE HUGGERS?

What should be the Christian's attitude and role in regard to our environment?

WE ARE STEWARDS. God made a garden and told man to tend it. We are to govern this planet under Him. We are to protect the animals, the plant life, the air, water, and the earth that God has given us. At the same time, we have a biblical mandate to subdue the earth, to take dominion over it, and we are to possess the earth. But nothing in the Bible says we are to rape the earth.

Unfortunately, we did precisely that. We gashed open mountains, cleared forests, polluted streams, and poisoned the air. We decimated whole species of animals. Think of the buffalo in the western portion of the U.S. or the egrets in Florida. We slaughtered them simply to obtain their feathers for some fashion-conscious lady to wear in a hat soon discarded. Such callous disregard for the earth and its creatures is a sin against God.

On the other hand, many extreme environmentalists have made a god out of nature. They think that nature and God are one. It is a Hindu philosophy which says that we are all part of this cosmos; the cosmos is "god," and there is no God outside of it all. Some people worship the wilderness, the trees, snail darters, and everything living, putting those things on par with man, or worse yet, on par with God! That is a nonbiblical notion, a false religion, and Christians shouldn't get hooked into it. The Bible makes it clear that man is a superior being, made in the image of God, and animals and plants are not. We are to worship the Creator, not the creation.

We can legitimately use animals for our garments and our shoes, and their meat and eggs, milk, and various other products. Animals are intended to serve mankind, not the other way around. Similarly, if we care for the forests and replenish them, there is nothing wrong with using wood to build our buildings, boats, and furniture. Using wisely the environment that God provided is biblical stewardship. Obsessing over the environment is foolishness or fanaticism.

IS CHURCH ATTENDANCE IMPORTANT?

Why do I need to go to church? Can't I just worship God every-where, anywhere I want?

IN A SENSE YOU CAN, but the New Testament tells us that we must "not for-sake our own assembling together."[12] As believers, we need to be in the presence of other Christians. Iron sharpens iron. We need the discipline, fellowship, com-fort, and understanding of other like-minded people. We are not hermits. God did not make man to live alone, but He made Him as a social creature. We need to gather together with those who share our faith and our point of view.

We also need to receive teaching from those who have been gifted in and com-mitted to those tasks by the Lord. Such biblical education is most frequently acces-sible in church. Can you worship God just as effectively out under the trees? Of course you can. He is the God of nature and the God of everything. You can defi-nitely worship God in environments other than church settings. But the com-mandment is that we not forsake "assembling together, as is the habit of some." Don't be unwise; we really do need each other.

CONDONING HOMOSEXUAL BEHAVIOR IN THE CHURCH

Certain denominations are beginning to condone homosexual behavior by members of the church. Do you feel it is for financial benefit, political gain, or social acceptance?

WE HAVE AN ENORMOUS PRESSURE in our society right now known as "political correctness." The "politically correct" think that it is inappropriate to criticize anybody for anything—including their religion (unless it happens to be evangelical Christianity), sexual preferences, lifestyle, or just about anything else. Furthermore, the multiculturalism being advocated today makes a bush native in a dugout canoe the cultural equal of a Ph.D. in physics; the German Nazis were the equivalent of the government of Israel. To the multiculturalists no culture is superior to any other—certainly not Christianity.

The Bible makes it extremely clear that homosexual behavior is sin, that the actions and the lifestyle are not acceptable for God's people. In the Old Testament, this sin was punishable by death.[13] Furthermore, the apostle Paul indicated that the

---

12   Hebrews 10:25
13   See Leviticus 20:13

acceptance of homosexuality by the society was a clear indicator of the decline of a civilization, the last stage before God gave people up to their own sinfulness. Scripture says, "For they exchanged the truth of God for a lie, and worshiped and served the creature rather than the Creator, who is blessed forever. Amen. For this reason God gave them over to degrading passions; for their women exchanged the natural function for that which is unnatural, and in the same way also the men abandoned the natural function of the woman and burned in their desire towards one another, men with men committing indecent acts and receiving in their persons the due penalty of their error."[14] God also gave them up to uncleanness through the lusts of their own hearts, to dishonor their own bodies between themselves. . . . God gave them over to a reprobate mind."[15]

In this same passage, Paul talks about women committing acts with women and men engaging in acts with men which are "unseemly," unnatural, indecent acts.[16] This is prohibited in Scripture, and the apostle Paul pulls no punches about it. He says bluntly that those who have engaged in homosexual behavior will not enter the kingdom of heaven, unless they are cleansed by the blood of Christ.[17] Those who continue a homosexual lifestyle after receiving knowledge of the truth run a similar risk.

For a church to accept homosexuals, to love them, minister to them, and help them find deliverance and freedom from bondage is one thing. For a church to accept homosexual behavior in the congregation or anywhere else and imply that it is normal is a craven surrender to political correctness, is contrary to Scripture, and it is wrong.

As for homosexual tendencies, certainly there may be people in the congregation who struggle with such feelings, just as people struggle against alcoholic tendencies or, quite frankly, heterosexual lusts. But we do not have to act on these tendencies. We can reject them as being contrary to God's best for our lives and move on without a sense of condemnation.

Someone who is tempted to engage in homosexual expressions but doesn't act on them has not committed sin in that area. Nor is it sinful for someone to experience a temptation toward immoral heterosexual activity, as long as it is not consummated. Both individuals need to be under the control of the Holy Spirit. There is nothing sinful about the tendencies, but to act on those desires and engage in homosexual activities, or to engage in fornication or adultery is blatant sin. Should a church accept that and put the imprimatur of Jesus on such activity? Absolutely not.

---

14   Romans 1:25–27
15   Romans 1:24, 28 (KJV)
16   See Romans 1:26–27
17   See 1 Corinthians 6:9-11

Like heterosexuals, many homosexuals are struggling to break free from the tendencies toward sexual sin in their lives. Many of these men and women love God and are truly trying to live for the Lord. For a relatively small number of people, sexual sin may even be demonically inspired. Such people who have had ungodly sexual relationships often need deliverance from the bondage of the past. For the most part, however, homosexuality is a learned behavior pattern. It may be the result of molestation in one's childhood or perhaps an unhealthy relationship with a parent, sibling, a relative, or another respected adult. Regardless of the cause, if a homosexual person honestly pursues counseling, it is possible to exit that lifestyle and live a full, normal life.

The Christian is to love the sinner and hate the sin. God loves everybody—heterosexuals, homosexuals, and lesbians. But God does not condone the homosexual or lesbian lifestyle. Nor does He condone sexual sin in any of us. The church's attitude toward the homosexual should be one of love and compassion, based on the truth of God's Word. We can say to the person who sins sexually, "We care for you and accept you, and we love you enough to help you get free of that sinful lifestyle."

KEEPING THE SABBATH

What does it mean for Christians to keep the Sabbath nowadays?

THE BIBLE SAYS that God labored for six days, and on the seventh day He rested.[18] God didn't rest because He was tired. He ceased from His labors because He had finished creation, therefore He hallowed the Sabbath day.

When Jesus interpreted the Sabbath, He said, "The Sabbath was made for man, and not man for the Sabbath."[19] Human beings require a day of rest. Working seven days a week with no break, followed by seven more days of work with no break will eventually destroy your mental, physical, and spiritual health. Any society that encourages people to work seven days a week, week after week, will ultimately destroy its people. We *must* have a day off for rest and refreshment.

Even many churches have missed this important truth. Some churches have Sunday school, two worship services, then an afternoon meeting, and an evening service of some sort. Then they have youth group, and more in the middle of the week. Although it is wonderful to have so many spiritual activities that people can

18   Genesis 2:3
19   Mark 2:27

enjoy, God's people must have time to rest and nurture family relationships, too. The Sabbath should be a day of rest, not more frantic spiritual activity; it should be a time to read the Bible, pray, talk to the Lord, when you have time to consider heavenly things, when you recharge your spiritual batteries. That's what keeping the Sabbath holy is all about.

The church used to emphasize keeping the Sabbath holy, but in recent years we have compromised. Now, government mandates dictate that we can't have closings on Sunday because this may violate the constitution. Nonsense! But these rulings are law, and as a result we have seven days a week of full-blown commerce in which people are flocking to malls, restaurants, and other places that at one time were closed one day per week. The people who have to work in the malls don't really have a quiet day of rest they can enjoy. No wonder we have so many emotional breakdowns and so much mental and physical stress in our society. We are in a self-destruct mode, ready to implode on ourselves because of our ignorance of this simple but vital truth.

It may not be easy, but practice setting aside one day each week for essential rest, prayer, relaxation, and close communion with the Lord. The remaining six days of your week will go much better!

KOOKY MINISTERS ON TELEVISION

Why are so many ministers on television and radio such kooks? I am a believer, but I must admit that I get embarrassed when my non-Christian coworkers mention Christian television programs. I have no defense for the foolishness I see and hear on some of these programs. What can I do to help turn the negative influence to a positive?

MAYBE YOU CAN WRITE THE KOOKS and tell them to shape up or get off the air. Amazingly, people are often attracted to the bizarre, and some of our television and radio personalities provide contemporary versions of yesteryear's traveling sideshows.

Outlandish ministers are often able to gain a following, since they become a magnet for people who thrive on the strange and weird. But valid ministries do not resort to or condone such unorthodox practices. That is why I have never appreciated the title "televangelist," because to me, it is a term of scorn created by the *Washington Post*. I am a religious broadcaster, but I am not a televangelist.

Certainly, many religious broadcasters are doing excellent work, presenting the gospel on radio and television, encouraging Christians, and building up the body of Christ. The outlandish will always have an audience, but that should not diminish our support and appreciation for those Christian broadcasters who are doing well.

IS IT OKAY TO GET ANGRY?

What expressions of anger are appropriate for Christians?

JESUS BECAME ANGRY at the Pharisees and priests who had allowed the desecration of His Father's house. He overturned the moneychangers' stands in the temple. He smashed open the cages containing doves and pigeons used for temple sacrifice. He said, "My Father's house is supposed to be a house of prayer, but you have turned it into a den of thieves!"[20] He made a whip and drove them out of the temple.

We talk about "gentle Jesus, meek and mild," but there was nothing mild about driving out a whole bunch of moneychangers. Jesus must have been an angry individual to have done that.

We should be angry at the abuse of the unfortunate, at the corruption of the powerful, and at the desecration of the things of God. We should rise up in righteous indignation against that sort of thing. On the other hand, we should be very careful that our anger is not merely because we have been injured or some interest of ours has been hurt, and we are therefore striking back. Ask yourself: Am I righteously angry because of a clear breaking of God's law, or am I angry because somebody hurt me? That is the defining point.

NUCLEAR WEAPONS—UNREPENTED SIN?

I believe that the invention and use of nuclear weapons is the greatest unrepented sin of our time. Where is your voice on the moral crisis of America's continued possession of nuclear weapons?

THE "NUCLEAR GENIE" has been out of the bottle for a long time. Since World War II, nuclear proliferation around the globe has continued, and the United States needs to maintain an arsenal to defend our nation against those who might use nuclear weapons against us. It's nice to talk about nations destroying

---

[20]   See Luke 19:46

their nuclear arsenals, but it is unlikely that will happen because of the sinfulness of people's hearts. Until everybody gets on board with the idea of getting rid of these weapons, we will have to protect ourselves.

Understand, the discovery of nuclear energy was not sinful in itself. One of the men who worked on the Chicago nuclear project thought that he was engaged in a process that would bring the world an inexpensive, safe, and unlimited energy source. The tragedy is that we did not pursue energy from the fusion of hydrogen atoms, but instead spent billions of dollars to create an arsenal of fantastically destructive hydrogen bombs.

WHAT MAKES A WORSHIP SERVICE?

Our church has begun a forty-five-minute "express" worship service to reach busy people. The service is mostly praise and worship, no preaching, no sermons. Attendance has doubled in a few weeks, and many newspapers and magazines are covering us. What are your thoughts?

I'M AN OLD-FASHIONED, Reformation-theology type, who still believes that the preaching of the Word should be at the center of the service. The idea of a quickie sermon or no sermon at all is like "Take 5 for God at 12," and seems almost an insult to the Lord.

Although I applaud the church's efforts to reach people through whatever means possible, what good is reaching them if we don't give them something of substance? The idea of an "express service" in which people sing and clap their hands a bit may be popular, and you may attract a large crowd, but it's not really a church service. We assemble ourselves together to pray, to have communion, to meet with and worship the Lord in reverence. That usually takes more than forty-five minutes. Our attitude should be "It is the Lord's day." It's more than merely talking or singing about God for a few minutes, so we can feel better before we rush out to a restaurant or the golf course or to watch a football game on television.

EVOLUTION VERSUS CREATION

It is almost certain that the world has been in existence longer than the Bible suggests. How much credence should we give evolutionary teachings, and where do we put the Creation story? I'm tired of

Christians sticking their heads in the sand as if there were not real contradictions to scientific explanations and biblical explanations for creation.

To DATE, SCIENTISTS HAVE GIVEN us at least ten cosmogonies, or theories, concerning the origin of the cosmos—ten different theories, and they all conflict with one another! Obviously, science likes to change its mind.

We don't have to worry that some things we believe in the Bible do not agree with so-called science. While today's science is much more accurate than in the past, it still doesn't have a definitive explanation for how the earth was formed. The current theory which I accept points to a big bang theory as the beginning of creation, when about 15 billion years ago an extraordinarily dense mass exploded, and out of that came an expanding universe. Part of the reason scientists believe this theory stems from the movement of the planets. Study of the cosmos indicates that the planets are still moving away from each other. Imagine that we took a big balloon that had not been expanded, put little dots all around it, and then began to blow up the balloon. As we blew up the balloon, the dots would get farther and farther apart. That is similar to what astronomers observe has been happening to our universe during these 15 billion years.

The big bang theory is not at odds with the belief in a creator or what is called intelligent design. The Bible neither supports or negates such a theory, since the Bible was not written as a science book. Genesis is the backdrop God uses to show that the Creator of the universe picked Abraham and his heirs, through whom He would bring forth the Messiah and the revelation of His salvation to mankind.

The Bible tells us that God created certain orders of life in the sea. He then created certain orders of life on the land, then mammals, and then human beings. That is exactly what the pseudoscience known as "evolution" has discovered. However, they then step beyond science to guess that higher life forms spontaneously evolved from the primitive ooze. The evolutionists' hypothesis is deeply flawed because they claim there was no divine creation. Evolution as currently expounded cannot explain at least one million missing links between the various classes and phyla of the biological order. These links would be absolutely necessary to explain the cosmos as it now appears. But these links don't exist! We just don't have them. There is no real evidence to support the theory that lower orders of life *evolved* into higher orders of life. We do not have a single case where one life form has been observed in the fossil remains evolving into another higher life form.

As a former farm boy myself, I found that one of the most obvious proofs against evolutionary theory is the mule. I used to drive a team of mules when I was a kid, so I learned a great deal about them. Mules are sterile. They can't reproduce themselves. They come from the mating of a male donkey with a female horse, yet they can't reproduce. Interesting, isn't it, that a mating of animals as close as the horse and the donkey produces sterile offspring. How, then, can it possibly be that we have an amoebae, which ascends to become a lizard out in the swamp, that ascends to become a snake on land, which in turn transforms into a bird, which settles to land to become a premammal, then an ape, and finally a human being? Anyone without a clear-cut antireligious bias would have to step back and say, "This is nonsense." These things don't happen and never have! It takes a great deal more faith to believe in "scientific" evolution than it does to believe that a wise God created life forms in ascending order, what I like to call "creative evolution."

Interestingly, we used to hear evolution discussed as a theory. When did the theory vanish and evolution become a fact? It never did. It is a refuge to those who refuse to acknowledge the truth. Evolutionists are trying to believe in what they think is true. They find one jawbone out in the forest someplace, and out of that they construct a whole apelike creature and say that this creature is a Cro-Magnon human being. Their science is a religion to them, and they are neither good at science or religion. It is possible to show, from many different sources, that the theory of evolution, as we know it, is wrong.

Unfortunately, the theory of evolution is taught in public schools as credible, and people laugh when you say we are going to teach creationism or "intelligent design" alongside it. But it is an attempt by man to downgrade God. Some human beings do not want to acknowledge that they were created. They would rather think that they came from a single-celled paramecium or an amoeba than to acknowledge that they have divine origins. It is astounding that some human beings would prefer to see themselves as the progeny of slime rather than admit that they were created by God, in the image of God, and for God's glory.

SPIRITUAL LEADERS AS RUDE, ARROGANT BULLIES

Why are so many Christian leaders rude, arrogant bullies and dictators in the way they lead their ministries? I understand being dogmatic when they have firm direction from God, but I have worked in several ministries where the leader is little more than a tyrant when he or she is out of the public eye. Shouldn't Christian leaders display

the fruit of the Holy Spirit in the way they manage people, maybe even more than the rest of us?

I CAN'T SPEAK FOR CHRISTIAN LEADERS who may be arrogant, but I have set for my own goal to stay humble before the Lord, because I know that at any time He could lift His anointing from me, and I would be nothing. I heard Billy Graham say years ago, "If God would take His anointing from me, my lips would turn to clay."

True Christian leaders recognize the greatness of God. Ministers recognize that we are nothing but servants. The word *minister* means "servant." The greatest among us are those who serve the most. I would aspire to be a servant, not a dictator.

Granted, some ministers get full of themselves and get used to the adulation of people who tell them how wonderful they are, but that can be a minister's downfall. D. L. Moody was coming out of a church when two women came up to him, and one of them said, "Oh, Reverend Moody, you are a wonderful Christian man!"

Moody looked at them and replied, "What are you trying to do, Madam, ruin my ministry?" Moody wasn't being rude; he just knew that ministers must turn a deaf ear to that sort of praise. If you are going to serve God and give Him the glory, you cannot be swayed by the applause of the crowd nor be moved by their criticism.

In some ministries, because of the lack of structure, discipline, or accountability, the leader tends to think of himself or herself as a little "pope," infallible, able to do as he or she pleases. But God will bring down those who think of themselves more highly than they ought. The most dangerous thing in the world for somebody who claims to be a servant of God is to act as a tyrant. He will get his just desserts from the Lord. I would counsel anyone in a position of spiritual leadership to walk very humbly, because those of us who teach God's Word and His ways will be held to a much higher standard than those whom we teach.[21]

STARVING CHILDREN ON TELEVISION

I hate to turn on the television and see pictures of all those starving kids. It's not that I don't feel compassion; I do, and I support as many charitable groups as I can. Yet, I feel that these groups who flagrantly depict young children in squalor are attempting to play on my emotions. Am I wrong for feeling this way, and if so, what can I do about

---

[21]   See James 3:1

it? I'm already maxed out on my charitable giving and my time working with local food kitchens.

YES, I THINK YOU ARE WRONG TO FEEL THAT WAY. You ought to think, *I am doing the most I can; there isn't any more unless God gives me more.* Begin to pray for those children and pray for the agencies that are attempting to help them. Regrettably, some agencies are frauds and have bogus orphanages, bogus feeding programs, and are basically stealing money under the guise of doing good. But there are many fine charities that are helping the poor, the needy, and the orphans and widows. Many people within these organizations are moved with great compassion toward hurting people, and they long to show Americans who are living in this affluent society how much need exists in the world. Perhaps that sometimes evokes a negative reaction, but it can also inspire the response that says, "I want to help them."

If you can't give any more, or as you say, you are maxed out, I recommend that you begin to pray for these charities, and encourage others to give to these charities, because it is noble to help widows and orphans in their inflictions. The Bible says, "This is pure and undefiled religion in the sight of our God and Father, to visit orphans and widows in their distress, and to keep oneself unstained by the world."[22] Surely that pure religion involves helping hurting people in their afflictions.

---

[22] James 1:27

CONTENTS

— CHAPTER 5 —

BAFFLERS ABOUT THE BIBLE
The Bible and the Spiritual Life

---

*T*HE WORD OF GOD is our guide for daily living, and it contains the answers to the most important questions of life: Where did we come from? Why are we here? Where are we going?

Interestingly, when tragedy strikes or troubles come, people turn to the Bible looking for answers; but even when times are good, the Word of God is the best-selling piece of literature in the world! It has sold literally *billions* of copies and has been translated into more than twenty-two hundred languages. People everywhere are excited to discover what God has to say about our lives.

In applying the Scripture to our lives, however, we need to keep in mind some basic Bible-study principles. First, allow the Bible to speak for itself. Don't come to it with preconceived notions of what the Scripture means. Let God's Spirit speak to your heart and mind through His Word. The same Spirit who inspired the writers to pen the words of the Bible will help you to understand what those words mean.

Second, take the Bible's total teaching on a subject rather than focusing on selected or isolated texts, or the texts you enjoy. We can learn practical lessons from the defeats and failures recorded in Scripture as well as the triumphs and victories.

Third, as you study the Bible, ask yourself practical questions such as, *What does this have to do with me? How can I apply what the Word of God says to my life?* Studying the Scripture merely for information or to gain knowledge is noble, but it will leave you disappointed unless you learn to apply what you have read. Ask yourself, *Is there an action I should take, an attitude I must change, an example I should follow or avoid, a command I must obey?* Look for God's promises on which you can rest your faith, and notice the conditions that pertain to it. In other words, allow God's Word to be the foundation on which you build your life.

I find guidance and direction for my life in God's Word. He speaks to my heart, mind, and conscience through the Bible, and I can communicate with Him through prayer. But a study of the Scripture often raises more tough questions, some that seem to defy answers. Here are some questions that sometimes baffle even sincere believers.

WHY BELIEVE THE BIBLE?

I get so disgusted when someone tells me I should believe something simply "because the Bible tells me so." That's nice for children, along with Santa Claus and the Easter bunny and fairy tales. But when I feel that I am truly seeking answers, it is patronizing and insulting to tell me to believe something simply because an old book includes that information. Why should I believe the Bible any more than the Book of Mormon, the Koran, or some other religious writings?

THE STORY IS TOLD of a woman standing in front of the *Mona Lisa* who said, "I don't understand what is so special about this picture."

The curator said, "Madam, this picture isn't on trial; you are." The painting had stood the test of time, and all the experts acknowledged it as a masterpiece. Similarly, the Bible has stood up under intense archeological, scientific, and philosophical scrutiny. It has been studied by the wisest people on the face of the earth, and it has proven that it is indeed inspired by God.

To say, "Here is a Bible verse, so do as it says," may seem insulting. Some people need a more rational approach to faith. Nevertheless, the Bible is a book of love from a holy God to His people. It is the story of the Jewish people, the redemption that God brought to their lives, and how God chose to save mankind and draw them to Himself by offering His Son as the sacrifice for their sins.

The Bible is also a practical guide for life. In terms of business, politics, and government, the Book of Proverbs is one of the best handbooks ever written.

The principles taught in the Bible still work today. A number of years ago, I wrote a book called *The Secret Kingdom*. It examined ten of the clearly stated, key principles that Jesus Christ enunciated. I pushed them as far as I could push them into human life and discovered that they were valid in every single situation—social contracts, church building, art, architecture, practical relationships, building a business—you name it. The law of use, the law of reciprocity, the law of responsibility—these were all there. In my opinion, these biblical principles are self-validating. If you live according to them, you will discover that they work!

So it is not a question of merely believing some ancient book. The Bible is relevant today; it is the best, practical guidebook for human life I have found anywhere in the world.

Much more importantly, the Bible tells us how to find God and how to be saved. It provides principles for living in our families, our relationships with our fellow man, and our government. It's all there.

Interestingly, the government of the United States of America is based squarely on the principles of the Bible. The relationship of man to God is the foundation stone of the liberties we enjoy. The Bible says, "Where the Spirit of the LORD is, there is liberty."[1] The founders of our nation considered such truths to be self-evident. The United States has been the most successful experiment in government of any nation in the history of mankind, and its laws—until recently—have been based on biblical principles.

The Bible is not simply an old book containing many interesting stories. It is the most important Book you will ever read.

SHOULD ALL BOYS BE CIRCUMCISED?

My wife and I are expecting our first child and our doctor says it is a boy. I feel we shouldn't alter the way God intended our bodies to be. My wife feels differently. Do you think all boys should be circumcised?

IN THE OLD TESTAMENT, circumcision was a sign of the covenant between God and His people. The idea was to dedicate yourself and your progeny to the Lord. It involved cutting off the fold of skin at the end of the male sex organ, and it was done on the eighth day of the child's life as a symbol that this child belonged to the family of God, and that God had promised this child a great future.[2] According to God's command, Abraham and his family were the first people in

---

[1]   2 Corinthians 3:17 (KJV)
[2]   See Genesis 17:14

the Bible to be circumcised, as were his male servants and all the male family members that followed. Years later, Moses demanded that the Hebrews circumcise their hearts;[3] in other words, that the true sign of their commitment to God would be internal rather than external, that they would open themselves completely to the Lord and obey His commands. Nevertheless, when God's people crossed into the Promised Land, they circumcised all the adult males, as well as the babies who had not been circumcised during the wilderness wanderings.

In the New Testament, however, circumcision is not commanded. In fact, Paul makes a strong point that circumcision or noncircumcision is irrelevant. Faith in God is a matter of the heart.[4] The earliest church council held in Jerusalem rejected circumcision as the sign of a Christian.[5] The only requirement of new converts to Christianity was genuine faith in Jesus Christ.

From a health standpoint, circumcision may have value. Apparently women who are married to uncircumcised men have a much higher incidence of cervical cancer than those who don't. Other than historical value and health aspects, circumcision has little meaning for twenty-first-century Christians.

IS CREMATION WRONG?

My wife and I are thinking about being cremated when we die. Is this wrong? I haven't been able to find anything in the Bible about it.

CREMATION CERTAINLY ISN'T BIBLICAL. In the Old Testament, burning of a dead person's bones was considered a disgrace, a sign of disrespect. The bones were taken out of the ground, burned, and then scattered around. None of the biblical patriarchs—Abraham, Isaac, Jacob, Joseph, or David—were cremated. All were buried in tombs of some sort. Even the location where a person was buried had great significance. Joseph, for instance, made his family members promise to take his remains out of Egypt and back to the Holy Land when they returned.[6] No evidence in either the Old or New Testaments indicates that a godly person was cremated. It may not be a sinful practice, but it is not biblical.

---

3   See Deuteronomy 30:6
4   See Galatians 5:15; Philippians 3:3
5   See Acts 15:1–29
6   See Genesis 50:22–25; Exodus 13:19

THE BIBLICAL STANDARD FOR DRINKING WINE

What is the biblical standard for drinking wine in moderation; for example, with a meal?

THE BIBLE SAYS that "Wine is a mocker, strong drink a brawler,"[7] and it says that kings aren't supposed to drink in excess because wine can cloud their understanding, their reasoning, and their judgment.[8]

In contrast, the apostle Paul advised the young preacher Timothy to "use a little wine for your stomach's sake and your frequent infirmities."[9] Water in many Middle Eastern countries was severely polluted, so wine was a commonly accepted drink. Moreover, the Bible speaks of wine's ability to "make glad the heart of man."[10] Jesus turned water into wine at a wedding in Cana of Galilee,[11] and undoubtedly, the Lord and His disciples drank real wine at the Passover meal we now refer to as the Last Supper. At that time, Jesus said, "I will not drink of this fruit of the vine . . . until that day when I drink it new with you in the My Father's kingdom,"[12] so it is obvious that Jesus drank wine while here on earth and plans to drink it in the kingdom to come.

The whole matter of drinking has to do with the effect drinking may have on your spiritually weaker brothers and sisters. My liberty is constrained by how the exercise of it will impact somebody else. The apostle Paul faced a similar situation regarding the eating of meat that had been sacrificed to idols. Paul personally felt no qualms about eating the meat, yet he said, "If eating meat would cause my brother to stumble, I will eat no meat."[13] In other words, Paul was saying, "I will deny myself a permitted pleasure if it might cause pain or spiritual confusion to a weaker person in the faith." While we cannot live our lives in legalism, a common-sense concern for other people should be maintained at all times.

In most countries outside of the United States, particularly the Mediterranean countries, wine with meals is customary for those who can afford it. Alcoholism is not a very grave problem for these people. However, in the United States we have as many as 10 million alcoholics and an estimated 30 million problem drinkers. To such people just one glass of wine could precede a drunken binge. We would not

---

7   Proverbs 20:1
8   See Proverbs 31:4
9   1 Timothy 5:23 (KJV)
10 Psalm 104:15
11 See John 2:1–10
12 Matthew 26:29 (NKJV)
13 1 Corinthians 8:13

want our influence to be the cause of destroying another person. In other words, our freedom is limited by the weakness of someone else.

That's why many Christians choose to willingly surrender their rights or privileges to do something that they do not personally regard as sinful or damaging to their health. Their concern for others is an act of love. The Bible does not prohibit drinking a glass of wine with your dinner or on some social occasion. But Scripture does command us not to be drunk with wine, but to be filled with the Holy Spirit.[14]

FORGIVING YOURSELF AFTER AN ABORTION

In my early twenties, I had an abortion. I'm now ten years older, a Christian, and still feeling horrible about the decision I made. I know I'm forgiven by God, but how can I forgive myself?

THE TECHNIQUE I HAVE USED and recommended for years involves writing down my sins. First, get alone with God and ask Him to show you your spiritual condition and to convict you of your sins. This may be one of the fastest prayers you'll ever have answered! As things come to mind, write them down on a piece of paper. Don't try to make excuses or rationalize your past conduct or attitudes. Just lay your sins out on the table so you can get a clear picture of yourself. The Bible says, "He made a show of them openly, triumphing in his cross."[15] Jesus openly died for your sins, now He's asking you to openly die to your sin.

Say to your heavenly Father, "God, I admit I am a sinner. I now take every one of these sins and lay them at the cross of Jesus. I ask You to cover my sins with the blood of Jesus; wash every single one away. I accept Your forgiveness, Father, and I ask You to help me forgive myself."

Say to Satan and his demonic entities, "I am guilty; I did these things, but because Jesus died in my place, I am free of all guilt. His blood has paid the price for my sins, and I am free of them. Satan, you lose. You cannot keep me bound any longer. I am free!"

Then, in a symbolic gesture of what Jesus did for you when He took away your sins, and as an act of faith, set fire to the paper listing your sins and burn it up. From that point on, simply believe and claim the forgiveness that God has for you. Do not allow the sins of the past to be resurrected. Anytime they rear their head, or the devil brandishes them in your face, say aloud, "I am forgiven. I am delivered. I am free!"

---

14   See Ephesians 5:18
15   Colossians 2:15 (KJV)

The Bible talks about having your conscience cleansed from dead works to serve the living God.[16] The Lord wants you to be confident in His forgiveness. He doesn't want you flagellating yourself over past sins. He knows all about your past, and He loves you in spite of it! Declare His forgiveness aloud and remind yourself of it frequently.

Realize that our unwillingness, even our inability, to forgive ourselves is not a compliment to God. It is really more of an insult, as if to say, "I believe that the blood of your Son, Jesus, can cover and cleanse the sins of the most vile offender, but my sins are too great. Sorry, God, what you did for me wasn't enough."

Don't insult God's character. Instead, begin praising God for forgiving you, and speak words of forgiveness about yourself, such as, "Based on the fact that the blood of Jesus is sufficient for me, and His grace is sufficient for me, I forgive myself, and I will live in that forgiveness from now on."

IS GOD A MAN OR A WOMAN?

What is God's gender? Is God a man or a woman?

THE BIBLE DESCRIBES GOD in anthropomorphic terms, stemming from the Greek word *anthropos,* which means "man" or "mankind." In Scripture, God is always portrayed as a patriarch, as a Father, as a man.

Yet the Bible is emphatic that God is a Spirit, so to say He is a man or a woman is inaccurate. Spirits don't have gender, or male and female characteristics. We describe Him as a Father because in human relationships, if He were a man He would fill the role of the father in a household, the provider and the head of the household.

God has combined in His character all the male and female characteristics that we have in humanity. We see this in Jesus, who was the perfection of God Himself. He had all of the qualifications of strong virility, yet at the same time He had the tenderness that would be considered a softer, female attribute. In that one Person was summed up the perfections of humanity.

DID JESUS MAKE WINE OR GRAPE JUICE?

Was the wine Jesus made at the wedding of Cana alcoholic or grape juice?

---

16   See Hebrews 9:14

THE BIBLE STATES that Jesus turned the water into real wine and not just high-quality grape juice.[17] Apparently, the wine Jesus made was much better than what had been served earlier at the wedding reception. In that culture, drinking wine at a meal or at a wedding celebration was not considered sinful. But there were biblical cautions against drinking too much: "Wine is a mocker, and strong drink is a brawler, and whoever is intoxicated by it is not wise."[18]

At the wedding in Cana, the guests had drunk nearly all the wine that the groom's family had available for the celebration. That's when Jesus' mother came to him and said, "They are out of wine."

Jesus wasn't being rude when He answered, "What do you expect me to do about it? My hour has not yet come." In other words, He had not yet begun His public ministry. Mary didn't push the issue; she simply advised the servants to do whatever Jesus instructed them to do.

Jesus told the servants to pour the water into large vats and then told them to draw some out and take it to the master of the feast. When he tasted it, he said, "This is fantastic! Usually at a wedding feast, the hosts bring out the best wine first, then afterward, when everyone is a bit tipsy, they bring out the 'rotgut' stuff, because at that point, the guests can't tell the difference. But you have saved the best till last!"[19]

No Jewish master of a feast would describe grape juice that way!

In ancient Middle Eastern cultures, as in many today, drinking wine was perfectly acceptable, as long as a person did not imbibe too much and become drunk. In American culture, however, alcoholism is a major problem. According to recent findings, more than 30 million Americans are "problem drinkers." The social damage of their conduct is appalling—they severely hurt their wives, husbands, children, associates, business partners, and others. This kind of alcohol consumption is not merely sipping a glass of wine socially. This is the consumption of high-alcohol-content drinks that will take you down. Excessive drinking can destroy your life and the lives of people around you.

Moreover, we are warned against being drunk. Scripture says, "Be not drunk with wine but be filled with the Holy Spirit."[20] Paul's contrast in this verse is a powerful word picture. Just as wine affects the entire body and personality of the intoxicated person, the Holy Spirit affects our total personality, filling our lives with supernatural

---

17   See John 2:1–11
18   Proverbs 20:1
19   See John 2:1–11
20   Ephesians 5:18

joy. As one Spirit-filled Christian quipped, "I didn't quit drinking; I just switched spigots!"

INSIGHTS FROM THE APOCRYPHA

Someone suggested that we purchase a Bible containing the Apocrypha. Does the Apocrypha have any spiritual wisdom for us?

THE APOCRYPHA are the fourteen noncanonical books, written between the time of the Old Testament and New Testaments, eleven of which the Roman Catholic Church includes in their Bible. These books contain a great deal of wisdom, but they are also loaded with all sorts of fanciful stories. Much of this material may be interesting to read but should not be considered on the same level as Scripture. Probably the most valuable of the books from a historical perspective are the four books of Maccabees, which inform us of the struggle of the Jews against their oppressors; particularly, Antiochus Epiphanes, the general who desecrated the temple in Jerusalem and is thought to be a type of the Antichrist.

LAUGHING GOSPEL

I've heard of a "laughing gospel" and other unusual responses to God's work in people's lives. I don't see any such expressions in the Bible, and I wonder if we are being deceived by our spiritual leaders. Or do I have a lack of faith?

GOD IS AN ALL-POWERFUL SPIRIT whose power far exceeds all the hydrogen bombs ever exploded. He is stronger than the sun; indeed angelic beings may reflect some of His holy brightness, glowing with light and filled with power.

In the Old Testament, when God's power came on individuals, they often were overcome and fell down in a swoon. The prophet Daniel was so overwhelmed by visions and angelic visitations that he was exhausted and sick for days and confined to his bed.[21]

It should not surprise us then that human beings sometimes have unusual

---

[21]   See Daniel 8:27

reactions when they come into the presence of such awesome power. Some may fall over in God's presence; others may emotionally express the joy of their heart in various ways. During the frontier revival meetings in America, it was reported that many people physically shook, danced, shouted, jerked, barked like dogs, and exhibited other unusual displays.

Some of these physical manifestations are sincere, flowing through a believer who is filled with the power of the Holy Spirit. On the other hand, many instances where people jerk, bark, or do other strange things while supposedly "in the Spirit" are nothing more than manifestations of the flesh.

Sometimes these kinds of reactions are actually caused by resistance to the Holy Spirit in one's life. If electricity is put through a resistance coil, such as the heating element of a stove, the coil will get hot. On the other hand, a house wire has conductivity and allows the power to flow freely through it. For instance, if electricity is put through a filament of a light bulb, a wonderful light appears without a great deal of heat. Nowhere in the Bible do we see Jesus jerking, jumping, or dancing under the power of God, although He had more heavenly power flowing through Him than any man who has ever lived.

We must not attribute every manifestation to God. When a person resists the power of God and is not totally yielded to Him, unusual manifestations may result. Instead of the Holy Spirit causing the response, however, the fleshly nature of the individual is responding.

On the other hand, unusual manifestations should not be discounted altogether. Someone once said, "Where I see a counterfeit ten dollar bill, I know there is a real ten dollar bill somewhere." There is such a thing as holy laughter. The Bible says, "The joy of the Lord is your strength."[22] When people experience joy in the Lord, they may clap their hands, sing, or dance. The Bible says, "Clap your hands, all you peoples! Shout to God with the voice of triumph."[23] This concept of shouting, dancing, and joy pulsates throughout the Old Testament. David danced before the Lord with all his might.[24] That is a good, valid expression of joy unto the Lord, and we should not condemn it as fleshly. It is a reaction of people before their Creator in which they show love the best way they can, with all of their being. They are worshipping God with their whole heart, and laughter may be part of that.

On the other hand, some manifestations are not of God, and we need to be

---

22   Nehemiah 8:10
23   See Psalm 47:1 (NKJV)
24   See 2 Samuel 6:14

careful that we are responding to the Holy Spirit, and not some other spirit—even our own fleshly desires.

People should be taught to seek the Lord Jesus and the power of His Holy Spirit. They should not be taught to fall down, to jerk, to laugh, or to do anything else, ostensibly by the power of the Spirit. If such manifestations do occur under the genuine anointing of the Holy Spirit, who are we to criticize? I have lived in Christian circles long enough to be quite tolerant, understanding, and patient, but I've also seen enough spiritual counterfeits to know we must be cautious that we are not deceived by Satan. We need to welcome God's power while being careful not to be seduced by what is counterfeit. By their fruit you shall know them.

DOES SAYING MAGIC WORDS MAKE A CHRISTIAN?

Does a person really become a Christian by simply saying some magic words and agreeing to some basic principles?

ACCORDING TO ROMANS 10:9-10, a person becomes a Christian by believing in his heart that God raised Christ from the dead and then confessing with the mouth that Jesus is Lord.[25] To believe in your heart is a commitment whereby you put your life into the hands of the One who died for your sins. When you confess Jesus as Lord, you are saying by the Holy Spirit that Jesus Christ is God, that He died for your sins and has risen again, and He indeed is the Supreme Being in your life.

Prior to that, in my opinion, there needs to be repentance. You must turn away from a life of selfishness and sin, and turn to God. It's as though you are going in one direction, serving your own interests. Now you turn around 180 degrees and begin moving in God's direction. The Bible uses the term *metanoia*, or "after-thought," to cause you to turn from your own course and begin to follow His course. As you turn, you open the door of your heart to Jesus and ask Him to come in and rule your spirit. His Spirit enters you, and you become a new creature. Scripture says, "Therefore if any man is in Christ, he is a new creature; the old things passed away; behold, new things have come."[26] You are a reborn individual!

Being a Christian is not merely knowing historical facts or learning some creed. Being a Christian is a new life; it is a life of faith in Christ, where you are now living in Him and He is in you. Paul says, "I have been crucified with Christ; and it is

---

25   See Romans 10:9–11
26   2 Corinthians 5:17

no longer I who live, but Christ lives in me; and the life which I now live in the flesh I live by faith in the Son of God, who loved me, and delivered Himself up for me."[27] I am dead to my old self and alive to God. That is what being a Christian is. It is a new life, a life of trusting God, a transformed life in Jesus Christ.

A BURNED-OUT SPIRITUAL MIDLIFE CRISIS

I'm a Christian, but lately I've begun to question truths that I have believed all my life. I just feel burned out. Does God understand this? Is there a biblical perspective on midlife crisis?

THE BIBLE SAYS, "Break up your fallow ground."[28] If you leave land fallow and don't plow it, the rains come and turn it to mud. Then the sun bakes it, and it becomes harder and harder. To get something growing in that sort of ground, you must plow it up, get rid of the weeds, and plant fresh seeds that will produce a good crop of fresh products.

Life takes a toll on us. Little things can creep in almost unnoticed: indifference, carelessness, lack of prayer and Bible study, or the absence of other spiritually invigorating activities. Sometimes it is helpful to lay aside several days to focus on God and break up your hardness of heart. In plowing up your fallow ground, start by confessing all known sin; including sins of omission, things you know you should have done but didn't. For instance, loving God with all your heart is the greatest commandment. Lack of love for God or loving Him halfheartedly is a sin. When you go before the Lord, admit your condition and say, "Lord, I confess that I have sinned against You in this area. I apologize. Help me, please."

Make a list of things you have thought, said, or done that you know are displeasing to God. Be brutal on yourself; don't allow any excuses. Write those things down and say, "Lord, I give all these things to You. I am sorry for my failures. I ask You to forgive me and to restore the joy of Your salvation to me.[29] Fill me afresh with your Holy Spirit."

Then burn your list, and start walking with God again in freshness. Pray openly and constantly. Bathe your mind and spirit with the Word of God. Surround yourself with the Word, in written form, in music, and in every way you can. Fill your life with

27   Galatians 2:20
28   Hosea 10:12 (KJV)
29   See Psalm 51

praise to the Lord, and get together with other people who love Him. These things will help to revive your heart, and keep it from being hardened again in the future.

WHY STUDY THE OLD TESTAMENT?

If the Old Testament is the old covenant before Christ came and died for us, why should New Testament Christians continue to study it?

THE WORD OF GOD remains the same, from Genesis to Revelation. Jesus said, "Do not think that I came to abolish the Law or the Prophets; I did not come to abolish, but to fulfill. For truly I say to you, until heaven and earth pass away, not the smallest letter or stroke shall pass away from the Law, until all is accomplished."[30] Granted, we now live under the new covenant, purchased by Jesus' blood, and we are no longer compelled to sacrifice animals to make atonement for our sins. Jesus is the complete, one-time sacrifice for all of us. Nor are we required to abide by many other ritualistic laws of the Old Testament. When the early church leaders gathered in Jerusalem for the first church conference, they dealt with the issue of how closely new Gentile believers should follow the old Law. The church decided that only a few simple rules needed to be carried over.[31]

Still, the Old Testament carries significant weight regarding the moral laws that Christians as well as Jewish believers are to keep. The Ten Commandments, for example, are almost all repeated in the New Testament in various forms; they have not gone away or been superceded, but rather are immutable laws of God. Similarly, Jesus often expanded on particular laws, but He never rescinded any of them.

The Old Testament also has great value to us in providing a deeper understanding of our origins and purpose. It answers such basic questions as: Where did we come from? Who is God? What is He like? Where did evil come from? What is the plan of redemption?

Without the Old Testament context, Jesus' coming to earth as the Messiah would be difficult to understand. Jesus came fulfilling the Old Testament prophecies, as the Son of David, in the family line of Abraham, to whom God promised, "Out of your seed shall all the nations of the earth be blessed."[32] As Christians better understand our Old Testament roots, we gain a greater appreciation for what Jesus did on the cross and God's plan of salvation.

---

[30]   1 Matthew 5:17–18
[31]   See Acts 15:19–29
[32]   Genesis 12:3

WOMEN IN MINISTRY

Can women serve as elders or even full-time pastors? What if I feel called to preach?

By ALL MEANS, PREACH! Women should have a prominent role in ministries. Think of Deborah in the Old Testament, who was a judge of Israel and a leader of God's people. In the New Testament church, deaconesses played key roles; Anna was a prophetess, speaking God's Word into a particular situation. The apostle Paul said that in Christ "there is no distinction between Greek and Jew, circumcised and uncircumcised, barbarian, Scythian, slave and freeman, but Christ is all, and in all."[33] We are all one in Christ.

On the other hand, the apostle wrote, "I do not permit a woman to teach or to have authority over a man."[34] In the early church, women served in many capacities, but always under the authority of a male spiritual leader. Women did not serve in the position of a ruling elder, presiding over the church. Nowhere in the early church do we have record of a woman pastor.

Today, women can preach, teach, serve on the mission fields, or do most anything else in the church, but God's pattern is for men to be the leaders, both in the church and in the family.

WHERE WAS GOD FOR JOB'S FAMILY?

We often talk about God blessing Job after his time of testing, that his material possessions were restored, and that God blessed Job with a new, larger family. But where was God for Job's original family; where was the blessing for them?

THAT'S A TREMENDOUS QUESTION, and I'm not sure I have a clear-cut answer, because the Bible doesn't say. All we know is that God allowed Job to be tested by Satan. Satan was walking up and down in the earth, and then he appeared before the throne of God.

God said, "Have you considered My servant Job? There isn't anybody like him on earth."

---

[33] Colossians 3:11
[34] 1 Timothy 2:12

"Sure, Job is righteous," Satan taunted. "Look at all the blessings you've given him. If You take them away, he will curse You."

God said, "Okay, he is in your hand; you just can't take his life."[35]

What ensued was the amazing story of how God allowed Job and his family to be attacked by Satan. Job lost everything he cherished, including his ten children, but he didn't lose faith in God. We must remember, though, if Satan takes the life of a loved one, that person isn't extinguished. The loved one will go to be with God. If a person knows the Lord and is part of God's family on earth, that person will be a part of God's family in heaven. Death isn't the worst thing that can happen to someone; losing eternity with God is far worse.

On another occasion in the Old Testament, a man named Achan sinned by taking some of the plunder from the victory at Jericho, resulting in the lifting of God's hand and defeat in the following battle at Ai. God revealed to Joshua what Achan had done, and when Joshua confronted Achan in front of all the people, he was stoned to death, as were his wife and children. Similarly, when Korah, Dathan, and Abiram, challenged the authority of Moses in the wilderness, God caused the earth to open and their entire families, as well as their donkeys, sheep, and all their possessions, and two hundred fifty men who had followed them were destroyed.[36]

When a parent is under attack by Satan, the wife and children often reap the repercussions. Many parents suffer more by seeing their children's pain than experiencing their own. The devil knows this as well. Often, when the enemy has attacked me and has been unable to gain any incursions, he has deflected the blows to my family members. Husbands and wives need to uplift each other in prayer. Parents need to be in continuous prayer for their children.

What was done to Job's family was done quickly. A terrible wind took the lives of Job's family.[37]

The greatest blessing Job experienced for his faithfulness wasn't the fact that God gave him more children, doubled his money, camels, and donkeys; the greatest blessing was that he saw the Lord. He said, "Up to this point, I have heard about you with the hearing of my ears, now I behold you with my eyes." And then he went on to say, "I abhor myself, and I repent in dust and ashes."[38]

The lesson of Job is this: Out of suffering and persecution comes a new

---

[35]   See Job 1:6–12
[36]   See Numbers 16:1–40
[37]   See Job 1:18–19
[38]   See Job 42:5–6

insight into God. The fact that you have material blessings as a result—or you don't have material blessings—is really irrelevant. Rest assured that God took care of Job's children in a far better world.

WHERE DID GOD COME FROM?

We know Jesus was born in Bethlehem, but where did God come from?

Jesus is the son of God. The Holy Spirit impregnated a young virgin named Mary and the baby conceived in her—Jesus—was God, as well as human. As the theologians say, He was "very God and very man."

As for the Father, the first line in Genesis says, "In the beginning God,"[39] so before anything else existed, God was already there. Then the record tells us what God did in relation to His creation. But there is never a mention in the Bible explaining where God came from. He says, "I am the Alpha and the Omega, the first and the last, the beginning and the end."[40] Scripture says, "From everlasting until everlasting, Thou art God."[41] There are many other descriptions of the ever-lasting Father. It is as if God has always been there. He is an ever-living Spirit. Concerning His origins, we don't know, and He didn't tell us.

In the Middle Ages, a group known as the Scholastics spent a great deal of time trying to figure this out. They came up with what they called the "Uncaused Cause." They said, "Everything has a cause until you get back to the Uncaused Cause," therefore God is the Uncaused Cause. That's great, but it doesn't answer the question of where God came from. The origin of God is a mystery, and we won't know the answer until He reveals it to us.

It's almost presumptuous for us, in our finiteness, to expect that we would understand who He is, let alone where He came from. Scripture tells us, "For My thoughts are not your thoughts, nor are your ways My ways," says the LORD. "For as the heavens are higher than the earth, so are My ways higher than your ways, and My thoughts than your thoughts."[42]

Modern scientists speak of the big bang theory, as a possible explanation for the origins of earth. They think a cataclysmic event took place about 14 or 15 billion

---

39   Genesis 1:1
40   Revelation 22:13
41   Psalm 90:2 (KJV)
42   Isaiah 55:8–9 (NKJV)

years ago. Supposedly, an enormous mass exploded and out of that came all of the planets, the solar system, and all of the galaxies in our universe. Now here's where it gets really interesting. Scientists speculate that if that mass had been off either too much or too little, by ten to the 120th power, (that would be like a tiny, tiny grain of sand), we would not have life on earth.

Whether or not there was a big bang, I don't know. But I'm astounded at the wisdom of God to project over 15 billion years the exact mass that would be necessary to sustain earth in an orbit around the sun, so human beings and the life we know could come into being! I stand in awe of His presence to learn of Him, whatever He will show me, and if He will show me more, I'll accept it gratefully, but other than that I don't know where He came from.

God said, "I am here, I AM."[43] That's His name, "I AM." He gave us His Son to tell us what He is like and how to be with Him forever. That's really all of us need to know in this life.

CAN WE KNOW FOR SURE THAT GOD EXISTS?

Scientist Carl Sagan said that he didn't want to believe, he wanted to know. How can I ever truly know that God exists?

WE CAN KNOW IT IN OUR HEARTS. I think the most intelligent thing any person can ever do is to surrender himself to God and to be filled with Him. Jesus said, "If anyone wills to do His will, he shall know concerning the doctrine, whether it is from God or whether I speak on My own authority."[44] If you will surrender your will to God's, then you will know. On the other hand, if you say, "God, I am not going to do Your will until You show me Yourself," He is under no obligation to show you anything. To know is to surrender. When we surrender, we begin to know. We enter into a relationship with the Creator in which we know that we know that we know.

The great mathematician Blaise Pascal said, "At three in morning as I was praying, [and] suddenly, fire!" He said, "Oh, God of Abraham, of Isaac and of Jacob, the world has not known Thee, but I know Thee, Father." He was a scientist, one of the greatest philosopher-scientists in the history of mankind, who suddenly ran into the fire of God and said, "I now know You."

---

43   See Exodus 3:14
44   John 7:17

That was a revelation from God. God reveals Himself to us as He chooses. In the meantime, we have the Scripture, the Bible, which tells us about God. We can read and believe the Bible out of faith. The apostle Paul wrote, "So faith comes by hearing, and hearing by the word of God."[45] If we expose ourselves to the Word, we will grow in faith.

God has not left Himself without a witness. The witness around us is the wonder of His creation and the inexplicable order of it all. Certainly, we're surprised that someone like Carl Sagan would not have recognized that and said, "There must be something behind this." But the wisdom of this world is insufficient to find God; it still takes faith.

The word in Greek for "wisdom" is *sophia,* from which we get our word *philosophy; phil -o-sophia,* the love of wisdom. Paul said, "When the world by wisdom knew not God, it pleased God by the foolishness of preaching to save them that believed."[46] When Paul got into Athens, he played head-games with some of the local philosophers. On Mars Hill, the local gathering spot for intellectuals, Paul said, "I see that you are a very religious people, and I noticed your statue to the Unknown God. Now, the Unknown God is the one I am going to declare to you."[47] He approached them from an intellectual standpoint, and most debaters would say that he won his points. Yet interestingly, to the best of my knowledge, he didn't win one convert from that debate in Athens. He went up the road to Corinth, and later he said, "When I got to Corinth, I was determined to know nothing among you save Jesus Christ and Him crucified."[48] And there he established a thriving church, because he talked about the cross and the necessity of knowing Jesus.

You can look at the world and see the wonder of a human being, the growth of a child, and all of the processes of life. The structure and order to it all is absolutely staggering! Any honest observer must conclude, "There has to be an order in this." Yet amazingly, some people choose not to see it.

I read an article on creation in *Encyclopedia Britannica* that said the genetic structure in one human being was the equivalent of a library of 1000 books, 500 pages per book, with closely printed, single-spaced type—yet the person who wrote that article said chance evolution brought that genetic structure into being! How ludicrous! If he walked into any library and saw the thousand volumes of closely printed text placed neatly on the shelves, that same person would never say, "My, I

---

45   Romans 10:17
46   1 Corinthians 1:21
47   See Acts 17:23
48   See 1 Corinthians 2:2, 1:18–31

guess this just happened by random chance." No, he or she would have to admit that someone put the order together and keeps it together. The order of the universe is one of the strongest "proofs" for God's existence.

IS JESUS THE ONLY WAY?

I am very uncomfortable with the idea that Jesus is the only way to heaven. What about all those devout Jewish or Islamic people? Will God condemn them to hell because they call Him by a different name?

GOD WILL NOT CONDEMN ANYBODY to hell because he or she uses a different name for Him. People will go to heaven or to hell according to how they respond to what they know. The deciding factor will be what you do in relation to the revelation that you have experienced. If a person sins against the revelation that he has received, then he will be punished. Yet, those who have accepted Jesus Christ as Savior will be forgiven, even though they have sinned. Jesus is the one true atoning sacrifice for sin, so those who come to Him will not enter into judgment, but will be passed from death unto life. They will be forgiven. That is the standard.

If you examine other religions carefully, you will find large doses of sheer superstition, fanciful thinking that often borders on nonsense. It does not comport with human experience. In books written about Buddha, for example, it is said that when he was born, he immediately was given twelve-league boots in which he began to take huge strides about the earth. But when you read about Jesus, He was a little baby born in a stable in Bethlehem to a couple who were descendants of David. You can read of His ancestors, from the time of Adam and Eve to His parents, Mary and Joseph, and see an unbroken line of the revelation of God. You see the historical preparation of the Jewish people for about two thousand years, and you see the promises of the prophets. In His birth, life, suffering, death, and resurrection, Jesus fulfills every one of the prophecies. It would be impossible for this many prophecies to be fulfilled in one life without it being ordained by God.

The history regarding Jesus is understandable, reasonable, and rational. Christians are not the ones attempting to escape from reason; those who ignore the evidence of Christianity choose to do so on the basis of their own prejudices, rather than the facts.

WHAT'S IN A NAME?

We talk so much about the name of Jesus, almost as if it is a magical "abracadabra" word. Yet obviously, in foreign cultures, "Jesus" is not even pronounced. What's so special about the name of Jesus?

WE BELIEVE it is the equivalent to a power of attorney. In law, for example, if a document is signed giving an individual power of attorney, that means he or she can conduct certain affairs on behalf of the person whose name is on the document. Jesus has granted His followers a similar power to use His name.

When we pray in Jesus' name, He is giving us access, first of all, to the Father. That is the only access we have to God, through Jesus, through His blood. Speaking and praying in Jesus' name is not a concept that man came up with. Jesus actually said, "Whatever you ask in My name, that will I do."[49] His name is a precious name to be revered and used appropriately.

Second, when we speak in Jesus' name, we are acting as His representatives to the world, and we are invoking His power and authority. He said, "All authority has been given to Me in heaven and on earth. Go therefore and make disciples of all the nations, baptizing them in the name of the Father and the Son and the Holy Spirit, teaching them to observe all that I commanded you; and lo, I am with you always, even to the end of the age."[50] When we go into the world to make disciples, we know that we have the grant of authority from the Son of God, the King of kings, the Lord of lords.

Moreover, healings can take place through the name of Jesus. When Peter gave account before the Jewish authorities after a man at the temple gate had been healed, he said, "If we are on trial today for a benefit done to a sick man, as to how this man has been made well, let it be known to all of you, and to all the people of Israel, that by the name of Jesus Christ the Nazarene, whom you crucified, whom God raised from the dead—by this name this man stands here before you in good health."[51]

Most important of all, it is the only Name, and the only Person that leads to salvation. "And there is salvation in no one else; for there is no other name under heaven that has been given among men, by which we must be saved."[52]

---

[49] John 14:14
[50] Matthew 28:18–20
[51] Acts 4:9–10
[52] Acts 4:12

Interestingly, in our culture, we don't hear anybody cursing by Muhammad or Buddha or by any other guru. It is always the name of Jesus that is profaned. The devil knows there is power in Jesus' name. He knows that the Name is precious to believers, so it's not surprising that he attempts to blaspheme and prostitute the name of Jesus.

WHAT IS THE UNPARDONABLE SIN?

What is the unpardonable sin, and how will I know if I've committed it?

THIS HAS BEEN A CONUNDRUM to Bible scholars. Jesus said that there is an unpardonable sin—"whoever blasphemes against the Holy Spirit there is no forgiveness for it"[53]—and people have worried over the centuries that they may have committed it. When I first became a Christian, a time came when terror gripped me that somehow I had committed the unpardonable sin. *Did I use the name of the Holy Spirit in some irreverent fashion in a conversation, and therefore, had I committed the unpardonable sin?* One afternoon, an attack came against my faith. I struggled in prayer. I said, "Lord, even if my destiny is hell because of this sin, in hell I will still believe in You and praise You." Then, as if by a miracle, God confirmed to my heart and mind that I had been forgiven, that my sin was not the sin unto death.

The sin unto death, or the so-called unpardonable sin, is to reject the Holy Spirit's wooing. The one sin that can't be forgiven is the sin of rejecting Jesus. If you do not accept Jesus, then you don't have forgiveness, and if the Holy Spirit is drawing you to Christ and you reject Him, then you have sinned against the Holy Spirit. But it is not unforgivable because of some formula or some words that you have said or didn't say; nor is the sin some atrocious act. It is an attitude of the heart that says, "I am going to turn away from God; I will not have anything to do with God."

That is the sin spoken of by John when he said, "I want you to pray for everybody, but the sin unto death I tell you not to pray for this."[54] Basically, he's saying that such a situation is irrevocable.

---

53   Luke 12:10
54   1 John 5:16

SELF-ESTEEM VERSUS SELF-PRIDE

What is the difference between having a good, healthy self-esteem, and being proud? Can't pride in oneself be a good thing, too?

IT CAN, BUT WE HAVE TO BE SO CAUTIOUS. Our nature tends to be proud, and pride resides at the heart of the first sin. Satan saw his own beauty and thought he could overcome God. Years ago, Frank Sinatra sang the anthem of the arrogant, "I Did It My Way," which sounds good in theory but actually exalts self rather than expressing honor and appreciation to God. Similarly, a classic poem says, "I am the master of my soul, the captain of my fate."[55] While extolling freedom and self-confidence, it does so at the exclusion of God. This is a human tendency, to think that we can do it our own way, that we are the captains of our own souls, that we are in charge, and we do not need to give God or anyone else any glory at all. As such, pride is the worst sin.

Conversely, humility is one of the greatest virtues a person can have, and one for which we should have greater appreciation. Humility, however, need not deny talent. If an athlete can run a 100-yard dash in 9.6 seconds flat, it would be silly to say, "Well, I am just an old slowpoke." That would be lying. The athlete's attitude should be, "God gave me an ability to run fast, and I give it back to God. The talent belongs to Him, and I will use it for His glory."

Scripture says, "If anyone boasts, let him boast in the Lord."[56] We can always boast in the Lord, giving Him credit for what we do. That kind of self-awareness is good. We need to have a certain confidence when we go out in His Name. I am confident that I can lift so much weight; or I can drive a car; I can ride a horse; I am confident that I can fly an airplane, or play golf, write a book, and host a television talk show. Confidence in acquired skills and God-given gifts is not sinful pride; it is an understanding of who we are in Him. Give God the glory for your achievements, for what He does in and through you, and you will not have to worry about sinful pride.

I make a habit of giving God credit for every good achievement. I take the blame for all of the mistakes. Then there is no confusion or occasion for pride.

WHAT DOES DEATH TO SELF MEAN?

What does it mean to die to myself?

---

55   Alfred Lord Tennyson, "Invictus"
56   2 Corinthians 10:17

THE APOSTLE PAUL SAID, "I die daily."[57] He also said, "I have been crucified with Christ; and it is no longer I who live, but Christ lives in me; and the life which I now live in the flesh, I live by faith in the Son of God, who loved me and delivered Himself up for me."[58] The idea of dying to self is that our "old man," our sinful nature, which is full of lust, greed, pride, envy and all those selfish things must die spiritually. When we surrender totally to Christ and receive His forgiveness and transforming power in our lives, that old man is dead. He is crucified with Christ.

Baptism is a good symbol of this. You are buried with Christ beneath the water, and you are raised in newness of life. The "old you" is dead so the new person in Christ can live. Now, the old man doesn't want to die—we want our own way—but for Christ to have His way in our lives, we must symbolically put our self nature in the grave and be renewed with the new man. The Bible says, "Put off, concerning your former conduct, the old man which grows corrupt according to the deceitful lusts, and be renewed in the spirit of your mind, and that you put on the new man which was created according to God, in true righteousness and holiness."[59] It is as if there is a transformation of the old to the new.

Certainly, the whole concept of being born again is the indication of that. "If any man be in Christ; he is a new creation. Old things have passed away and behold all things become new."[60] The Bible is filled with thoughts of dying to self, and the self-life, and coming alive to Christ.

The benefit to dying to ourselves is that Christ lives in us, and we are no longer reliant on our own power to live the Christian life. We can relax and allow Christ Jesus to be Himself in us!

It is the unwillingness to die to self that causes jealousy, hurt feelings, shyness, greed, party spirit, marital discord, and so-called wounded spirits. I have little sympathy for people who tell me they have been "wounded." My answer: How can you be wounded when you are supposed to be dead?

Regrettably, most of us aren't too keen to see the rotten old self die. For that reason, a loving God sends along enough trials and anguish to speed along the process. His blows, if we embrace them as good, can free us from bondage and lead us to a whole new liberty in our life in Christ.

---

[57] 1 Corinthians 15:31
[58] Galatians 2:20
[59] Ephesians 4:22–24
[60] 2 Corinthians 5:17

CONTENTS

— CHAPTER 6 —

HOT POTATOES
Moral, Social and Ethical Issues

W E LIVE IN A WORLD where absolute values are hard to find. For more than a half-century, the message has been trumpeted: "Everything is relative, there is no right or wrong, only what is right or wrong *for you.*" People trying to find ground to stand on quickly find the slippery slope of contemporary "morality" a treacherous place to maintain their footing.

Consequently, many people try to make the Bible line up with their choices, rather than aligning their choices with the Bible. That is a dangerous approach to Bible study, and it often reaps confusion, guilt, and pain in our lives. While we may occasionally have trouble applying the Scripture to our day-to-day decisions, especially in areas where no clear answer is available, the Bible is extremely specific about moral, social, and ethical issues. The real question is not, "What does the Bible say?" but, "Will I obey God's Word?"

CHOOSING SEXUAL ORIENTATION

Why do you feel that homosexuality is a sin? Did you choose your sexual orientation? Did you wake up one morning and tell yourself that you were attracted to women? Neither do gay people.

GRANTED, I AM HETEROSEXUAL in orientation. Like most young men before marriage, from my teens I engaged in a number of heterosexual dating relationships. Now after almost five decades of marriage, my wife, Dede, and I have four children and fourteen grandchildren. My sexual orientation, however, gave me no license to commit fornication before marriage or adultery since being married. Regardless of an individual's sexual orientation, God expects him to control his appetite.

It is ludicrous for a person to say, "I'm attracted to someone of the same sex, so I can legitimately commit sex acts with him or her because I have an urge." The Bible calls that fornication, a word that stems from the root word, *pornea*, from which we also get the word *pornography*. It implies improper sexual activity between two unmarried people, and it is soundly condemned in the Bible. This is not a matter of opinion or preference; it is what the Word of God says.

For instance, the apostle Paul asked the rhetorical question, "Can you take the members of Christ and join them to a harlot?" He explains, "Your body is the temple of the Holy Spirit."[1] If you are a Christian, your body is not your own. You belong to God, and your body is His temple here on earth. You are not free to do as you please, regardless of whether the immoral activity is heterosexual or homosexual.

Although reliable evidence is almost nonexistent, there may be some genetic predisposition on the part of a tiny fraction of the 2 percent of our population who are homosexuals and the 1 percent who are lesbians. The truth is, almost all of the homosexuals and lesbians become so not because of genetics, but because of the influence of others.

Let's not soft-pedal the issue, though. The Bible clearly labels all forms of homosexuality as sin. In Paul's letter to the Romans, the moral decline toward homosexuality and lesbianism is considered the last step in a society that has willfully walked away from God. Scripture says, "They exchanged the truth of God for a lie, and worshiped and served the creature rather than the Creator, who is blessed forever. For this reason, God gave them over to degrading passions; for their women exchanged the natural function for that which is unnatural, and in the same way also the men abandoned the natural function of the woman and burned in their desire towards one another, men with men committing indecent acts and receiving in their own persons the due penalty of their error."[2] The Bible also says that no one who is an abuser of mankind or a homosexual is going to enter the kingdom of heaven.[3]

You can talk about sexual orientation all you want, but that will not alter the Word of God. The Bible does not compromise its standards to comply with current

---

[1] 1 Corinthians 6:15, 19
[2] Romans 1:25–28
[3] See 1 Corinthians 6:9

opinions, or the fickle, waffling positions of so-called political correctness. The Bible says homosexuality is wrong.

Do Christians love homosexuals and lesbians? Absolutely. Just as we love anyone who has been deceived by the devil and caught in the grip of harmful addiction. We love homosexuals, we pray for them, and we are willing to help them find Christ and discover freedom from their destructive behavior. The church should not, however, condone homosexual behavior any more than it should condone the behavior of an adulterer, a fornicator, a thief, or a murderer.

Can such conduct be forgiven? Certainly! Will there be consequences of their past lifestyles? Probably so. Sexual sin, whether heterosexual or homosexual, always reaps a bitter harvest sooner or later. Thankfully, God's love and forgiveness extend to every one of us, to anyone who will honestly seek Him and call out to Him to be saved.

CROSS-DRESSING

I have been married for thirty-one years. Soon after our wedding day, I discovered that my husband enjoyed dressing up in women's clothes. A recent test shows that he has an extra X-chromosome. We are both Christians and have prayed for deliverance from these feelings, but he continues this behavior. Please tell me if it is okay to condone this in our marriage.

AFTER THIRTY-ONE YEARS, condoning his conduct is rather a nonissue. You've already been condoning it by default if he's been doing it that long! As for an extra chromosome, who can really tell how much that has to do with his conduct?

Regardless, for those who are mentally competent and physically able, conduct stems from choices. If your husband is choosing to dress in women's clothing, even after you have prayed for deliverance, he is obviously hooked on some sort of fetish. But it is a choice.

The Old Testament condemns wearing the opposite sex's clothing. The Bible says, "A woman must not wear men's clothing, nor a man wear women's clothing, for the Lord your God detests anyone who does this."[4] Based on this passage alone, the behavior of a cross-dresser should not be condoned, regardless of the reason.

---

4   Deuteronomy 22:5

Seek out a Christian counselor who will pray with you, work through deliverance, and help your husband walk out of this lifestyle. It may take some time—a thirty-one-year habit is rarely overcome in an instant—so commit yourselves to a long-term program, and rejoice with each bit of progress.

CLONING

Why should Christians encourage or discourage cloning?

SCIENCE IS ON THE VERGE of making a subclass of human beings. Christians believe that a human being is created in the image of God, takes on some of the attributes of God, has a spirit that can commune with God, has a mind of great potential, and has a destiny designed by God.

Speaking to Jeremiah, God said, "Before I formed you in the womb, I knew you; before you were born I sanctified you; I ordained you a prophet to the nations."[5] Notice, there was a preexisting reality of this person before he was even formed in the womb!

We say that life begins with conception, but in truth, life begins with the concept in the mind of God. God said, "I formed you in the womb." Now we are saying, "The Jones Clinic is going to form you in a petri dish; we are going to manipulate a little piece of genetic material and make an exact copy of the person from whom that genetic material came." This is monstrous and it does violence to the whole concept of human dignity. Most civilized nations are repulsed by the thought of human cloning. They regard it as an abomination. It most certainly is detestable to God.

DO CLONES HAVE SOULS?

If scientists can take a piece of genetic material from one human being, put it in a test tube, and produce a duplicate person, would the clone have a soul?

I WONDER VERY STRONGLY if God is going to allow human beings to get that far in our efforts at playing God. No doubt, that which is precious, which is made in the image of God, would be farmed and used for body parts—it is a

---

5　　Jeremiah 1:5 (NKJV)

horrifying thought! It would be a real-life version of Aldous Huxley's *Brave New World*, and it may well bring on the judgment of God.

Would life created in a lab have a soul? I doubt it, but I really don't know.

SPERM BANKS

Christian singles are waiting much longer to marry these days, by choice and by circumstance. Many singles would like to have families of their own. Adoption is an option, but what about the woman who wants the experience of giving birth to her own child? Is it wrong to go to a sperm bank for in vitro fertilization?

IT MAY NOT BE WRONG, but it may not be smart, either. A child needs an intact family—a father and a mother. That is God's plan, not society's or even the church's. The nuclear family, complete with a father and a mother, was designed by God. Sadly, one of the big problems with today's teenagers is the absence of fathers in their lives. Many women are having children out of wedlock. In other cases divorce has devastated the family. In other situations some men have simply dismissed their responsibilities and walked away from their families. In fewer numbers, women are abdicating their responsibilities and "dumping" the children on dads to raise. As young people grow up in these homes without the appropriate family structure, the negative psychological manifestations are widespread. Rebellion, inability to compete fairly, low self-esteem, almost a self-loathing, and many other ramifications can often be traced back to the absentee father or mother in a child's life.

Sure, you can go to a sperm bank, become impregnated, and have a baby. But motherhood for you will not be the supreme act of love and altruism you believe it to be; instead, it may be the epitome of selfishness. The child's birth will be more to satisfy your own selfishness, your desire to have a baby, your desire to be fulfilled as a woman. It will not be the best or most intelligent decision for the child.

Besides willfully and purposely joining the ranks of single parents, you will probably place undue strain on those around you. Childcare will be a constant hassle; your child's identity will also be a question throughout his or her life. "Who was my daddy? What was he like? What did he look like, what sort of man was he?" These are just a few of the many questions that are bound to come up, and for which you will have woefully inadequate answers. "You came from a test tube. I didn't know your daddy, I didn't even know his name. I just bought some of his sperm." Have you considered the issue of nurture, finances, and education for this child? Ask yourself, "Am I condemning this child to poverty even before birth?"

Bringing a life into this world is a precious matter. Nowadays, we can scientifically help create life in God's image, but the care and nurture of children should take place in a stable home environment, and that includes both a father and mother.

Moreover, you should consider whether you are attempting to manipulate God's plan for your life by trying to have a baby outside of marriage. Is there an underlying lack of faith in your heart and mind? An impatience with God, or even a resentment toward Him? "God, You haven't provided a husband for me, and I really want a child, so I'm going to take matters into my own hands." If you truly want children—and want the best for them—pray that God will give you a family in which to raise them.

OWNING STOCKS IN COMPANIES DOING GENETIC TESTING

As a Christian, should I be investing in a company that does genetic testing?

GENETIC TESTING takes many forms, and some of them are quite beneficial for people. For example, mapping the human gene has proven extremely helpful in leading to medical breakthroughs and sometimes even cures for certain diseases. No doubt, some people invested in the genetic testing companies to finance the research on such discoveries. It is not immoral that they should profit from such research. DNA testing has helped law enforcement catch criminals and exonerate the innocent.

The water gets murky, however, when you consider immoral and unethical uses of genetic research such as stem-cell research on aborted babies or buying body parts salvaged from fetuses. Christians cannot in good conscience willingly invest in companies doing research that runs counter to biblical values; particularly, that which looks to the destruction of unborn human beings.

IS SELF-INTEREST SINFUL?

What's the difference between being self-centered and selfish, and being self-interested—watching out for me—and self-protecting?

WITH MAD BOMBERS and snipers on the loose, every wise individual will take precautions. We applaud airport screening of people and baggage. We want metal detectors to keep weapons out of our schools. The Book of Proverbs says, "The wise man sees the danger and hides himself, the fool goes on and is punished."[6] However, the emphasis in a person's life should be on God. He should be in the center. We should be focused on Him, on His pleasure and His Word. The Presbyterians in the Westminster Confession say, "Man's chief aim is to glorify God and enjoy Him forever." I believe that is where our center should be—to glorify God and to enjoy Him.

If our focus is building our safety, our own fortune, our reputation, how we can experience more pleasures, or acquiring more material possessions for ourselves and our families, that is self-centeredness. On the other hand, knowing God causes us to want to be better people. We become aware that we could do better in school, at work, that we could be a better athlete or musician, we could work harder, we could study and learn more. Sure, we have certain failings in life, but it's not wrong to have a feeling of joy in our accomplishments. That is a perfectly legitimate human emotion.

IS ABORTION SOMETIMES A BLESSING?

If God has a plan for every life, what is the purpose of carrying a baby nine months, only to have it be stillborn or born with a terrible defect that keeps the child from functioning as a normal person? Wouldn't terminating that child's life before birth be a kinder thing to do for all concerned?

THE STORY IS TOLD of a son born to an alcoholic father who had some kind of genetic problem. This child became deaf as an adult and was otherwise afflicted with a number of other physical problems. Yet, inside him was music that has thrilled the ages with its majesty and splendor. That deaf musician was the great composer Ludwig van Beethoven.

The normal thinking might have been, "Let's abort this child because he will be a burden to us." He has bad antecedence and his birth is certain to bring nothing but problems." Wouldn't abortion have been better?

No, the world would be minus the great concertos and other masterpieces written by Beethoven. None of us is able to play God, to say, "This child is a mistake," or "This child is okay; this child is worthy to live. This one is not."

---

6   Proverbs 22:3

The late Dale Evans Rogers wrote a book called *Angel Unaware* about her daughter with Down syndrome, who turned out to be a great blessing to her. Was that child a mistake? Dale thought of her baby as an angel. I hesitate to say in anybody's case that it would be better to abort a baby who might have some birth defect or some problem.

Also, as believers we attribute all children to God and we trust that He created them the way that He did for a reason. He allows human beings to participate in that creative process by having children. He also permits us the opportunity to damage some of our cells and chromosomes before we conceive children. We could contract diseases, or we could do things to damage ourselves, or our parents could have done things that have wreaked havoc in our lives and in future generations. Is God responsible for that? No, He is not.

Where did that child's birth defect come from? Maybe it was caused by something that the parents did. But does that mean that we have the liberty to kill the child? The answer in my opinion is no.

Part of the problem lies in our ideas of what is valuable and what is not. Often our concepts of value are contrary to God's standards. Consider a woman such as Helen Keller, who was blind and deaf, and yet she learned to communicate through sign language and was a great inspiration to the world. Was her life worthwhile? If you simply looked at the fact that she couldn't run and jump, play basketball, tennis, or golf, and do all the things that we consider so important in life, you might say, "Well, she wasn't worth much." But Helen Keller made an immeasurable contribution to our world that inspires us even to this day.

IS AIDS A CURSE FROM GOD?

Is AIDS a modern-day curse from God or some sort of punishment for our sin?

My reading has led me to believe that AIDS is the result of a tragic mistake made in the early 1950s by scientists who were working for a research institute, which later became part of the World Health Organization. The disease actually began in a laboratory where scientists were trying to develop a polio vaccine using monkey serum. They gave the serum as an oral spray vaccine to about two hundred thousand volunteers in Zaire.

The researchers did not realize that the monkey serum carried a virus for which human beings had no defense mechanism. The virus caused a shutdown of a person's immune system, making him or her susceptible to a host of debilitating diseases. Because the virus attacked the immune system, it was given the name "acquired immune deficiency syndrome" or AIDS. The AIDS virus is transmitted by blood and some secretions of human mucus. Ironically, this occurred just as society entered a "sexual revolution," purporting a newfound sense of sexual freedom of expression. The AIDS virus moved from the jungles to the urban areas, then overseas by international travel. It was initially a disease of homosexuals and intravenous drug users. Soon it jumped into the heterosexual community. It is now a curse upon participants in promiscuous sexual activity.

AIDS is now spreading out of control and there is no known cure. To say AIDS is a plague of God is a bit overstated. AIDS is a disease that man has brought upon himself. Obviously, the flagrant sinfulness of human beings is spreading AIDS primarily in three ways: homosexual activity, unprotected heterosexual activity, and intravenous drug use. Granted, some people get AIDS from infected blood through the normal course of blood transfusions. It can also be passed from infected mothers to their unborn children. But the major cause of AIDS these days is promiscuous sex. Yes, it has become a curse. According to reports presented at the 2002 International AIDS Conference held in Barcelona, Spain, more than 40 million people worldwide carry the AIDS virus. Currently, 11 million children in Africa have lost one or both parents due to the virus, with that number predicted to nearly double by 2010.[7] Epidemics are being forecast in China, Russia, and India as well as the sex capital of the world, Thailand. But it is not because God is punishing our world; it is because men and women continue to engage in activities that God has prohibited, thus causing the rapid spread of this plague, and bringing a curse upon themselves.

---

[7]   "More AIDS Orphans," *New York Times*, "World Briefs," 11 July 2002.

CONTENTS

— CHAPTER 7 —

YOU ARE WHAT YOU EAT
Health and Diet

WHILE I AM NOT AN EXPERT in the field of health, exercise, and diet, I have studied extensively on the subjects. Furthermore, I've had the privilege of interviewing many nutritional and fitness experts on our television program, and I have benefited greatly from their knowledge and wisdom. Still, I readily acknowledge that I am not a physician, so my advice on these subjects must be considered with that caveat in mind.

Almost on a daily basis questions come to me concerning how we can live better, longer, and more productively. I'm convinced that most of us could improve our energy level and effectiveness at work, play, or with our families simply by improving our diets.

Unquestionably, our diet impacts our lifestyle immensely. "You are what you eat" is more than a book title or slogan; it is an indictment for many Americans. Most of our diets are atrocious! We consume enormous amounts of junk food, caffeine, and sugar, while ignoring much-needed proteins, nutritious fruits, and vegetables. Worse yet, most of us have better alternatives that we simply are not using to our advantage.

We can also glean insight from the Old Testament, in particular, where God's people were commanded to refrain from eating certain foods. Granted, some of the restrictions were ceremonial, but we can't help but wonder if there were not good health and dietary reasons behind the rules.

In this section, I'll answer some representative questions that have been e-mailed to us, and offer a few suggestions that have proved helpful to my family and to me. These practices have worked well for me, and I'm convinced they will help you, too. Certainly, you should always check with your doctor before embarking on any new fitness program or diet, but as a rule, we can eliminate many health problems by making wise choices about how we treat our bodies.

MY DOCTORS TREAT SYMPTOMS, NOT CAUSES

I feel like the woman in the Bible who spent all her money on doctors, but was not any better. My doctors simply treat my symptoms rather than searching for and treating the causes for my sickness. How can I take a more proactive approach to my health?

MOST DOCTORS are well educated in pathology, treating physical problems, rather than striving for wellness and wholeness. Only within recent years has the medical profession begun to place more emphasis on studying the effects of vitamins and minerals and other "nutriceuticals," or all-natural substances, as preventatives against disease. Prior to that, most medical schools concentrated on teaching doctors to use drugs and chemicals to deal with pathology and on teaching surgeons how to operate on diseased or broken organs of the body. While all of us are grateful for hospitals and doctors and their wonderful efforts at helping to fix what hurts, we'd be less dependent on their services if we could build up a healthy cell structure in our bodies to prevent the physical problems from happening and to help God bring about the natural healing of our bodies when problems occur.

I'm a strong advocate of vitamins and health foods. Although many frauds exist within the vitamin and health food industry, and some substances do not live up to the claims made on their labels, the real, truly beneficial products can be found in most reputable health food stores. Judy Lindberg McFarland's book *Aging Without Growing Old* (published by Western Front, Ltd., 2000) is an excellent book on health and nutrition and can help you make intelligent purchases of products that actually work. Drs. Ronald Klatz and Robert Goldman's book *Stopping the Clock* (Keats Publishing, 1996) is another extremely helpful book about aging, longevity, and proper nutrition.

Most health food stores can provide information about supplements that help to guard against some of the more common maladies, as well as information about age-defying antioxidants. Gailon Totheroh, our science and medical reporter at CBN, has been on the cutting edge of investigating the effects of substances such as glucosamine and condroitin, substances that actually restore cartilage and joints that have been ravaged by arthritis. These amazing, natural substances are available at most health food stores. Similarly, at CBN we sent out more than five hundred thousand pamphlets describing age-defying antioxidants. We had a similar number of requests for a health shake recipe that I make and take personally that provides adequate nutrition and a good start to each morning. I am including these materials for you in the appendix of this book. You can take charge of your life and ward off the ravages of disease and old age by making simple, relatively inexpensive changes in your diet and taking available health supplements.

Besides ingesting things that are good for us, we must also avoid eating and drinking substances that are known to be harmful to our bodies. For instance, we once did a major television focus report at CBN on the dangers of NutraSweet™, a substance found in many diet soft drinks. NutraSweet reduces visual acuity, and has been tagged as a cause of headaches, stomach cramps, and even partial blindness in some people. Stay away from anything that contains aspartame as a sweetener. Other cell killers include trans fatty acids found in the grease used to fry many foods, turning good foods into dangerous poisons which are damaging to your heart and cholesterol levels.

You needn't become a fanatic about health issues, but wisdom dictates that we will live better, longer, healthier lives if we give our bodies the nutrients they need while avoiding the substances that destroy our cells, arteries, and vital organs.

IS ADD A REAL DISORDER?

Do you think ADD is a real disorder, and why are so many kids labeled with it?

I'M A VITAMIN AND MINERAL BUFF, so I believe that many disorders that are being treated chemically could be better dealt with naturally. Ritalin™, used to treat children and some adults who have been diagnosed as having attention deficit disorder (ADD), is a potent drug that should not be given to children indiscriminately. Yet because so many children seem hyperactive, Ritalin is commonly prescribed. In truth, part of what may be causing our children to be so hyper is their diet. The diets of most American children are atrocious. You cannot live at fast-food restaurants ingesting a regular diet of soft drinks, pizza, doughnuts, crackers, pretzels, and all sorts of other sweet and salty products without having a reaction in your body. There are so-called excitotoxins such as MSG (found in Chinese and much spicy food), trans fatty acids (most hard fats), and aspartame, all of which can probably drive your children's nervous systems into overdrive. Before pumping our children full of Ritalin and other drugs, we ought to carefully examine their diet and exercise regimes.

Concerning ADD, again I highly recommend Judy McFarland's extremely helpful book *Aging Without Growing Old*, in which she advocates minerals such as potassium, magnesium, and others that will help cure the symptoms associated with ADD. Check your local health food store for other helpful resources, but don't buy into the idea that because a child is unusually energetic or lacks the ability to focus, he or she must have some disease. That's rubbish.

WHY AREN'T CHRISTIANS THE HEALTHIEST PEOPLE?

Shouldn't Christians be the healthiest people in the entire world? If so, why do so many die of the same diseases nonbelievers die from?

BECAUSE MANY BELIEVERS INDULGE in the same unhealthy habits as nonbelievers!

The Seventh Day Adventists, however, have remarkable physical constitutions. Autopsies done on members of that religious group have revealed internal organs similar to teenagers because the members of that church don't smoke or drink alcoholic beverages. Beyond that, many are vegetarians and most maintain extremely healthy diets.

On the other hand, if we eat burgers and fries, soft drinks, pretzels, and potato chips, we are asking for trouble. Many snack foods on the market today are extremely unhealthy. Originally, many snacks were promulgated by beer companies and were known as salt snacks, because they were meant to induce a taste for beer. The snacks were salty, so people wanted a drink after they had eaten them. It was a double whammy—a double dose of unhealthy products.

We once had Dr. Russell Blaylock, author of *Excitotoxins: The Taste That Kills*, as a guest on our program. His premise was that the food industry purposely puts many of these chemicals such as aspartame (sweetener), monosodium glutamate (MSG) found in many spicy Chinese and Cajun foods, excitotoxins, as he called them, into our food to enhance the food's taste. Once a person has grown accustomed to these more intense tastes, it is almost impossible to be satisfied with the more bland, soy products and other natural foods that don't artificially stimulate our taste buds. The problem, of course, is that these excitotoxins are extremely dangerous to our health!

Greasy food is also unhealthy, especially trans fatty acids, which are in certain types of margarines. If some of these products are fried, they can be carcinogenic and can do serious damage to your health. Similarly, bacon is cured with nitrate, which is bad for your health. Also, if you barbecue certain foods at the improper temperature, it can turn carcinogenic.

If we do the same things that everybody else does, we will we will be just as sick as everyone else. We will not be healthy, no matter how godly we are.

I try to be circumspect in what I eat. I read a lot about nutrition, watch my diet carefully, and I ingest a large amount of minerals, vitamins, and amino acids. I have cut down on eating red meat, and as a result have reduced the danger of plaque in my arteries and have enjoyed good health.

Ironically, when a baby begins eating soft foods, many parents make the mistake of inundating their child with sweets, trying to get the baby to eat. We assume that since such food tastes good to us, it must taste good to them. But babies have an acute sense of taste, and often food that may be bland to adult tastes would be quite satisfying to an infant.

Unfortunately, if we insist on coating the baby's food with salt or sugar, before long the child will begin craving those tastes and will not be satisfied otherwise. But children don't normally desire megadoses of sugar and salt. We teach our children to crave those substances that can lead to ill health later in life. On the other hand, a child's palate can be trained to enjoy fruit and vegetables and sugarless products, and can be quite content and much healthier.

IS THERE A BIBLICAL HEALTHY DIET?

What is a better, more "spiritual" diet that God prefers His people to maintain?

GOD'S PROVISION FOR ADAM AND EVE was fruit and grain. Most dieticians today recommend a diet replete with fruits, vegetables, and natural grains.

To me, soybeans are almost the perfect food; they have twenty out of twenty-two essential amino acids, making them an almost complete protein. They have the right balance of fats and carbohydrates, and they contain the substance genistein that fights cancer. The soybean is a remarkable source of protein, and it doesn't cause the allergies that can be caused by certain milk products.

According to the Bible, the ancients ate meat. However, their livestock weren't fattened in pens and shot full of growth hormones. In Jesus' day, the people ate a great deal of fish, lentils, and olive oil. They also ate yogurt—they called it curds—which is also very healthy. Diets low in fat may reduce cholesterol, but they also sharply reduce testosterone. We need animal proteins and healthy fat from fish or vegetable sources such as flaxseed.

Scripture mentions certain foods that were considered ceremonially unclean and were avoided. Interestingly, many of these are not healthy foods.

God did not prescribe a specific diet that all people should follow, but in Ezekiel 4:9, God gave the prophet directions for a loaf of bread that consisted of a number of types of grain mixed together, including barley, beans, lentils, spelt, millet, and wheat. My *700 Club* cohost and I tasted bread made from this mixture, known as Ezekiel's fasting bread. It tastes absolutely wonderful, is extremely healthy, and could be a fabulous replacement bread for people wanting to lose weight. Following our feature on "Ezekiel's Bread," Full Cup Coffee House, the Atlanta-based company that produces it, was inundated with calls from around the world.[1]

In contrast, at the beginning of the twentieth century, many American milling companies began removing the wheat germ and other essential minerals from the flour used to make bread. The result was processed white flour, which had almost no nutritional value but looked "cleaner." They then artificially replaced some of the vitamins and labeled the resulting mess "enriched." Such flour and bread are not enriched at all! Quite the contrary! These breads are deprived of the basic nutritional value that God put into grain in the first place.

Many people fail to realize that our bodies react to simple carbohydrates, such as white flour and sugar much as they do to alcohol. These foods evoke a craving for more because they do not satisfy the body's basic need for proteins and minerals.

Too often, many of our "Christian fellowship" opportunities are frequented by silent killers. At many church suppers or pot luck dinners, you can usually find a wonderful assortment of biscuits, rolls, fried foods, cakes, pies, ice cream and other delicacies loaded with sugar. Those foods are killers! They will poison your system and can lead to cancer, high blood pressure, heart disease, and obesity. How ironic that in the midst of plenty our bodies are being starved of vitamins and minerals! Sadly, such American starvation shows up most often in the form of fat rather than the malnutrition we've seen in places such as Ethiopia.

---

[1]   For more information on Ezekiel's Bread, contact: Full Cup Coffee House Ministry, 3232 Cobb Parkway, #214; Atlanta, GA 30339 (Phone: 770-805-8826; Fax: 770-433-1135), or contact them at www.Fullcup.org.

To live healthier, you must shift your diet to include more complex carbohydrates found in fruits, vegetables, and whole grains such as oatmeal. Beware of anything that includes hydrogenated fats or oils found often in margarine and bread, crackers, and peanut butter. Changing to a more healthy diet will indeed be a more "spiritual" diet, since you will be taking better care of the temple of the Holy Spirit, your body!

My good friend Dr. James Carraway is one of the nation's leading plastic surgeons and skin-care experts. He is also an expert on diet and nutrition. He has written an outstanding article in the *Cosmetic Surgery Times,* November/December, 2001 issue entitled, "Foods from Biblical Times—Are they still healthy for our patients?" This article was so complete and well done that I have requested permission to include it in the appendix to this book. See Appendix 2, page 327.

WHEN IS COSMETIC SURGERY APPROPRIATE?

When is cosmetic surgery appropriate?

COSMETIC SURGERY is becoming more common today because of our quest for youth. Some people would say that it is a terrible thing, because it smacks of pride and an obsession with physical beauty. Certainly, if cosmetic surgery is sought simply to enhance your sex appeal, you may be dissatisfied no matter how many body parts you change.

On the other hand, if cosmetic surgery makes people feel better, if they have more self-confidence, if they can do their job better, if they feel more accepted by people, then cosmetic surgery can be a good thing—especially for those with some sort of physical disfigurement. If a person has an unattractive growth on his or her face that would be better taken away, or some terrible birthmark, or other facial deformity that attracts unwanted attention, cosmetic surgery can prove a liberating blessing.

Cosmetic surgery is expensive and is mostly affordable for the affluent. We did, however, have a team of plastic surgeons with us on CBN's "Flying Hospital," a medical missions team that traveled to many poor nations of the world aboard a plane equipped with hospital gear. The team offered free medical help to as many people as they could treat.

The plastic surgeons on that team were incredibly gifted. One girl in El Salvador had been badly burned. Her skin had grown back on one of her arms in such a way that her forearm was attached to her chest and was, therefore, useless. One of the plastic surgeons examined her, smiled and said, "I can fix it. No problem."

He went to work and reattached the tendons in a way that allowed the girl to move her arm, eventually allowing her complete mobility. A young man in the Philippines had a large goiter about the size of a melon extending from the front of his chin, horribly disfiguring his face. We paid for his ticket to come to Virginia Beach, and wonderful plastic surgeons removed the goiter and literally gave the man a new life. One poor young fellow was so badly burned that he wore a ski mask so people wouldn't have to look at his face. A team of volunteer plastic surgeons shaped a new ear for him, reshaped his nose and mouth, and did a near miraculous job of helping to repair the skin on his face. I can't say enough about plastic surgeons who use their skills to alleviate the sufferings and humiliations of other people.

Granted, much cosmetic surgery in America is precisely that—cosmetic. I don't see anything wrong with it any more than combing our hair, putting on makeup, or wearing contact lens to make oneself look more presentable.

One caution: Keep in mind that plastic surgery cannot magically transform you into somebody else. Some people with emotional or self-esteem problems are obsessed with cosmetic surgery in the vain hope that they will be more popular, successful, or happier with themselves. That is a dangerous illusion. A good cosmetic surgeon will not permit people to undergo surgery after surgery in a quest to satisfy their unrealistic expectations.

Sooner or later, we must face the fact that this body is deteriorating, no matter how much touching up we do. It is not our final home. Our true home is in heaven, where we will live eternally with God, and our bodies will be spiritual rather than physical. In the meantime, as long as your focus is on Jesus, if cosmetic improvement makes you feel more comfortable, more power to you. But if you can't do it in faith, don't do it.

DEPRESSION'S PREVALENCE IN MARRIED WOMEN

Why does depression (especially among married women) seem so common nowadays?

SINGLE WOMEN AND MEN can become depressed as well as those who are married, but it does seem that an inordinate amount of depression is showing up in young mothers. A condition known as postpartum depression sometimes occurs after the birth of children. Giving birth places an enormous strain on a woman's body. To carry and nurture that baby for nine months exacerbates normal emotions, not to mention the enormous physical strain. Nowadays, largely for insurance reasons, women are hustled out of the hospital before their bodies have had a chance to adapt; they have a baby one day and they are out of the hospital the next. They don't have a chance to rest or recuperate. Many of them are back to work in a couple of weeks, which is extremely taxing. A woman and newborn child need to rest, and the mother needs time to nurture her child. The birthing process is such a shock to a woman's system that depression could easily follow. Imagine compounding the strain by forcing the young mother to undertake normal household duties *plus* returning to the pressure cooker of office demands!

Recently, I read of a woman who did violence to her young children. It was inexplicable, except, perhaps, when you consider the effects of depression or some type of psychosis. Certainly, motherhood puts an enormous strain on women. There is a prolonged strain on their bodies if they don't get enough sleep and rest. For young mothers trying to maintain a career, keep their husbands happy, take care of their children, and be active in the church or community, the load often becomes overwhelming, and depression can be the result.

Proper nutrition is an extremely important preventative against depression. I remember one woman who was in a near suicidal state. I could see cracks at the sides of her mouth, which indicated a deficiency of vitamin B-2. She was biting her nails, and her eyes were bleary. I asked, "What are you eating?"

She said, "I don't eat much, but I do drink a lot of soda, and I eat potato chips and snack food."

"How many soft drinks do you usually consume in a day?"

"Eight or nine," she replied, "plus I usually have some coffee with my sweet rolls in the morning." That was her "regular" diet!

I said, "I want you to start taking a therapeutic vitamin with minerals. Stop ingesting all that junk food, caffeine, and sweets, and begin eating proteins, fresh fruits and vegetables, and get a lot of exercise and fresh air." A few months later, I saw her again. She was emotionally stable, had begun a successful business venture, and was doing extremely well. She was a happy woman, free from her former depression.

Certainly, not every case of depression can be cured so easily, but if you or someone you love is battling depression, look for physiological causes first. Check for low blood sugar by having a glucose-tolerance test. If you catch it early enough, before diabetes sets in, the antidote for this is simply to stop eating sweets and start eating proteins. Make sure the person is exposed for lengthy periods to early morning sunshine in order to replenish the levels of the neurotransmitter serotonin in the brain.

Of course, exercise can release the body's mood elevator, the endorphins. Look for a doctor who is trained in nutritional medicine instead of pathology, someone who can help you take positive, preventative steps, rather than simply dealing with the negative symptoms after the problem exists.

I believe that a leading cause of depression and attempted suicide is guilt. An individual is engaged in conduct which he or she knows to be wrong. The conduct causes guilt and shame, but the individual refuses to stop. Feelings of frustration and self-loathing set in, which can deepen into depression. The flip side of this same syndrome involves the person who knows something must be done but is afraid or unwilling to do it. Self-deception follows, then self-loathing, then depression.

Until the spiritual and psychological causes are dealt with, depression will deepen. This is one reason that the confessional of the Catholic church is so beneficial. A depressed person can unburden his soul in confidence and, in the process, receive words of encouragement, comfort, or admonition.

CONFRONTING ADULT MALE HORMONAL CHANGES

My husband of more than twenty years has withdrawn from me and appears no longer attracted to me physically or emotionally. What can we do?

ONLY IN RECENT YEARS has science acknowledged the changes that take place in a man's body beginning during his midlife years, and extending into his late forties, fifties, sixties, and beyond. Regrettably, many wives misunderstand or misinterpret what is happening to their husbands during these years.

First of all, don't rule out the possibility of blockages in the heart, the arteries, and other parts of the circulatory system, and don't ignore the pressures and failures at work that can leave a man despondent and withdrawn.

His testosterone level is dropping, his sexual drive is diminishing, and his muscle mass is deteriorating, while at the same time, the level of fat in his body is increasing. Consequently, without an extremely vigorous exercise program, his body is becoming flabby, and his vitality is going downhill. Overall, he feels as though he is no longer the man he used to be. And he's right! This is a major change for a man, similar to the transition a woman goes through during menopause.

What does this do to a man's ego? How is his self-esteem affected? His self-worth plummets because he can no longer function in the way he once did. In a speech at Regent University, Lech Walesa quipped, "The only male thing that I used to do that I do now is shave!" Lech could make light of his age, but to most men, their loss of virility is no laughing matter.

Some men attempt to compensate for these changes by wearing their hair in a younger style, dressing in a more youthful fashion, engaging in extreme sports, or driving a shiny new sports car. While they may look somewhat foolish, at least they aren't hurting anyone.

Unfortunately, other men try to compensate for their lost virility by seeking out a new relationship, often with a younger woman who strokes his ego. While we cannot condone his actions, let's try to understand what is happening.

Several basic hormones that have operated in a man's body since puberty begin to change as a man ages. In his mid-twenties, a man may have had an abundance of testosterone, the hormone primarily responsible for his sex drive as well as his energy and vitality; and DHEA, a hormone that gives energy and protects against disease; and the human growth hormone secreted by the pituitary gland, which helps build and maintain muscle tissue throughout the body. But as his body ages, these vital hormones dwindle, so by the time he reaches his sixties, these hormones are almost nonexistent in his system.

Many men don't realize the changes they are experiencing are physiological in nature; others simply don't want to admit that they are aging, so they take desperate steps hoping to reclaim their youth. It is almost as though they are going through a second childhood.

Even though he may love his wife immeasurably, without testosterone, a man's sex drive cannot possibly be what it was when he and his bride first married. Similarly, without DHEA, he is more susceptible to disease and an overall lack of vitality; without human growth hormone, the adipose tissue in his body will accumulate, creating the dreaded "middle age spread." Ironically, all three of these conditions seem to occur at about the same time, tossing the husband and wife into an emotional tailspin.

Can these hormones be replenished? Yes, they can! Testosterone can be replaced with injections or by wearing doctor-prescribed transdermal patches, similar to those worn on the arm by smokers attempting to quit.

DHEA is available in pill form at most health food stores. Human growth hormone injections are available at a high price from some physicians. Arginine, niacin, glutamine, alpha lipoic acid, choline-inositol, and tyrosine are helpful for stimulating the brain and muscles. For those men who are able to exercise vigorously, heavy weightlifting—especially using one's legs—can stimulate the release of human growth hormone. Of course proper diet combined with regular exercise is extremely beneficial. Certainly, before taking any of these steps, a wise man should see a doctor for a thorough physical examination.

Unfortunately, when these changes are not acknowledged, a wife may feel that a man's inability to function is due to a lack of love, that "he doesn't love me or want me anymore" or "the fire has gone out in our marriage" or worse yet, that he has someone else. In fact, the problem may be nothing of the sort! His body is betraying him and he doesn't know what to do about it.

For many men, it is easier to retreat from a meaningful relationship with their wives or to bury themselves in work or some other activity (even religious activities) rather than confronting the problem.

As intimacy becomes little more than a fading memory of glories past, some men succumb to living vicariously, watching racy television shows, viewing dirty movies, or engaging in Internet pornography. Meanwhile, their wives become increasingly dissatisfied with their relationships. Many women retreat into their own worlds of mental fantasies. Too often, couples who have been happily married for years sit by idly while they watch their God-ordained marriages going down the tubes right before their eyes.

This can be prevented easily if couples will seek a medical solution to their physiological problems and a spiritual solution to their emotional problems. Beyond that, we must recognize that aging does have its many incontrovertible effects on our bodies, and we should develop realistic attitudes concerning our expectations of ourselves and our spouse. Seek the Lord's wisdom for how you can maintain a healthy, growing relationship with your spouse all the days of your life.

GLUTTONOUS, FAT CHRISTIANS

I know that sin is sin, but why do we tolerate overweight, almost gluttonous Christians, yet we turn our eyes from drug addicts or alcoholics? Is one sin more acceptable than another?

THERE'S NO DIFFERENCE between one and the other, except that illicit narcotics are against the law, so people ingesting them are breaking the law. Alcohol can lead to more direct consequences than gluttony. Gluttony takes a while before its full effects are felt. It harms the individual but doesn't necessarily harm others. Alcohol can lead to rage, it often leads to erratic driving, possibly endangering the lives of passengers and other people on the road. It causes some people to carry out acts of violence or immorality that they wouldn't normally do. So, from society's standpoint, drugs and alcohol are worse. But from God's standpoint, one sin is as damning as another. One self-indulgence is as damaging as another; if we sin against God, it is a serious matter. He doesn't have classes of sins, with mortal sins, venial sins, and peccadilloes all meriting certain degrees of punishment. The Bible teaches that all sin is destructive, offensive to God, and must be repented of and forgiven.

Beyond that, our bodies are the temple of the Lord, but the testimony we have before the world is often compromised by our external appearance. I recall a Bible teacher who weighed nearly four hundred pounds! He was so short of breath, he huffed and puffed and sounded like a freight train when he tried to walk up a hill. His obesity had stressed his heart, capillaries, lungs, and his skin. Sadly, his condition was due almost entirely to his overindulgence and gluttonous eating habits. He could consume an entire pie at one sitting! How could such a man possibly be a positive witness for the Lord? He obviously disregarded the temple of the Holy Spirit, and his gross obesity could hardly be considered a recommendation of the Christian lifestyle.

Many Christians tend to excuse gluttony as an acceptable sin. For proof, simply attend the next church supper or gathering of believers where food is served. Often, at such gatherings gluttony is the norm. Well-meaning women exhibit their fine culinary skills, then stand back and watch as their men dig their graves with their teeth!

Gluttony has become a national epidemic, especially among children, and it is bringing with it a host of related illnesses and unhealthy conditions. A Christian should reject gluttonous habits, just as we do other addictive actions or compulsions that are harmful to our health and to our testimonies before the world.

BENEFITS OF BREAST-FEEDING

I've heard of health benefits to breast-feeding, and I want to breast-feed my baby; but because of my job, I have to bottle-feed. Am I doing my baby a disservice or contradicting God's natural way by bottle-feeding my child?

BREAST-FEEDING A BABY provides an incredible amount of protective substances from the mother during the initial six months of the baby's life. The mother passes on to the child antibodies and enzymes that help strengthen the baby. Recent studies indicate that a substantial increase of diabetes among the young may be caused by babies drinking cow's milk instead of mother's milk. I'm also aware of numerous medical studies concerning the increased risk of breast cancer in women who do not breast-feed their babies. Moreover, babies aren't ready for cow's milk. When they drink it, the milk creates a reaction that causes problems with the pancreas and the endocrine system and can lead to serious complications. Clearly, breast-feeding is God's designed means for mothers to feed their babies, and to do otherwise, you are definitely doing your baby a disservice.

Many baby formulas are convenient but are simply not the best for your child. If at all possible, use the milk that God has made available to you. Many businesses, churches, and schools now designate a private area where nursing mothers may breast-feed their babies without being exposed to the public. Other lactating women prefer to use a breast pump to draw and store mother's milk ahead of time for their babies. This milk can then be given to the baby, even when the mother is not available.

Beyond the health benefits of breast-feeding for the child, the emotional bonding that takes place between mother and child during breast-feeding is invaluable and should not be missed if at all possible.

MY HIGH-TECH JOB IS STRESSING ME OUT!

I'm under horrendous stress in a highly complex work environment. The demands are more than I can possibly get done, so I spend long hours trying to satisfy my superiors. I'm on call constantly, living with my computer and cell phone almost surgically attached. I never seem to have any peace. I feel that I'm cheating my family, but I can't afford to quit my job, and I'm good at what I do, but how much longer can I keep going this way?

NOT LONG! You need to do something quickly, before it is too late!

I am frankly not sure that the demands of high-pressure jobs are worth the physical, emotional, and social price they exact from us. Before I became a Christian, I worked for a very large multinational corporation. The pressure and the demands were horrible. At age twenty-five, I had developed arthritis in one ankle (from which the Lord later healed me), and I was heading toward an executive ulcer . . . all for the princely wage of $125 per week.

I left that job to start a business with a couple of friends from law school. From there, I met the Lord and started the adventure of a lifetime. Before it is too late, there may be a better way for you.

However, here are suggestions if you decide to stay with your current job. Begin by examining your priorities carefully. Life works best when our priorities are:

1. God

2. Family

3. Career

Each of us needs to spend time alone with God in prayer and meditating on His Word every day. As you spend time communing with the Lord, basking in His love, and allowing Him to show you His priorities, it's amazing the peace that comes to your heart and mind. You'll discover something that has been eluding you for some time—rest!

Certainly, we are busy; nearly every productive person I know is busy! But the most productive people I've met are those who consistently keep God in first place in their lives.

You also need to take time to relax. Budget your time and money in such a way that you plan for periodic "getaways," some time for your family, and especially with your marriage partner. Short mini-vacations—times when a husband and wife can go off for a day or two by themselves, just to enjoy each other—are invaluable boons to any marriage and family. These excursions need not be expensive. A day at the park, hiking, swimming, canoeing, or a walk on the beach or in the woods, a weekend spent away from home at a nearby hotel; any activity that takes you away from the hustle and bustle of everyday life will help you relax, and will also reap huge dividends in your relationship with your husband or wife.

These husband-wife times should be separate from family vacations, which are sometimes more stressful than work itself! Take time for yourself, and take time for your relationship with your spouse. Your children will thank you.

But don't fool yourself. These stress-relieving activities will not happen unless you plan them into your calendar and budget. Don't rely on happenstance to relieve your stress. There will always be another phone call to return, another project that needs to be done, or something that will rob you of your special time together if you allow it.

When you keep the Lord first in your life, and your family second, your career will suddenly seem far less stressful. You will be better at what you do, less stressed, and your superiors will be pleasantly surprised at your performance in the workplace.

VALIDITY OF GOVERNMENT VITAMIN STANDARDS

I take a daily multivitamin. Is that enough to maintain good health or should I be taking other supplements?

I HAVE RECOMMENDED what I consider to be the essential antioxidants and B-vitamin complex in the material at the appendix of this book. The so-called minimum daily requirements of vitamins as determined by government standards are extremely inaccurate and insufficient, as far as I am concerned. I do not recommend most "grocery store" brand daily vitamins, because they don't have enough minerals to really improve one's health, especially if you are looking for something to help you fight the effects of aging.

Instead, I have found the Varsity Pack 2 multivitamins and minerals sold at Lindberg Nutrition Express (800-338-7979), for example, to be reasonably priced and conveniently prepackaged in the right combinations and dosages.

ARE ANTIDEPRESSANTS UNBIBLICAL?

I am currently under a doctor's care and taking antidepressants. My church leaders feel that taking such drugs is not biblical, and have advised me to stop taking them. They say that God made me the way I am, and these medications interfere with my ability to hear from Him. What does the Bible say, and can I be healed of this depression?

DEPRESSION AS WE KNOW IT today is not specifically discussed in the Bible, but see my discussion earlier in this chapter under "Depression's Prevalence in Married Women." Certainly, Job was depressed after losing everything he had. The prophet Elijah experienced a deep emotional trough after his victorious rout of the prophets of Baal on Mount Carmel. Perhaps the closest illustration of the emotional roller coaster many people are on today can be seen in the life of Saul, the first king of Israel. King Saul had some bizarre experiences that we might diagnose as manic-depressive or possibly schizophrenic behavior. Saul's depression may even have been demonically inspired.

A person who is manic-depressive has a chemical imbalance in the brain that can lead to severe delusion, terrible bouts with depression, or even suicide. Often, in a severe manic state, a person may knowingly or unwittingly inflict harm on others. In one case, a man who worked at CBN became completely deranged, out of his mind with manic delusions. We referred him to a Christian psychiatrist who was able to treat the chemical imbalance with appropriate antidepressants, and the man began to function normally and resume a normal life.

The human brain operates by a series of electrochemical impulses called synapses. If the chemical balance is not correct, or if the impulses do not fire properly, it's possible for a person to experience all sorts of strange, erratic reactions. Consequently, I see nothing wrong with someone taking antidepressants under the watchful care of a good doctor.

On the other hand, I do not concur with the psychobabble espoused by Freudian psychologists and psychiatrists who seem obsessed with finding some experience in the person's past to excuse the person's present condition.

The Bible says that we are "fearfully and wonderfully made."[2] In dealing with people who exhibit bizarre behavior, we must determine the root cause of their malady. Is it low blood sugar or an improper chemical balance in the brain? Is it a lack of oxygen to the brain? Has there been a severe emotional trauma? Has there been mental or physical abuse or extreme stress? Or is the condition due to demonic oppression or possession?

Only people with extraordinary skills should be dealing with people who exhibit erratic mental behavior. I strongly caution Christians to pray for God's intervention and healing, but to leave the treatment of mental illness to those who have been trained in the field.

One further caution: Some people in our society believe that they should never endure pain or emotional discomfort. As a result, doctors prescribe powerful drugs such as Valium™, Librium™, Xanex™, Prozac™, and others. This is totally unrealistic, and it is unconscionable for doctors to indiscriminately attempt to treat people simply by giving them "feel good" medications. Life is difficult and at times stressful. We do experience pain, suffering, and heartaches. We often must bear up under sorrows.

Yet we dare not go through life medicated! Such flagrant indulgence in the "pharmacopia" available nowadays is improper and dangerous. Reputable doctors should have the courage to resist the cravings of their patients for such drugs. For a tragic example of what can happen when the dangers of these practices are ignored, review the life of Elvis Presley, who died after years of misuse of drugs—almost all of which had been prescribed by a doctor.

---

[2]   Psalm 139:14

NATURE'S REMEDY FOR POOR CIRCULATION

I suffer intense leg pains from poor circulation. Can you suggest any natural remedies that might relieve my discomfort, rather than over-the-counter drugs?

IN MY OPINION, THE BEST WAY TO IMPROVE your circulation is to start by engaging in some mild form of aerobic exercise such as walking. A brisk thirty-minute walk every day will often do wonders for one's circulation. As you grow stronger, you might also try something more vigorous such as bicycling, tennis, or join an aerobics class at a gym.

Vitamin C which includes the citrus bioflavonoid complex, a substance derived from the rinds of various citrus fruits, is extremely beneficial in building up the arteries and capillaries. Vitamin A with beta carotene builds veins and capillaries. I strongly recommend a substance known as alpha lipoic acid, which is a powerful antioxidant to help circulation. Glutamine, a tasteless white powder, is also helpful for quicker cellular and muscular recovery after strenuous exercise or after surgery. Vitamin E has been recognized for its excellent work in promoting blood flow. The best natural painkiller is calcium. Recently, attention has been directed to the beneficial effects of coral calcium from Okinawa.

Wrapping an Ace bandage around your legs or wearing support stockings can also aid in supporting the arteries and capillaries, and helps to improve circulation.

HERBOLOGISTS, YING AND YANG

A family member is going to a herbologist for high blood-pressure treatments, and it seems the herbs are working. Many of the herbs are not FDA approved and are actually illegal in the U.S. The doctor opens the session with prayer and suggests meditation. From a Christian perspective, what are your thoughts regarding this type of therapy?

MANY ORIENTAL HERBALISTS combine their treatments with mystical beliefs such as "ying and yang," the concept of positive and negative energy flows in the body. I have personally observed in China the remarkable effects of acupuncture, which uses the concept of energy flow at key points in the body. On the other hand, some lead patients to repeat prayers or "mantras," which are unwitting prayers in a foreign language to a demonic power. In my opinion, you should stay away from such "doctors" who practice pseudospiritual medicine.

Many herbs are quite beneficial to our bodies. Wisdom accumulated for thousands of years from other cultures regarding the medicinal benefits of these herbs can indeed enrich our lives. Echinacea, for example, is an herb that can help your immune system fight off a cold if taken for about two weeks following the onset of the sickness. Others are natural relaxants, help indigestion, and can fight disease. After all, some of the best known remedies had their origins from God's wonderful pharmacopoeia of the forest.

Some herbs are beneficial, others are benign, and others can be extremely dangerous. For instance, ma huang, an herb which is being banned in the U.S., contains the powerful stimulant epinephrine, also known as "speed." This substance, used in many popular diet pills, should be avoided because it can cause heart attacks and even death. Other herbs sometimes used by less-than-ethical "herbologists" have not been clinically tested, nor have they been cleared by the FDA. Some are absolutely worthless; others have dangerous unintended side effects.

I'd urge considerable caution before taking any untested product; do some research to find information regarding tests done on the substance before ingesting any herbal medication.

OBESE—I WANT SURGERY

How do you feel about obesity surgery? I'm 160 pounds overweight. I've tried every diet known to man and have prayed for God's direction over this area of my life. I know there are risks involved, but I think they're worth it. What are your thoughts?

MEDICAL PROCEDURES NOW EXIST whereby a portion of the stomach can be stapled in such a manner that it shrinks the capacity and restricts the amount of food that gets through the system. Other operations involve removing a portion of the intestines. Many people who have undergone such surgeries are quite pleased with the results.

Obviously, operations of this sort are frankly unnatural and can be extremely dangerous, possibly even life threatening. But being 160 pounds overweight can also be extremely dangerous! In your case, you must balance the risks of such a medical procedure against the danger of dropping dead from a heart attack due to your obesity. Nevertheless, I recommend that you secure the professional opinions of several specialists in the field before going forward with a medical operation to treat obesity. There are medical quacks in this field, and the horror stories coming from their mangled patients will curl your hair.

I'd also fully explore the possibility of treating this condition with a combination of diet and exercise, which, if pursued with diligence over a few years, would have life-long benefits with minimal risk to your health. You didn't become 160 pounds overweight in a few weeks, and you won't lose that much weight quickly. But with determination and a workable plan with some accountability, you may save your own life without the expense and risk associated with extreme surgery.

NOT ADDICTED, BUT ENJOYS A SMOKE

I enjoy having a cigar, pipe, or cigarette on occasion. It's not an addiction, just a pleasure. Is this wrong?

THE GREAT PREACHER Charles Spurgeon used to smoke a cigar or a pipe, but when he realized the negative witness his smoking was having toward others, he felt compelled to stop smoking because of the impact he was having on weaker believers.[3] In Spurgeon's day, science had not yet discovered the dangerous results that nicotine and nicotine tars could have on the lips, larynx, and lungs of a human being. Unquestionably, smoking or chewing tobacco has led to hundreds of thousands of cases of cancer, many of which have been fatal. I can see no reason someone who is armed with that knowledge would expose himself or herself to that risk or expose those people nearby to the dangers of secondhand smoke. This past year I attended the funerals of two people who died of lung cancer as a result of secondhand smoke. These were not joyous occasions for their grieving loved ones.

Fifty years ago, when we lacked scientific evidence about the harmful effects of tobacco, smoking or chewing tobacco was considered a harmless pleasure. Today, we know better, that use of tobacco is a deadly pastime. Consequently, no Christian should indulge in the willful destruction of his or her body by using tobacco in this fashion.

---

[3] For a clear discussion of liberty versus the effects of our actions on a weaker believer, see Romans 14:13–23.

FIGHTING THE "BATTLE OF THE BULGE"

I'm in my middle-age years, fighting the "battle of the bulge." I know I can't do many of the things I did when I was younger, but what can I do to regain my physical fitness?

THE ROAD TO FITNESS is not nearly as arduous as some people might make it seem. Certainly, you should start easy, and work up gradually to more rigorous activity. Don't go out some Saturday and try to run three or four miles in the hot sun, only to end up with heat stroke, shin splints, and a possible heart attack!

Before beginning any exercise program, have a complete physical examination to make sure of what you can and cannot do. Then, when you begin exercising, start by stretching extensively for ten to fifteen minutes to limber all parts of the body before any vigorous activity. Stretching tends to alleviate many aches and pains, as well as preparing your muscles for action.

The best beginner's exercise I can recommend is simple walking. A brisk walk of twenty to thirty minutes three to five times each week will do wonders for you! Ideally, you can walk outdoors in the fresh air, but walking indoors on a treadmill is beneficial also. As the weeks go by, your body will become conditioned to the exercise.

I also recommend the use of light weights that you can use at home or in a gym. You needn't lift large, heavy weights to tone your body. In fact, often the strain of lifting too much can be damaging to your muscles and back. Perhaps you know a trainer who can advise a series of simple exercises with the weights. If not, many books are available on the subject nowadays. Again, start small, and as your muscles become more firm, you will gain strength. Beyond that, you will be much less likely to suffer arthritis, and you can continue activity well into your seventies, eighties, Lord willing, or even your nineties. It's never too late to start!

I started working with weights regularly a few years ago while I was in my late sixties. I began with light weights, and now bench-press up to 235 pounds and leg-press over 1,500 pounds! Not bad for a fellow in his early seventies! With exercise, the law of use is important. If you exercise what you have and add a little each time to what you are doing, you will get stronger, bigger, and better. The more you do, the better you will be. Beyond that, exercise is fun, especially if you enjoy things such as jogging, golfing, bicycling, rowing, mountain-climbing, horseback riding, or swimming, which is especially good for those who cannot put stress on your joints. Women who are hoping to prevent osteoporosis, however, need some weight-bearing exercises that involve some concussion. Your bones can be strengthened by light weights, jogging, or running.

For those looking for a disciplined approach to diet and exercise, I highly recommend Bill Phillips's best-selling book *Body for Life*. This proven twelve-week program provides recipes, as well as exercises that can bring about dramatic results in an amazingly short time. Phillips sets up the proper rotation and rest for muscle groups and also cautions against overexercising which can actually keep muscles from growing and lead to ill health. Regardless what exercise regime you settle on, however, the most important exercise you can do is to start.

CONTENTS

— CHAPTER 8 —

DO MIRACLES REALLY HAPPEN?

Sickness and Healing

Some of the toughest questions in life begin with *why?* Such questions are especially difficult because clear-cut, bona fide, meaningful answers often elude us. These questions taunt us in the middle of the night and challenge our faith in the light of day.

Why has this disease or tragedy struck our lives?

Why didn't God protect us from this evil?

Why did God let me be born in the first place if He knew that I was going to experience so much grief?

Why does God allow these things to happen, especially to those of us who love Him?

The "why" questions keep popping up like weeds in a garden. And just as we need to constantly weed a garden if we hope to enjoy the harvest, we must constantly keep our hearts free of insidious "why" questions. Not that God can't handle them; He simply chooses to refocus our attention on "how" questions: How are we going to get through this? How can we learn from this? How can we grow stronger as a result of this experience?

Every person who has ever sat by the bedside of a friend or family member with a debilitating disease, or has grieved the loss of a loved one, has grappled with the "why" and "how" questions. Despite our faith, sometimes the best we can do is cry out to our heavenly Father, "God, it hurts!"

Can God heal our bodies? Yes, He can!

Does He heal everyone, every time we ask Him? Apparently not.

Why?

God is not offended by our questions concerning sickness and disease; He does not punish us for questioning, but at the same time, we dare not allow our questions to turn to unbelief. In seeking for answers, keep believing that God knows best, that He is not immune to your pain. As a loving Father Himself, He knows what it feels like to watch His Son die a horrible death, and that His ultimate plan is to cause all things to work for good to those who love Him.[1]

DO MIRACLES REALLY HAPPEN TODAY?

Are there any real miracles today? I know we talk about various things as being miraculous, but many times, I think these things are merely coincidences or the normal processes of life. For example, when we pray for someone to be healed, and they are not immediately healed, yet over six months time or so, they feel better. That doesn't seem like a miracle to me.

WE MUST DEFINE THE TERM *healing* and the term *miracle*. If I cut my finger and I put a bandage on it, and someone says, "How is your finger?" I could say, "Well, it is healing." Indeed, in a week or two, apart from some additional infection, the skin will heal. God has placed within my body recuperative powers that He has given to every human being. So we expect our fingers to heal if we cut them. We expect our faces to be healed if we cut them shaving. That is a type of healing.

If a person has some contagious infection and the source of the contagion is eliminated by antibiotics or otherwise, he will begin to get better. The normal, natural processes within the body will cause it to become well. That is a natural healing, and God has certainly put within us natural healing potential.

Now, let's assume that someone has a serious illness, and instead of the healing being gradual, God's people pray and the healing process is accelerated; instead of waiting two weeks, three weeks, or a month, healing is instantaneous. The condition goes away as does whatever was causing it. Suddenly the person is well. That is still a healing.

---

[1] See Romans 8:28

However, let us assume a person had his leg cut off. No amount of healing can bring that leg back. But God can do the miraculous. I'm aware of a case involving T. L. Osborne at a meeting he held in Ghana. Osborne preached from the Bible about the healing power of God. A man whose leg had been cut off at the knee was standing at the periphery of the crowd of 200,000 listening to the message. The power of Jesus Christ touched him, the word of God brought faith in his heart, and miraculously, spontaneously his leg began to grow, his foot and toes grew, his entire leg was restored like new! Now, that is a miracle!

In one case, we see the acceleration of the natural healing processes. The other is an instantaneous, miraculous healing that can only be attributed to God. Both are valid forms of healing. Does He do miracles today? Yes, He does, all around the world.

A DRUG ADDICT IN DENIAL

How can I help a friend who I know is on cocaine but who refuses to admit it?

I THINK THERE IS NO MORE SKILLFUL CLASS OF LIARS in the world than drug addicts. They live in denial themselves, and they will cheat, lie to, and steal from others to feed their habits and avoid detection.

Intervention can be helpful, if you know what you are doing, and if you know for sure that this person is a drug user. You can get a group of concerned people together and confront the user; don't let the addicted person leave until she or he acknowledges what is going on and begins to cry out to God for help. That is an extreme measure, but it is sometimes effective.

Both secular and Christian drug-rehabilitation programs are helpful, but a determined addict will beat the system and con the people trying to help him or her and come out of such a program as addicted as ever. There needs to be an anointing of God to set the addict free.

Apart from prayer for that person, there's not a whole lot you can do, unless you are involved with his or her family members. Together you can bring an intervention in that person's life. You can say, "Look, we know you are doing drugs, and we are going to help you come clean." Then take whatever steps are necessary. Understand though, little will be accomplished until the user admits, "Yes, I am an addict and I want help." Once that is done, there needs to be a break from the environment, the acquaintances, and the pressures that have brought on and nurtured the addiction. Remember, for hard-core users it takes as much as five years of being clean to ensure against a relapse.

WHY DID GOD SEND ME AN AUTISTIC CHILD?

I'm a single parent with no help from my family. My autistic child has seizures and is violent at times. Why would God let this happen?

GOD ISN'T THE AUTHOR of our problems. Many physical or mental maladjustments relate to genetic imbalances. This problem could also stem from nutritional deprivation, radiation, or an accident. Medical science hasn't come up with a definitive consensus. Why does God allow these things to happen? I don't know. Maybe it is a way of bringing us closer to Him. Dale Evans Rogers had a Down syndrome baby, whom she wrote about in her book *Angel Unaware*. Dale said that this special-needs child was an angel to her and brought her much closer to God.

Why your family wouldn't help to raise this child is beyond me. But both secular and religious agencies exist in most American cities that offer help and training for autistic children. Reach out to them and to caring people in your church to help you raise this special-needs child. Don't try to do everything yourself; don't be too proud to ask for help. And at the same time, don't be bashful about asking God for healing and deliverance from this affliction.

Jesus encouraged us to persevere in prayer, even when all hope seems lost. He instructed us to "keep on asking, keep on seeking, keep on knocking," and indicated that our persistence will pay off.[2] It is entirely proper to beseech heaven for healing of an autistic child, either through dramatic spiritual means, or through a revelation of some technique to the physician that will cause a change in the child's condition.

Do not rule out the possibility of demonic activity or influence, but don't assume demons are causing the condition. I'm cautious about attributing mental illness or physical abnormalities to demonic oppression or possession.

Certainly, we know demonic influence is real; demons sometimes bring strange curses upon people, which are often manifested in unusual mental problems. To discern whether these conditions are demonically inspired or not requires that we have the full panoply of resources available, including emotional, physiological, and spiritual expertise.

---

[2]   See Luke 11:5–10

Love your child and continue to pray for wisdom. As you pray that God will change your child's condition, pray also that He will change you and draw you closer to Him through these circumstances.

WHY DO CHILDREN SUFFER INCURABLE DISEASES?

Why does God allow children to suffer with incurable diseases like cancer? Why doesn't He just heal them?

PERHAPS THE QUESTION COULD BE, why does God allow *anybody* to suffer with cancer or other debilitating diseases? We wish we knew more about these things, but frankly we don't. I've prayed for many people with cancer; some have been healed while others have not been healed. Sometimes they live to a ripe-old age, and others die in their prime. We just don't know why.

We do know that God does not put cancer on anybody. Cancer may be caused by genetic problems, or it may stem from the many pollutants and carcinogens in our environment and in our food. People's immune systems are weakened because they do not nourish their bodies properly, then they cannot withstand the daily onslaught of tobacco smoke, polluted air and water, and carcinogens put in our food.

My wife's father had an eye disease, iritis, and the doctors treated him with a certain medication that led to his developing leukemia and an early death. Did God cause that? No, the medical community made a mistake.

Why doesn't God simply heal everyone for whom we pray? We don't know. Sometimes He seems to be waiting for us to truly lay hold of Him and see Him as our source. At other times, and for reasons we do not yet understand, He chooses not to heal, as He did when the apostle Paul prayed three times that the "thorn" in his flesh would be removed.[3] We do know that He is *able* to heal. We know that Jesus said, "With God, all things are possible."[4]

That's why when a child is suffering from some disease, it is completely appropriate for believers to storm heaven's throne with our prayers on his or her behalf. Ask God to touch, to heal that sick child. But keep in mind, physical death in this world is not the worst thing that can happen to a child. Jesus said, "Their angels always behold the face of my Father in heaven."[5] If a child dies from cancer or any other disease before they reach an age of accountability, they

---

3   See 2 Corinthians 12:7–9
4   Matthew 19:26
5   Matthew 18:10

are taken to live eternally with the Lord in heaven.[6] To us the child's death is a tragedy. To the child it is an eternity in paradise.

SHOULD A CHRISTIAN AVOID USING MEDICINE?

Many Christians avoid using medicines, even to the point of allowing a child to be sick or, in rare cases, to die. What role should faith play in those situations?

THE GOOD DOCTOR SAID, "I bind the wound, but God heals." We should consider medicine and the medical profession as blessings from God Almighty. Many dedicated Christians are in the healing arts, and they are great servants who strive to bring to us the latest in technology to alleviate our sickness and suffering.

To think that we shouldn't avail ourselves of medical science is ludicrous. At CBN, through "Operation Blessing," we have taken medical teams to many impoverished areas, and have helped hundreds of thousands of people with debilitating diseases. For instance, in El Salvador a man had been shot and the bullet had lodged in the jawbone. A surgeon with our team was able to remove the bullet and save the man's jaw. In Ecuador, at least 40 percent of the people we treated had intestinal parasites. Others are weakened by malaria. Some cannot see properly and need the eyeglasses we give for free. Some babies are born with cleft palates and our volunteer doctors repair them. Some have skin eaten up with scabies. Simple medication can kill the fungus and their skin is restored.

God blesses the work of doctors, hospitals, and medical science. On the other hand, He can also heal without medicine. It is a question of how God chooses to work in the hurting person's life.

I do not agree with those groups who discourage the use of medicine, who let children die while they wait for divine healing. These groups sometimes refuse to receive inoculations against infectious diseases such as diphtheria, whooping cough, and tetanus. While their faith may be real, their actions are foolish. Certainly, God can heal independently of doctors, but He also chooses to work through the medical profession. The centuries of accumulated medical knowledge given to our generation should be considered a priceless legacy and a gift from God. Anyone who refuses to use it hurts himself.

---

[6]   Matthew 18:10

WHY DO THE GOOD DIE YOUNG?

Our thirty-three-year-old son, who had studied for years hoping to become a Third World doctor, died of a brain tumor. He was a believer who took good care of his body, never drank or smoked. Why would God take such a fine young man who could have done so much good in the world?

SCRIPTURE SAYS, "Precious in the sight of the Lord is the death of his saints."[7] The comforting thought is that the young person in this question is with the Lord.

Another passage says, "The righteous perish and no man takes it to heart, not knowing that they're being spared from the evil to come."[8] In 2 Kings, we read that King Hezekiah of Judah was near death, and he prayed, "Oh, God! How could you be so terrible to me? How could you let this disease kill me? I've served you, and tried to do your will all my life. Please! Please extend my life."

God granted Hezekiah's request and gave him fifteen more years on earth. During that time, Hezekiah fathered Manasseh, who grew up to be the most wicked king in Israel's history![9] The evil spawned by Manasseh led to the ultimate downfall of the nation of Judah. Only God knows what the future holds. Keep in mind that sometimes when righteous people die, God may be shielding them or us from future disasters that only He knows about before they happen. Just think, if only Hezekiah had died on time, the history of his nation would have been dramatically different.

On the other hand, it's important to emphasize that God does not send cancers or brain tumors on His people. Granted, in the Old Testament, God was said to be in charge of everything, both good and evil. From a New Testament perspective, however, sicknesses and disease are often attributed to the activity of Satan. Other diseases seem to be the results of natural forces. In recent years, scientists have discovered that many cancers come because our man-made products, such as asbestos and pesticides, contain carcinogenic materials implicated in cancerous tumors.

Your son died young, but although it is correct to say that God allowed the cancer that killed him, it is not correct to say that "God took him." One day you will learn all the reasons, but not now.

---

7   Psalm 116:15
8   Isaiah 57:1
9   See 2 Kings 20:1–6, 21

WHY ISN'T EVERYONE HEALED?

I was wondering why some Christians get healed and others don't. Is it a matter of faith or sin?

WHEN JESUS CHRIST WALKED THE EARTH, there is no record of anyone who came to Him for physical healing who did not get healed. If Jesus Christ was the perfect expression of God on earth, then we must presume that spiritual healing is in the perfect will of God.

But Jesus differed from us in that He had absolute power and total discernment. He could tell if paralysis was caused by sin or if a crippling infirmity was caused by demon powers. He knew when there was enough faith for healing or when the individual needed a faith-building challenge. He sometimes healed with a word or a touch. In another instance He prayed, applied a mud poultice, then spoke a word of healing. He did not operate merely on what His physical senses told Him, but what His heavenly Father showed Him.

Some people don't get healed because of lack of faith. They really do not understand God's power or the principles of divine healing. Some people are not healed because of sin in their lives—the most common and deadly is the harboring of grudges, hatred, and the unwillingness to forgive. Some are not healed because their physical problem stems from an underlying psychological problem, what is called a psychosomatic (soul/body) disease. Some are not healed because they have been attacked by a spirit of infirmity which needs to be cast out.

Jesus Christ could deal with all the causes and treat them accordingly. Imagine the damage a well-meaning counselor could inflict on a suffering person by telling her that her psychosomatic asthma is caused by demons, or the automobile accident was the result of sin, or the sickness of a child is caused by a parent's lack of faith.

Right now, we see through a glass darkly. We learn more as we grow closer to Jesus Christ and become more mature in our understanding. In the meantime, I advise great humility in describing the causes of sickness and the reasons some Christians are not healed.

MY PRAYERS AREN'T ANSWERED . . . IS IT ME OR GOD?

When I pray for healing and don't see or feel any immediate results, should I pray again, pray a different way, or just pretend that everything is okay, that God heard my prayer and will answer someday in His time? I believe that heaven is a place of ultimate healing, but

when I pray in Jesus' name for someone to be healed and they are not, I feel that God is either lying to me or that I am doing something wrong in the way I pray.

THAT IS A TREMENDOUS QUESTION. I remember Kathryn Kuhlman said, "One day I am going to ask God, 'Why do some people get healed, and some don't?'"

Kathryn couldn't fully answer that question; nor could I without having the same wisdom, anointing, and discernment that Jesus had. To the best of my knowledge, He never turned down anybody for healing. Everyone who came to Him seeking help went away healed. He sometimes tested their faith, as He did with a Canaanite woman in Matthew 15:22 who said, "'Even the dogs feed on the crumbs which fall from their master's table.' Then Jesus answered and said to her, 'O woman, your faith is great; be it done for you as you wish.' And her daughter was healed at once."[10]

Jesus told his disciples to "keep on asking," "keep on seeking," "keep on knocking."[11] Those who did would receive, find, and have the door opened. He taught almost desperate perseverance in prayer. Much of our praying is halfhearted and desultory, not desperate.

We are to keep on banging on the gates of heaven until we have an assurance in our hearts of one of two things: either God says no, or God says yes. If He says no, then we must receive His will and get on with our lives. If He says yes, we should begin praising Him for the answer which we know is on the way.

God honors persistent prayer, and it is not wrong to bring the same issue to Him repeatedly until you know His will. Once you know what God wants, then pray accordingly. Sometimes in the process He will show us things that need to be fixed in our own lives before the answer comes.

We need to realize that we just can't shake a little tree and expect blessings to shower us. God is not a genie in a lantern that needs only to be rubbed three times and *poof!* We get what we want. We must be willing to surrender ourselves deeply in prayer to the things of God. He will withhold no good thing from them that walk uprightly.[12]

---

10 Matthew 15:27–28
11 See Matthew 7:7
12 See Psalm 84:11

212 BRING IT ON

MEDICALLY SUBSTANTIATED HEALINGS AND MIRACLES

Have you ever seen any genuine, "medically substantiated" healings and miracles?

We HAVE RECEIVED at CBN tens of thousands of reports of healings from all over the world! I recall one woman in Calgary, Alberta, who had been deaf for about fifteen years. As I prayed and spoke a word to that condition, God opened her ears instantly, and she could hear!

Another woman came to CBN headquarters when we were located in Portsmouth, Virginia. She had a large growth on her neck, so I prayed for her. The growth went down under my hand as I prayed!

One man had been addicted to nicotine for years. He had been smoking one or more packs of cigarettes every day of his life for more than twenty-five years. I prayed for him and commanded a spirit of nicotine to leave him. He coughed once, belching forth an awful, foul smell. In a moment of time, his desire for nicotine left him, and he was free!

I believe that our responsibility is not so much to pray and ask God to do things, but to pray and ask God what is going to happen. Then speak with the power of the Holy Spirit directly to the demon, or the disease, or sickness. With the authority given to us in Jesus' name, we can demand ears or eyes to open, we can speak to the leg that needs to be knit together, we can speak to the growth and demand that it dissolve.

At CBN, we regularly see the manifestation of the word of knowledge. The Holy Spirit reveals conditions of people in the audience, some of whom are suffering from severe illnesses. It thrills me to hear the testimonies of people who have been healed while sitting in the audience or watching at home on television when someone has spoken a message based on knowledge revealed by the Holy Spirit.

"I came here with a severe muscle injury . . ."

"I was suffering with arthritis of the spine . . ."

"I've been battling a kidney disease . . . and you spoke that word that described my condition exactly, and now I am healed!"

We have seen literally tens of thousands of people who can bear witness to God's healing power. I've seen too much to doubt the marvelous power of God! His power is available to all believers today because of what Jesus did on the cross. For almost all of the filmed testimonies we carry on *The 700 Club*, there are medical backups, x-rays, etc., which validate the authenticity of the reports.

The Bible says that Jesus bore our sicknesses and diseases upon Himself. Isaiah the prophet wrote, "Surely He has borne our grief and carried our sorrows; yet we esteemed Him stricken, smitten by God, and afflicted. But He was wounded for our transgressions, He was bruised for our iniquities; the chastisement for our peace was upon Him, and by His stripes, we are healed."[13]

Clearly, the suffering of Jesus was not limited to the time He spent on the cross. Prior to being nailed to the cross, He endure ghastly beatings with the dreaded Roman scourge, a thirty-nine fanged whip with pieces of metal or rock attached to the ends of each cord. As the whip lashed across His body, it literally ripped the flesh of Jesus, leaving bloody stripes across His back. Isaiah implies that something about the price He paid with these stripes not only purchased our forgiveness, but also our physical healing.

The Bible is replete with incidences of men, women, and children being healed by the power of God. Moreover, Christians are instructed to pray for each other when we are sick, and to believe God for healing. James, the brother of Jesus, wrote, "Is anyone among you sick? Let him call for the elders of the church, and let them pray over him, anointing him with oil in the name of the Lord. And the prayer of faith will save the sick, and the Lord will raise him up. And if he has committed sins, he will be forgiven."[14]

The price for your healing has been paid in full! You can come to God boldly, asking in the name of Jesus, and believing to be healed.

MY PERSONAL HEALINGS

Have you experienced healing personally, or have any of your family members ever been healed?

WHEN OUR OLDEST SON, TIM, was about four years old, a terrible fever came on him, and grew progressively worse. My wife is a nurse, yet nothing she or I could do seemed to help. Instead, the fever intensified. Suddenly, our son's eyes rolled back in their sockets, his body twitched from the fever, and he lost consciousness.

I dropped to my knees beside Tim and cried out to God to save my boy. I acknowledged to God my failings as a father. Now, as I was agonizing in prayer,

---

13   Isaiah 53:4–5 (NKJV)
14   James 5:14–15 (NKJV)

God showed me that if I, an imperfect father, could love my son, God our heavenly Father loved Tim thousands of times more than I did. It wasn't necessary to beg Him to do something that He already wanted to do.

I consciously surrendered Tim to God in prayer, lifting him up to the love of God with full assurance that God's love for my son was far greater than mine. No longer was I begging and pleading; I was surrendering to God's love for my son. As I did, the love and power of God surrounded Tim, and the fever broke. Tim got up, and the following morning he showed no trace whatsoever of the sickness. He was completely healed!

This was the first of many healings we experienced in our family. Beyond that, as I praised and worshiped God, He used this incident to take me deeper with Him than I'd ever been before, and I received the baptism of the Holy Spirit and began functioning at an entirely different level in my Christian experience.

HINDRANCES TO HEALING

What are some of the main obstacles that might prevent me from receiving God's healing in my life?

JESUS SAID, "If you stand praying, and you have ought against any, forgive, that your heavenly Father might forgive you."[15] The single greatest hindrance to receiving miracles of any kind in our lives is the lack of forgiveness toward those who have offended us.

When you trusted Jesus as your Savior and were born again, you received God's forgiveness. Now God expects you to live in an attitude of forgiveness and to extend forgiveness to others. In His model prayer, Jesus instructed us to pray, "Forgive us our trespasses as we forgive those who have trespassed against us."[16] According to this word, we set the standard for how we can expect God to forgive us. If we refuse to forgive others, we are limiting the forgiveness that God will extend to us! This is a startling truth that many people miss as they pray the model prayer.

Following a meeting in Jerusalem, a woman approached me and asked me to pray that she be healed of the bursitis in her shoulder. I gladly complied, prayed, but the woman was no better.

"Please, tell me a little about yourself," I said.

---

15   James 5:14–15 (NKJV)
16   See Matthew 6:9–13

The woman told me that her husband had just died.

I probed a bit into their relationship, and she told me that he had been an abusive, drunken man, and she harbored deep resentment toward him, even now that she was widowed.

I asked her to pray after me, "God, I thank you . . ."

"God, I thank you . . ." she repeated.

"For giving me a drunk for a husband," I said.

The woman gulped hard, and slowly said, "For giving me a drunk for a husband."

"Who abused me during our marriage . . ."

The woman tearfully repeated my words.

"Because that brought me closer to You."

She echoed my words.

I continued, with the woman repeating each phrase of my prayer, "And God, I forgive him, and I forgive You. And I praise You for everything that has happened in my life."

Following this prayer, I said, "Now, let me pray for you." I prayed, and instantly she was healed. The bursitis was completely gone! "Raise your hands," I directed her. Prior to our prayer, she had not been able to lift her hands higher than about forty-five degrees, but now she raised her hands high above her head and began praising the Lord.

The woman simply had to get that resentment out of her life before her miracle could come. I've seen many similar situations, in which someone is holding onto some area of bitterness or unforgiveness, and it stymies the Holy Spirit's further work in that person's life.

Other people suffer a shock or a severe grief from which they have difficulty recovering. They seem unconsciously to turn off their will to fight and in the process their immune systems no longer function. Malignant cells begin to multiply in their bodies and soon there are outbreaks of cancer. Certainly, a fatalistic attitude—one in which a person believes that God cannot or will not intercede in his or her life—or a secret death wish will hinder all attempts at healing.

Often we don't pray as we should. In Mark 11:22–24, Jesus explained the basis on which we can dare to ask and believe God for miracles. "Jesus answered and said to them, 'Have faith in God. For assuredly, I say to you, whoever says to this mountain, "Be removed and be cast into the sea," and does not doubt in his heart, but believes that those things he says will come to pass, he will have whatever he says.

Therefore I say to you, whatever things you ask when you pray, believe that you receive them, and you will have them."[17]

Jesus gave us a pattern that we should pray and acknowledge the heavenly Father's power and willingness to help. Then we are to speak to the obstacle, or the sickness, and command it. Jesus spoke directly to people in need of healing; to the little girl who had died, He spoke, *"Talitha Kum,"* or "Little girl, get up!"[18] Jesus spoke to Lazarus, who had been dead for four days. He said, "Lazarus, come forth!"[19] Jesus didn't pray, "Heavenly Father, would you please heal my brother Lazarus." No, He spoke directly to the situation.

Similarly, we are to speak to the mountain and make it move; we are to speak to the demon and cast it out. You don't ask cancer to leave a body, you must command it to go in the name of Jesus! In Jesus' name, we can command that the financial resources be released; we can speak to the sickness or disease and demand that it leave. God's power is transmitted from the mind of God, to the Spirit of God, to the Spirit of man, to the mind of man, to the voice of man, and then to the world around us. We will never see miracles until we realize the power that exists in the spoken human word energized by the Spirit of God. Jesus said that if you speak to the problem, believe that you have already received the answer, and don't doubt in your heart, you will have the thing that you say.

Remember, you can't doubt in your heart. In other words, your spirit must be in agreement with the Spirit of God or your words will be powerless. James wrote that we should "ask in faith without doubting, for the one who doubts is like the surf of the sea driven and tossed by the wind. For let not that man expect that he will receive anything from the Lord, being a double-minded man, unstable in all his ways."[20]

You must listen in prayer and hear what the Holy Spirit is telling you. When the Holy Spirit witnesses to your spirit that something is going to happen, you must agree with Him if you expect a miracle.

When you give assent to what the Spirit is telling you, agree that the miracle is going to take place, then you must speak it aloud by faith. "I command this tumor to dissolve, in the name of Jesus." "I command this knee to get better." Begin to speak to the condition in the name of Jesus, and it must obey you, assuming that you do not harbor bitterness, resentment, or unforgiveness toward another person.

---

17   Mark 11:22–24 (NKJV)
18   See Mark 5:41
19   John 11:43
20   James 1:6–8

CONTENTS

— CHAPTER 9 —

SPIRITUAL GIFTS AND SPIRITUAL COUNTERFEITS

THE OLD ADAGE "use it or lose it" is certainly applicable when we consider the gifts and talents God has given to each of us. The parable of the talents, a story told by Jesus, illustrates the truth that He expects us to use what He has given to us, that He anticipates a return on His investment, and that He *notices* whether or not we are good stewards of what we have been given.[1]

Moreover, we do not simply receive spiritual gifts and manifestations of the Holy Spirit for our own enjoyment, but for the benefit of the kingdom of God. In 1 Corinthians 12, Paul says, "But the manifestation of the Spirit is given to each one for the profit of all: for to one is given the word of wisdom through the Spirit, to another faith by the same Spirit, to another gifts of healings by the same Spirit, to another the working of miracles . . . But one and the same Spirit works all these things, distributing to each one individually as He wills."[2] What does this mean? Certainly, it means that God, by His Spirit, is doing something special in each of our lives. But it also means that when you experience the work of God in your life, don't assume that what He is doing is purely for your own consumption, blessing, or edification. On the contrary, as part of the body, the blessings you receive from God and the lessons He is teaching you are to be shared with others in the community of believers.

---

[1] See Matthew 25:14–30
[2] 1 Corinthians 2:7–11 (NKJV)

Obviously, not every one of us is gifted in the same areas. Some of us have gifts of healing, some have gifts of prophecy, and others the discerning of spirits. The same is true of our talents. Some of my friends are wonderful singers, while others need to be mixed in with a choir. Some of us are talented as teachers, preachers, evangelists, pastors, business leaders, or homemakers. We don't all have the same gifts and talents, but all of us can use what we have been given for God's glory.

Furthermore, ability or expertise is not prerequisites to service in Christ's kingdom. All it takes is a dedication to Him, and a realization that He can use your life to touch others. Look at the people God has used throughout history. Most of them were rather unspectacular on their own—but they believed in God. And they believed in themselves, in that they were willing to let the Lord use what little bit they had to offer.

Consider the little boy who figured so prominently in the feeding of the five thousand, the only miracle other than the resurrection of Christ that is included by all four gospel writers.[3] Everything Jesus used to perform that incredible miracle was really quite small in itself. It was a *little* boy who brought five *little* loaves of bread and two *little* fish to Jesus. Yet this little boy also had a little bit of faith, enough to present what he had to Jesus. The Lord took it, blessed it, broke it, and was able to supernaturally minister to the needs of thousands of people. All because a little boy gave what little he had to the Master.

Certainly our talents and spiritual gifts can be misused. The key to exercising spiritual gifts correctly and wisely is to use what God has given you to build up Christ's church, and to bring honor and glory to His great name.

SPIRITUAL GIFTS . . . FOR THE APOSTLES, OR FOR NOW?

Help! I'm so confused about spiritual gifts. My church teaches that these things were for the original disciples only, but many other Christians claim to have all sorts of gifts of the Spirit. Are these gifts for today, and if so, how do they function?

Yes, THE MANIFESTATIONS OF THE HOLY SPIRIT are for today. Granted, some Christians believe that miracles, healings, and the other manifestations of the Spirit ceased when the last apostle died. They base that teaching on a misunderstanding of 1 Corinthians 13:8, where Paul said, "Whether there are

---

3   See Matthew 14:13–21; Mark 6:30–44; Luke 9:10–17; and John 6:1–15

prophecies, they will fail, whether there are tongues, they will cease; whether there is knowledge, it will vanish away." Paul goes on to explain, "For we know in part, and we prophesy in part; but when the perfect comes, the partial will be done away."[4] Paul's point is that love—God's agape type of unconditional love—is the only thing that will last forever. Everything else, no matter how good or useful, pales in comparison.

The epitome of that love is the Person of Jesus Christ, not His church, not even the Holy Bible. Only Jesus is perfect, and Paul says when the perfect has come, the manifestations of the Holy Spirit will no longer be necessary. We will be with Jesus, in His presence, and He will abide with us eternally.

In the meantime, God has provided various manifestations of His Holy Spirit, the Spirit of Jesus, that believers have available to help them do the works of God on earth until Jesus returns in power and glory for His church.

In 1 Corinthians 12:4–11, Paul lists nine of these manifestations of the Holy Spirit. The Greek word he uses is *charismata*, from which we derive our word, "charismatic." This word is often translated as "gifts," but might be better rendered as "manifestations."

For discussion purposes, it's helpful to view these manifestations in three groups of three. The first group of manifestations has to do with *revelation*, which is the showing of truth. The *word of wisdom* is a revelation by God to an individual about events that will take place in the future. Next is the *word of knowledge*, which is a revelation of a present condition which is not observable or discernable by the senses. Third is the *discerning of spirits*, which is the Spirit-imparted ability to see the invisible world of human spirits, demonic spirits, or angels.

Group two is associated with gifts of *power*. For example, a person with a gift of *miracles* may actually be used of God to restore limbs, redirect or calm storms, and even raise the dead! Other believers may demonstrate the manifestation of *healing*, which is effective when dealing with disease and sickness. While all genuine Christians are saved by faith in Jesus Christ alone, some believers have an additional manifestation of the working of *faith*. Often this gift comes into play when there is a need for divine protection, but also when God's people have need to believe for some extraordinary accomplishment, far beyond our human ability or our resources can provide.

The third grouping includes manifestations of *utterance*, or those involving speech. This includes bringing messages in tongues in a public assembly, the ability

---

[4]   1 Corinthians 13:9–10

to *interpret* such messages, and the bringing forth of *prophecy*. The manifestation of tongues has often been misused, but when the real manifestation is experienced in a Christian assembly, it should be interpreted, preferably (but not always) by someone other than the person who spoke the message in an unknown tongue. The message should be presented to the body for consideration.

Prophecy is given to the church for exhortation, edification, and comfort. These prophecies are not necessarily predictive in the sense of foretelling the future. Rather, they are intended to strengthen the church family with the knowledge of the presence of God and His power in their lives. A word of prophecy can be coupled with the word of wisdom, so an utterance comes forth about a future event.

In the Bible, true prophets exhorted the nation or the church about the condition of their lives, and the commands of God to them. Prophets spoke forth the word of the Lord to the contemporary conditions, often speaking of the sins of the people and impending judgment if the people refused to repent and live rightly.

Christians today would do well to study carefully the role and function of the manifestations of the Holy Spirit, and the spiritual offices such as apostle, prophet, pastor, teacher, and evangelist that God has designed for people to fill in His church. These manifestations are real, and the church often languishes when we lack these manifestations in our midst.

ARE MY PROPHETIC DREAMS THE GIFT OF PROPHECY?

Ever since I was young, I've had prophetic dreams, dreams that have come to pass, sometimes within days. Do you think I could have the gift of prophecy?

PROPHECY IN THE BIBLE does not usually come in the mode of prophetic dreams. Certainly, God uses dreams to speak to individuals, and He often reveals future events through dreams. Consider Joseph. He had dreams that his brothers and his father would one day bow to him. When Joseph revealed his dreams, his brothers made fun of him. "Behold the dreamer," they mocked sarcastically. "Do you really think *we* will bow down to *you*?"

But Joseph's dreams eventually came to pass, and the brothers were no longer laughing. Then, while Joseph was in prison, he became the interpreter of other people's dreams. God used these dreams to bring Joseph to the attention of Pharaoh, the ruler of Egypt. When Pharaoh told Joseph the content of his dreams, Joseph replied, "God has told to Pharaoh what He is about to do."[5] Then Joseph explained to Pharaoh the meaning of his dreams and encouraged him to conserve food and resources during the prosperous times, and to save for the tough times that were coming. Pharaoh recognized the wisdom of Joseph's advice and promoted him to the second-highest position in all the land of Egypt, second only to Pharaoh himself.

Nebuchadnezzar also had a dream and sought interpretation from Daniel, another young Hebrew. God gave Daniel the correct interpretation of the dream and Daniel passed along the information to the king.

God, who knows everything, who knows the end from the beginning, can indeed reveal future events to His people through dreams (or any other way He chooses). Receiving information in dreams, however, is not the same as having the gift of prophecy, or as I prefer to refer to it, the *manifestation* of prophecy, which is intended for exhortation, edification, and comfort. God may speak to you and give you some sort of revelation through your dreams, some insight or understanding, and it may have prophetic overtones, but that is not necessarily a manifestation of prophecy.

Additionally, God speaks to us through His Word, through the still, small voice of His Holy Spirit speaking to our hearts and minds; He speaks through circumstances and events. At times, He also gives a "word of wisdom," through which God opens the future and lets you see into it. And, yes, God does sometimes speak to His people through dreams.

A few cautions: Dreaming is such a subjective experience, it allows great room for error in the interpretation. Most psychiatrists view dreams as a manifestation of the human unconscious mind rather than a revelation from God. If you are receiving spiritual revelations that are manifested through dreams, handle this information carefully. Enjoy what God is giving you and avoid getting caught up in some sort of psychic phenomena that might cause you to drift away from Him.

Beware, too, of charlatans and others who might encourage you to exploit the gift you have. Many dreams and interpretations of dreams are silly to ridiculous. For instance, a person might dream of a black hand floating around through space. In a matter of days or weeks somebody dies or a tragedy occurs. I question the source of these spooky intimations of disaster. However, if God shows you something in advance of its happening, hold this in your heart, as Mary, the mother of Jesus, treasured the information given to her. If it is meant to be shared with others, the Holy Spirit will guide you. Above all, be sure that your dreams, if predictive of future events, have God as their source, not Satan.

---

5 Genesis 41:5

PSYCHIC POWERS

I believe the words of knowledge you receive are psychic abilities in operation—yours and God's. When you're spiritual and intend to help others, then psychic results happen. I challenge you to disprove me.

I CAN'T DISPROVE IT, but it helps to understand three words in the New Testament Greek: *pneuma*, which means "spirit, wind, or breath;" *psuche*, which means "soul." This is the word from which we get the word *psychic*. And *soma*, which is "body." Human beings are tripartite creatures, comprised of body, soul, and spirit.

The Bible says that the *psuchikos* man, the soulish man, receives not the things of the Spirit of God, for they are foolishness unto him. Neither can he know them.[6] So if a person is operating on the soulish, psychic level, he is not dealing with the Spirit of God. The information received may be merely human, or it may come from a spirit, but it is not directed by the *Holy* Spirit. When you delve into psychic things, you inevitably discover that it is soulishness and demonic as opposed to God's Spirit.

In 1 Corinthians 12 and 14, the enablements of the Holy Spirit are described. These *charismata*, or manifestations of the Holy Spirit, come about through the operation of the Holy Spirit in a human being. For instance, when we receive a word of knowledge, it is the Holy Spirit speaking to our spirit the things God wants to reveal. That is not psychic. The psychic attempts to imitate many of the things the Spirit of God does through His people.

Certainly, most of us have powers in our minds that we may or may not exercise. Our minds send out both FM and AM radio waves. We can do amazing things in the psychic part of ourselves. The full potential of the human mind and soul has never been realized. But the Bible never tells us to stir up our psychic part or our soulish powers, because the psychic part of unredeemed humanity will ultimately lead to worship of the devil and rebellion against God. Scripture does instruct us to stir up our spirit. It says, "For the one who sows to his own flesh shall from the flesh reap corruption, but the one who sows to the Spirit shall from the Spirit reap eternal life."[7]

Sincere Christians who have been baptized in the Holy Spirit and those through whom the various manifestations of the Spirit are operating should not be afraid to express these manifestations for fear of entering the psychic realm. The

---

[6]   See 1 Corinthians 2:14
[7]   Galatians 6:8

angel of God told Joseph, "Do not be afraid to take Mary as your wife; for that which has been conceived in her is of the Holy Spirit."[8] We need not fear what is conceived of the Holy Spirit.

Yet we should stay far away from any psychic phenomena that is not under the control of the Holy Spirit, including psychics on television, tarot card readers, fortune tellers, and other occult practices the devil uses in an attempt to seduce us from God into falsehood.

FILLED WITH THE SPIRIT, BUT NOT SPEAKING IN TONGUES

How is it possible for a person to be unquestionably filled with the Holy Spirit, yet never speak in tongues? Should such a person seek to speak in tongues? Are they living below God's privilege if they don't speak in tongues?

I FULLY RECOGNIZE the wonderful contributions of Christian leaders who do not exercise this particular manifestation of the Spirit. Nevertheless, from what I can read in biblical accounts, when the Holy Spirit filled ordinary people with supernatural power, the usual consequence was that they began to express the joy in their hearts by speaking in tongues, in languages they had never learned.

On the day of Pentecost, the Holy Spirit came in power upon unlearned Galileans and they began glorifying God in languages they had never learned.[9] Described scientifically, the higher cortex of their brains which controlled their speech centers had been placed under the control of the Holy Spirit. The Bible tells us that if anyone can control his tongue, he is a perfect man. So we can see how dramatic Pentecost was.

To say that a person is living beneath his or her spiritual privileges if he or she does not speak in tongues would be condemnatory. But I do know that a world of spiritual wonder is available to the Christian through the baptism of the Holy Spirit and the manifestations of the Holy Spirit, not only speaking in tongues, but the interpretation of messages in tongues, prophecy, the working of miracles, the gifts of healing, discerning of spirits, and miracles. These manifestations lead us to participate in the New Testament ministry of Jesus in a way that those who remain outside of this realm rarely experience.

Certainly, it is possible to serve the Lord without speaking in tongues. Many people

---

8   Matthew 1:20
9   See Acts 2:1–8

whose primary focus is on evangelism have been mightily used by God and blessed beyond measure. Yet I'm also aware that in many cultures, the demonstration of the power of God in signs and wonders wins people to the Lord. In an evangelistic meeting in which I preached in India, three to four hundred thousand people responded to an invitation to receive Jesus as their Savior, and they did so in the context of miracles. In that wonderful meeting, not only were there manifestations of healing, but spirits of fear that had enslaved large numbers of the people were cast out by the power of the Holy Spirit.

When Christians confront people who are under Satan's control, it is crucial for us to be possessed by God's Spirit as fully as the unbelievers are possessed with demonic power.

WHY DO CHARISMATICS SEEM PREDISPOSED TOWARD IMMORALITY?

Why do so many Christians who seem predisposed toward more charismatic types of spiritual expressions (going under the power, speaking in tongues, receiving words from the Lord, etc.) also seem predisposed to immorality?

SOME PEOPLE BY NATURE are more inclined to combine sensuality and spiritual power. David, for example, was a man after God's own heart. He was filled with the Spirit. He brought forth the design of the temple by the Spirit. He sang songs and wrote psalms, obviously under the anointing of the Holy Spirit. He was a warrior of great renown who destroyed enemy armies. He took over the government of the nation and led God's people to greatness.

On the other hand, he had a number of wives, sired a number of children, and yet wanted more. He lusted after Bathsheba, a woman he saw bathing from his rooftop. He not only committed adultery with her, but he also had her husband Uriah killed. What was it about David—a man after God's own heart—that triggered such foolish passion and clumsy cover-up?

What is it in our society that allows powerful leaders to be flagrantly lustful, as though sexual immorality has become an expected—and accepted—perk that goes with prominence? Why does the animal sensuality of movie stars, rock musicians, famous athletes, flamboyant preachers, or politicians such as Bill Clinton make them particularly attractive rather than abhorrent to women? I believe it was Henry Kissinger who said that political power is the ultimate aphrodisiac. These people have more opportunity because women literally throw themselves at them. Nor should we discount the fact that Satan literally stalks effective men of God in an attempt to destroy them through sex, money, or pride.

I do know that the people who are moving into the gifts of the Holy Spirit and the demonstrations of the power of God are those who are inclined toward the love that comes from God. They express their love more openly, and they are not as reserved in their worship. So, would that make them more open to improper expressions of affection? Although it is a possibility, it certainly is not widespread as your question implies.

SPEAKING THINGS INTO EXISTENCE

Some Christians give the impression that God has given us creative power with our words. Can we really speak something into existence?

JESUS SAID, "Whoever says to this mountain, 'Be taken up and cast into the sea,' and does not doubt in his heart, but believes that what he says is going to happen, it shall be granted him. Therefore I say to you, all things for which you pray and ask, believe that you have received them, and they shall be granted you."[10] Proverbs says, "A man shall eat good by the fruit of his mouth."[11] Your confession is extremely important, and, indeed, your words do have creative power, if they are energized by the Holy Spirit.

Throughout Scripture, we can find incidences of God speaking things into existence. For instance, if we look at the origin of this universe, it was the spoken word of God that brought it to pass. We read again and again in Genesis, "God said, 'Let there be . . .'" and it happened according to His Word. Moreover, the apostle Paul reminds us that God "gives life to the dead and calls those things which do not exist as though they did."[12] He has given us the energized Word through the Holy Spirit, and with His power, amazing things can take place if we speak them into being.

Paul said, "If you confess with your mouth Jesus as Lord, and believe in your heart that God raised Him from the dead, you will be saved."[13] Apparently, something about confession, acknowledging verbally that Jesus is Lord, validates your spiritual experience. Power flows from the creative mind of God to the Spirit of

---

10   Mark 11:23–24
11   Proverbs 13:2
12   See Romans 4:17 (NKJV)
13   Romans 10:9–10

God, to the spirit of man, to the mind of man, and to the mouth of man. God's thoughts will be transmitted by the Holy Spirit to our spirits, and if we speak them forth, things will begin to take shape and change.

On the other hand, human beings simply blabbering away will not bring about anything good or creative. It is the Holy Spirit of God that must do the work. We become the instrument of His divine will, if we will yield ourselves to Him.

Jesus also said, "For by your words you will be justified, and by your words you will be condemned."[14] When we stand before God in judgment, we will give account for every idle word we utter. Our words are extremely important. Scripture warns that the tongue is like a rudder that steers the ship. "Look also at ships: although they are so large and are driven by fierce winds, they are turned by a very small rudder wherever the pilot desires. Even so the tongue is a little member and boasts great things."[15]

Similarly, it is a flame of fire, and no man can contain it.[16] When a person is filled with the Holy Spirit, and his or her entire life—including the tongue—comes under the control of the Spirit of God, his or her speech will be affected. When a person speaks in tongues under the direction of the Holy Spirit, even though it may be in an unlearned language, it is nonetheless the spoken word.

In my experience, the way I've seen healings take place has been to speak the word, to see creative miracles, to command storms to cease. That is what Jesus did. He spoke to the waves. He said, "Peace, be still."[17] And that is the way you deal with demons, too. You speak to the demon, commanding it to obey. When you exercise the authority of Jesus' name, and command evil spirits to be gone, they must obey. Taking authority over demons is a scripturally sound activity. It is not some hocus-pocus, mind over matter or some weird magic.

Similarly, agreeing with God's Word, and speaking to our circumstances is not a "name it and claim it" game of "let's see what we can get from God." We are not talking about magic, formulas, tricks, or games; we are talking about the power of God having real results in our everyday lives according to clearly annunciated biblical teachings.

14　Matthew 12:37 (NKJV)
15　James 3:4–5 (NKJV)
16　See James 3:6–8
17　Mark 4:39

PROPHETS AND THEIR FUNCTION

What position do prophets have in the church today?

THE BIBLE SAYS that God set in the church "apostles, some prophets, some evangelists, and some pastors and teachers, for the equipping of the saints for the work of ministry, for the edifying of the body of Christ. . . "[18] The job of the apostle is to lay the foundation of the church in areas where the gospel has not gone or in areas of endeavor where there has been nothing before. Apostles are foundation layers. John Wesley, for example, the founder of the Methodist church, was an apostle. Others have had an apostolic calling from God to be the founders of a new work—not necessarily an individual church, but a denomination or some other ministry.

The office of "prophet" is to bring forth the Word of God to people. A prophetic ministry doesn't necessarily mean telling the future. That is where we get the terms confused. Most prophets are to be *forthtellers*, more than foretellers. Prophets speak forth the Word of God about a situation that exists today. And they should speak about gospel doctrinal messages that come from God.

We sometimes confuse the "word of wisdom" with "prophecy." The word of wisdom can speak of future events as well as having prophetic overtones to it. But prophecy is for edification, exhortation, and comfort.

The Old Testament prophets were called seers; they could see into another world. They heard the Word of the Lord, and they spoke it forth to the people. That is what a prophet should do. There are people who occupy that office today. God reveals things to them, which they speak forth. This ministry is not something that is taught from a book, but something they have received from God for a particular situation. Apostles, prophets, pastors, teachers, and evangelists are the gifts of God to His church. We need these ministers to be active throughout the church today.

PROPHETIC PREDICTIONS THAT DON'T COME TRUE

I read in the Bible that when a prophet's prophecies didn't come true, he was executed. Understanding that we live under New Testament grace teachings, shouldn't someone who says, "Thus saith the Lord," bear responsibility when his or her predictions don't come true?

---

[18]   Ephesians 4:11–12

ARE YOU SUGGESTING that we should execute them, perhaps?

Seriously, the surest test of a prophet is whether or not what they have said comes to pass. The Bible says that you are not to fear a prophet whose word does not come to pass.

When attempting to evaluate the ministry of a prophet, ask some basic questions: What is their track record? Over the years, have they said things that have had validity, or are they speaking out of their own ideas? This is not to say that a young prophet cannot speak authoritatively under the guidance of the Holy Spirit, or that an "experienced" prophet cannot make a mistake. But with spiritual maturity and reliance upon the Holy Spirit, a prophet should not misrepresent God's message to His people.

Should there be some discipline against people who claim to have a word from the Lord, but don't? Yes, but unfortunately we don't have an ecclesiastical structure that is capable of bringing such discipline. An individual church could do it, a pastor, a church board, or the entire congregation. But it would take a great deal of courage to stand up in the pulpit and say, "Sister Smith has spoken three messages prophetically, and none of those messages has come to pass. Therefore we proclaim that she has no standing as a prophetess." Nevertheless, a good pastor should be willing to offer gentle reproofs when inappropriate messages are expressed in a public assembly. So-called prophetic messages must be judged by those in authority, not allowed to stand if they are invalid.

Jeremiah was faced with a false prophet who was speaking lies to the people of Judah. Within a few months after the false prophet's words failed to come to pass, the false prophet died. No judicial proceeding took place; God simply took care of the matter Himself.

Now that the Holy Spirit has been poured out, God has invested His people with the spiritual wherewithal and the spiritual authority to deal with false prophecies. The Bible says that "the spirits of the prophets are subject to the prophets."[19] Scripture also says that in a church meeting, "let two or three prophets speak, and let the others judge."[20] In other words, the other prophets in attendance should judge whether something that is said in a public gathering is truly of the Lord or not.

I was presiding over a meeting, when one or two people brought forth prophetic messages that did not comport with the Scriptures. I did not feel that the words

---

19   1 Corinthians 14:32 (NKJV)
20   1 Corinthians 14:29 (NKJV)

were appropriate, so I brought a gentle word of rebuke and correction to the word that had been given.

Later, other leaders in the assembly confirmed to me that they, too, had considered the "prophetic messages" to be off-target. This is a New Testament corrective pattern—prophets judging prophets—and if we use it sensitively when prophetic messages are inappropriate, they can be easily corrected with minimal disturbance to the congregation.

PROPHETS OR CHARLATANS?

Many ministers say things on television, radio, or in conferences that stretch credibility. Recently, a major evangelist said that Jesus would physically manifest himself on stage with him during an upcoming crusade. How can that be possible? Is such prophecy credible? How can I discern God's messengers from false prophets?

SOME OF THESE SPIRITUAL CHARLATANS say things that are simply nonsense. They've been doing it for years—since biblical times, really—and they will continue doing it until Jesus comes.

God does speak to people today, just as He always has. All over the world, He is revealing things to His people. But not everyone who claims to be speaking the truth from God is on the level.

As I said above, the best way to discern whether one who claims to speak for the Lord is real or not is to look at his or her track record. If a person glorifies Jesus Christ and is true to the Bible, and if the so-called prophetic words come to pass, that person should be heeded in the future.

Today, we simply disregard foolish or false words purportedly from God. I recall a fellow in New York some years ago who said, "God spoke to me, and told me that my next child is going to be a son." He and his wife had one child already, and that child was somewhat ill.

His wife gave birth not long after that—to a beautiful little girl.

"Well, God said that it wasn't the *next* child; it was the child after the next who will be a son," he said.

He and his wife had another baby—another daughter.

On another occasion, this man said that God was leading him to go to a particular street address in New York where he'd see his prayers answered. He went. And when we got to the address "that God had given him," the house had been demolished, and there was nothing there but a big hole in the ground. It was obvious that God was not the one speaking to this man!

Foolish "prophetic" claims can be discarded without too much peril. False prophets, however, should be taken much more seriously. False prophets exalt themselves rather than Jesus. Many exalt themselves *above* Jesus. Scripture says that we will see an increase in the activity of false prophets as the time for the Lord's return draws nearer.[21]

Some false prophets operate under the direct influence of Satan. More often, an inflated ego is at the root of the problem. For a preacher to say, "Jesus is going to physically appear on the platform with me" sounds like confusion and exalted ego. Jesus can appear whenever or wherever He chooses, but to appear on stage, visibly, with a modern preacher? . . . I would have to see it to believe it. When you see that inflated ego exalting the minister rather than the Lord, you can usually disregard that message.

This is another reason why it is so important that Christians know the Word of God, rather than being influenced by every new doctrine that comes down the pike. Yes, the ministry of prophets can be valid, and we dare not discount them. The apostle Paul warned, "Do not despise prophetic utterances. But examine everything carefully; hold fast to that which is good."[22] No doubt, many charlatans were at work even back then, causing confusion for many people. Some believers probably concluded that prophecy itself was suspect, and Paul had to remind them that the genuine manifestation of the Spirit was a good thing and should not be thrown out with the imposters.

We have a similar situation today with many mobile, itinerant preachers claiming to have a special word from God, when, in fact, they may have no such thing. Despise not prophecy, but be wise as well.

When somebody says to you, "God spoke to me," you can say, "Okay, let's talk about it. What did He say?"

A fellow came to me once and said, "God told me that He's coming back on Sunday, and I need to go on television to tell everyone about it."

"Well, brother, as I read the Bible, it indicates that nobody knows the day nor the hour when the Lord is going to return, not even Jesus Himself," I replied. "I really don't think God gave you a special insight into Christ's return."

"God's going to smite you if you don't give me access to television," he threatened.

---

21   See Matthew 24:24
22   1 Thessalonians 5:20–22

"I'm sorry," I answered. "I guess I'll just have to take that chance."

Sunday came, and Jesus didn't. The erstwhile "prophet" wound up in the mental ward of the local hospital.

Don't despise prophecy, but weigh it against God's Word, and hold fast to what is good.

DIRECTIVE PROPHECY . . . BOON OR BANE?

A prophet came to our church recently and "spoke into" various people's lives words of rebuke and encouragement. Much of it was vague and general, but some of the prophet's words were very specific. Is it possible to "speak into" someone's life, and if so, what place should we give such instructions as compared to the Bible?

THE BIBLE SAYS, "Despise not prophesying."[23] Why would the early church have despised prophecy if everything about it was good? Early Christian leaders were extremely cautious about prophecy because there were charlatans who were serving themselves, not the Lord.

In modern times, there are those I term "gospel bums," who travel from place to place, living off the saints, claiming to have prophetic words for them. Frankly, I'm leery of directive prophecy by one person to another. God does not give people authority over others in that fashion. The word of prophecy is much broader than that, dealing with a manifestation to a congregation or to a people or to a nation. Prophets do not normally tell a person to "sell your possessions and to go to Canada and live in the woods," or, "God told me that you should divorce your wife," or, "God is telling you to take a boat trip to Fiji." I have no use whatsoever for that kind of "prophesying."

But I was in India having a meal with a man who has proven himself to be a great leader in the church, a person who is highly respected by others and by me, when he told me, "Jesus appeared to me and He has a message for you."

"What is the message?" I asked somewhat skeptically.

My friend said, "He has given your son Gordon a message for America, and he must go to America and deliver it. It is his anointing now, but if he delays, and is disobedient, that anointing will lift, and that message will be gone."

I thanked the man, pondered the matter in my heart, but took no action to get

---

[23]   1 Thessalonians 5:20–22

Gordon back to the States from where he was ministering in the Philippines and throughout Asia.

A month or two later, I was in a prayer meeting at our headquarters when a lady who has a prophetic ministry in the United States was praying. She said, "God says your son is going to return home to America."

To me, that was a confirmation of something that I had personally felt was going to happen in a number of months, but I did not want to accelerate it. This was a confirmation by two people who were clearly respected Christian leaders, who did not know each other or have knowledge of what the other had said. Because it came in such a supernatural fashion and it was something that God had already expressed in other ways to me, I received it as a prophetic statement and acted on it with remarkably positive results.

When prophetic words are spoken, it is necessary to judge whether that word was really from God. Take it as Mary did, and ponder it in your heart whether these things are true.[24] Listen and hear the prophecies, and then let God work it out. He will give you confirmation if you ask. Let every word be confirmed in the mouth of two or more witnesses.[25]

---

[24] Luke 1:29, 2:51
[25] See Matthew 18:16

CONTENTS

— CHAPTER 10 —

CURSES AND BLESSINGS, DEMONS AND ANGELS

A SURVEY RECENTLY RELEASED in the United States indicated that a majority of the American people do not believe in the existence of the devil, and a substantial minority of so-called born-again Christians agree.

Believe me, the devil is real. Jesus Christ said he was, the apostle Paul said he was, the apostle Peter said he was, and if you visit Asia you may have occasion to meet him or one of his representatives face to face.

Satan and his demonic cohorts present a formidable foe, but Jesus defeated Satan when He died on the cross, was buried, and then rose victoriously three days later. Yes, there will be battles that remain to be fought; but remember, the war is already won! If you trust in Jesus, you needn't fear the enemy. Never forget that "He who is in you is greater than he who is in the world."[1]

The big question is, where did these evil, supernatural beings come from? God created various orders of angels to serve Him in heaven and to serve as messengers on earth. There were cherubim, archangels, and seraphim. Apparently, prior to the creation of man, a rebellion took place in heaven. A mighty angelic creature, one of the cherubim, whose name was Lucifer (the name means "the light one"), became intoxicated with his own beauty and wisdom and decided that he could run the universe better than Almighty God. Lucifer then led one-third of the angels in this

---

1 1 John 4:4 (NKJV)

rebellion. We don't know how long the Lord tolerated Lucifer's rebellion, but we do know that one day Lucifer and his angels were cast out of heaven, down to earth, where he came to be known as Satan, the "adversary," and the former angels are known as "demons." He is also referred to as Diabalos, the devil or deceiver; Apollyon, the destroyer; Abaddon; and the Great Dragon.

The details of how Lucifer was transformed from a shining, high-ranking angel into the liar, thief, and murderer he has become are not told in the Bible. Any stories you might read, sermons you may hear, or movies you may view which purport to describe this event are based on sheer conjecture or someone's vivid imagination, and should be regarded as such. Obviously, God did not intend for us to dwell upon the devil's demise, or He would have provided more information.

Nowhere in Scripture is there even the slightest hint that Satan and his demons will ever be saved, reformed, and allowed to reenter the kingdom of God. On the contrary, the Bible is replete with references to Satan's eventual destruction, as well as that of anyone who follows him.

SHOULD I PLAY VIDEO GAMES WITH OCCULT AND DEMONIC SYMBOLS?

I received a video game for my birthday that has demons and occult symbols in it, and I was wondering if I should be playing it. It's just a video game.

THE SHORT ANSWER is *no!* Many modern video games are based on demonic activity, real or imagined. Similarly, the baleful effects of the game Dungeons and Dragons are well known in terms of teen role-playing. For some people, games such as these are the doorways through which they enter deeper, more devious, demonic prison chambers. Christians should not be playing these games. It's like giving an invitation to the enemy of your soul to find a way to destroy you. If you open wide the door, believe me, he will try to enter.

Demonic forces are real; they are not to be trifled with; they are not frivolous, childhood games. These video games can lead to demonic oppression, then demonic possession, and in some instances result in suicide or the type of tragic killings that took place at Columbine High School, shocking America. For many, these video games are the gateway to the occult, and that is reason enough to stay away from them.

ARE DRUGS AND LYING CAUSED BY DEMON POSSESSION?

If someone is struggling with drug abuse and pathological lying, is there an actual demonic spirit that gives these urges, or could the addict be demon possessed?

DRUG ADDICTS AND ALCOHOLICS will lie with the most convincing faces! They will profess that they are going clean, that they'll never touch the stuff again; many will even claim to have had an experience with God. Then a short time later, they are right back where they were—or worse. Until they have a genuine encounter with God in which He sets them free, they'll most likely continue their destructive habits. Lying is often pathological when it is spurred by alcohol or drugs. The addicted person will lie, cheat, steal, and take advantage of his or her own family members or best friends to satisfy his or her cravings. Nothing is sacred, and no one is considered untouchable when an addict is scavenging for something to sell or trade for drugs or alcohol. An addict lives for that next fix, so the preeminent thing in his or her mind is how to obtain it. Nearly everything an addict says or does is dominated by that desire.

Is that demonic? It can be. Certainly, it is obsessive behavior. The desire for drugs or alcohol obsesses the addicted person's mind until nothing else matters.

Not all drug addicts or alcoholics are demon possessed, but I do know that there are demonic spirits behind most addictions, including nicotine, alcohol, and narcotics. They need to be delivered. Christians can pray and in Jesus' name cast out the spirit behind the addiction, but the addicted person will still need a tremendous amount of help to rebuild positive patterns in his or her life.

Any continued, willful, sinful behavior creates an environment where lying can become not only pathological, but demon controlled. Consider the man or woman trying to cover up a sexual affair. One lie breeds another, until the person can hardly tell the truth, even when he or she wants to do so. It's a downward spiral, because sin blinds the person to the reality of God and His Word. The Bible talks about people who wouldn't come to the light because their deeds were evil.[2] They want to cover up, rather than confess and come clean. But that cycle can be broken when the sinner truly reaches out to Jesus. In the meantime, Christians should saturate that situation with prayer.

---

2   John 3:20

BREAKING GENERATIONAL CURSES

I'm confused about the term "generational curse." Isn't it true that when we come to Christ, He forgives all our sins? Why then do I have to ask forgiveness for the sins of past generations, or be responsible for them?

GOD DOESN'T HOLD PEOPLE ACCOUNTABLE for the sins of their ancestors. The Bible makes it clear that if a person sins, he or she will die because of his or her own sins, not those of somebody else. That is true even if the person's parents and grandparents and generations before them were all godly Christian people. Likewise, our ancestors cannot keep us from God if we truly seek Him. Even if a person has scoundrels in his lineage, if he trusts in Jesus, God will receive him. That is the standard.

Yet it does appear that what seems like a curse has been attached to certain families, and it transmits from one generation to the next. As such, the spiritual action that is necessary may require asking forgiveness for something your ancestors did, then seeking deliverance, and demanding that the curse that may have descended through your family be broken in Jesus' name.

Scripture says that the sins of the fathers are visited on the heads of their children for generations to come.[3] Perhaps you had a great-aunt who was dabbling in the occult; perhaps someone else in your family tree was a witch or fortune-teller; perhaps they were slave traders or murderers. The impact of these relatives may have come down through the family for years. That bondage can and must be broken in your life or it can serve to do you harm. The term "generational curse" refers to the lingering effect of the sins of previous generations that seems to bring on unexplained tragedies to the present members of a family.

On the other hand, we can pass on good, godly influences, as well. For example, in a practical matter, if I am diligent and I accumulate several hundred thousand dollars in savings, when I die it will pass on to my children. They in turn will be able to take it and do even more with it. Down the line, my prudence, wisdom, and godliness will be transmitted to my children and grandchildren. At the present time, every one of my children and grandchildren knows the Lord. They have an inheritance of eternal salvation. To me, that is the greatest legacy that my wife, Dede, and I can bequeath to our family when we leave this world.

---

3   See Exodus 34:7

Had I lived my life as a criminal and wound up in jail for the various crimes I might have committed in that role, and had I brought my children up without God's Word, without moral values, and without a biblically based lifestyle, it is much more likely that my legacy would be one of lawless, impoverished children and grandchildren.

We see this frequently with children of divorce. They are much more likely to get divorced than people from intact nuclear families. The same is true of child-abuse situations; abusive fathers often produce sons who grow up to be physically abusive as well.

The good news is that our godly legacy goes on for thousands of generations; whereas the sins of the fathers are visited on the second or third generations. That's due to God's grace. As I look back in my lineage for hundreds of years, I see men and women of God, praying people, ministers of the gospel. Did that legacy have an influence in my life? Absolutely!

Of course, we can start a new lineage by trusting in Christ. Scripture says that all the old things are passed away and new things have come.[4] You can break free from the effects of sin.

If there is a curse in your lineage, gather your family together and bind the curse and cast it away. Take authority over this enemy. Whatever sins may have existed in your parents' or grandparents' past, confess them, take authority over them, especially anything of occult practices or leanings, and command Satan to release your family from their effects. Remind him that he has no dominion over God's property, that he has no authority over your household, over your children or grandchildren. You have done nothing to deserve a curse. The Bible says, "A curse without a cause shall not remain."[5]

PALM READING

I'm terrified of the occult and want to stay away from it at all costs. I had my palm read a few years ago, and now I'm concerned that I may have been dabbling in something I shouldn't have been. Is there any truth to this, and does God place lines on our hands that can influence our destinies?

---

[4]   See 2 Corinthians 5:17
[5]   See Proverbs 26:2

Palm reading, discerning your character and your future by the lines on your hands, has, in my opinion, no validity. The real danger, of course, is the magnetic draw of the occult. Palm readers, fortune-tellers, and other so-called psychics may indeed be used of the devil to draw people into a dependence on them for information about the future, rather than trusting God one day at a time. This is dangerous and wrong. The Bible never says that there is no reality in the occult. It commands God's people to avoid those who practice it.[6]

Every human being wants to know the future. A few years ago, CBN commissioned pollster George Gallup to do a study of questions Americans would ask God if they could ask just one question. One of the top ten questions was, "What does the future hold for me and my family?" We'd all like to peer into the darkness to see what lies ahead. This is a normal human desire.

God's Word gives us what we need to know concerning the past, present, and the future. Scripture says, "We have a more sure word of prophecy,"[7] that we can live successfully, trusting in Him. God not only knows the future, and holds the future, He is our future! If we trust in Him, we needn't fear what is to come.

Nevertheless, don't allow the devil or your own guilt feelings to haunt you about something in your past for which you have already repented. You needn't be overly concerned about the fact that you formerly read the horoscopes looking for signs, or visited Madam Swami or whatever her name was. Simply ask God to forgive you for not trusting Him for guidance, rebuke any strongholds the enemy may have tried to establish in your heart through the visit to the palm reader, and from now on, trust the Lord for the direction you need in your life. He has promised that if you will trust Him, He will guide your steps in the right path.[8]

I was in Pakistan several years ago, and as my traveling companions and I prepared to leave the airport, one of the local businessmen with whom we were dealing asked my aide if he knew his astrological sign. The Pakistani said, "I'm a Sagittarius; what are you?"

With a twinkle in his eye, my aide quipped, "I'm a Mexican!" His answer indicated that he was totally unconcerned about the signs of the zodiac, or the alignment of the stars on the day he was born. He is a born-again believer in Jesus Christ, and that is all that matters to him.

Children and those who don't know Jesus sometimes unwittingly dabble in the

---

6   Deuteronomy 18:10–15
7   2 Peter 1:19
8   Proverbs 3:5–6

occult by reading horoscopes, by going to a fortune-teller, or by having their palms read. God understands the desire to know the future, and it is unlikely that these chance encounters with the occult inflict permanent, irrevocable damage. Nevertheless, He also warns us to stay away from such purveyors of darkness who pretend to cast light on the future.

Magazines that offer psychic predictions for the future, horoscope columns, prophecies of Nostradamus, or the writings of Jeanne Dixon or Edgar Cayce hold an amazing magnetic appeal to most people. Often such activities begin superficially, but the magnetic power, energized by Satanic forces, grows in intensity and draws the innocent seeker deeper and deeper into the occult, to the point of offering prayers and worship to Satan. Such activities are extremely dangerous and should be avoided at all costs!

The best policy is to stay away from spiritism, psychics, fortune-tellers, tarot card readers, Ouija boards, or anything else that hints of the occult. Even those seemingly innocuous things such as games, horoscopes, and carnival palmists should be avoided. Instead of turning "to spirits that peep and mutter,"[9] we can ask God concerning our present and our future, and He has promised to direct us in the way we should go.

SEEING ANGELS

Have you physically seen heavenly angels? If so, how can I begin to see them?

I PERSONALLY DO NOT SEE ANGELS. I have dealt with demons and cast them out, but I've done so through the word of knowledge that the Lord revealed to me. But I haven't seen them and I'm glad I don't.

One of the manifestations of the Holy Spirit described in 1 Corinthians 12 is that of discerning of spirits. Notice, this is not simply discerning devils or angels; it is seeing into the invisible world, including the ability to discern human spirits. It is generally recognized that we are surrounded by an invisible world in which spirits operate. For instance, in the Old Testament, Elisha and his servant were facing the Syrian army, complete with chariots and soldiers in battle array. But Elisha instructed his servant not to fear, because the number with them was far greater than the number opposing them. Elisha prayed that the Lord would "open the servant's eyes."

---

[9]   Isaiah 8:19 (KJV)

God answered that prayer, allowing the servant to see that the entire mountain was filled with horses and chariots of fire![10] This was an angelic host ready to intervene on Elisha's behalf. The heavenly force had been there all the time, but only when the Lord opened the servant's eyes was he able to see it.

So it is today. Angelic and demonic activity swirl all around us, and for the most part, we are oblivious to it. Only as God opens someone's eyes, giving him or her an ability to discern spirits, can these entities be seen.

It is not necessarily wrong to pray for this manifestation of the Spirit. If the Spirit of God grants you this manifestation, you must always use it to glorify Christ. Use caution, however, since this gift comes with tremendous responsibility. Some years ago, I was told of a woman in Pennsylvania who received the manifestation of the discerning of spirits. She could see the hideous spirits at work behind the masks most people wear, and it overwhelmed her. After a few days, the revelations became so horrible she asked the Lord to remove her ability to see them.

As a general rule, it is unwise to focus your attention on angels. Angels are ministering servants, doing the Lord's bidding. That's all. We are to keep our hearts and minds centered on Jesus. While every believer has at least one guardian angel, we are to worship God alone. Beyond that, the Christian life is one of faith, not sight, so seeking to see angels may actually indicate a lack of faith rather than spiritual maturity.

TALKING TO THE DEAD

A man on TV talks to the dead, and my wife and I are intrigued. We can't believe that he knows so much about the person he is asked to contact. Is this wrong?

CERTAINLY WE CAN BE INTRIGUED by psychic activity. Psychic activity possesses a strong pull toward the occult realm for ordinary people. This pull is motivated by Satan and his cohorts. It is fascinating, but it is also extremely dangerous, so don't let your curiosity get the best of you.

I'm aware of the television personality of whom you speak, and he is indeed a brilliant reader of human clues. Most of these clues are revealed unwittingly by the subject, and the "reader" is highly skilled in piecing the details together to provide a composite picture. The naive seeker who is so desperate to contact his loved one is easily duped into believing that the man on television is actually in touch with the

---

[10]   See 2 Kings 6:16–17

dead. Listen carefully to the patter and you will see how he sets up clues calculated to dupe the unsuspecting into revealing facts which are then later given back as if from the departed loved one.

Similarly, conductors of séances and their modern counterparts, the psychics on television, are extremely skilled manipulators. Much of their "ability" is mere showmanship, complete with echo chambers, wires, electronic effects, and a behind-the-scene operator. That which is not fake, however, is motivated by Satan, incorporating demonic assistance. These people are possessed by "familiar spirits" and have knowledge about the dead person and are able to communicate it. But it is not the dead person speaking; it is a demonic spirit.

In the Bible, the one confirmed instance of someone seeking information from the dead and receiving it took place when King Saul went to a female medium in Endor, and asked to speak to Samuel.[11] The woman called up Samuel, and when he appeared, the witch was shocked and feared for her life! No doubt, she was as surprised as Saul that anyone actually responded to her incantations.

Samuel spoke to Saul and reaffirmed God's judgment on him. This is the only time in Scripture that such information was imparted through a medium. Moreover, the message was not one that Saul wanted to hear and may actually have indicated that he'd reached the final rung in a series of steps downward in his life. The next day, as Samuel predicted, Saul died an ignominious death.

I believe the person on television is a skilled showman and a fraud, but whether or not he is a fake, I don't believe that the dead talk to us. People may talk to *someone* during these psychic sessions, but it is a "familiar spirit," controlled by demons. Stay away from spirits that, according to the Bible, "peep and mutter."[12] Speaking to the dead, and attempting to hear from them is forbidden in the Bible.[13] We should never attempt to contact people "on the other side."

The Scripture teaches, "Shall not a people turn to the living God?"[14] that they should seek advice from the mouth of God Himself. If we as God's people will seek Him, He will tell us all we need to know!

WHO IS THE DEVIL, AND WHERE DID HE COME FROM?

Where did the devil come from, and how much power does he really have? Can he be everywhere, for instance, or does he operate as a

---

11   See Samuel 28:1–19
12   Isaiah 8:19 (KJV)
13   Deuteronomy 18:11
14   See Acts 14:15

general, commanding troops of demons to attack human beings, yet not personally entering the battle? Is the devil a person or merely a catch-all term for evil in our world?

We DON'T KNOW EVERYTHING about the devil, but we do know a certain amount that has been revealed to us in the Old Testament and the New. He has a number of names. He was called Lucifer, which means "the shining one" or "the light one."[15] As for where he came from, Lucifer was a created being. He was the highest of the angelic order. He was beautiful in all his ways. He was called "the anointed cherub that covers,"[16] which was to say that he stood by the throne of God and covered the very holiness of God. He had the highest position that one could have in the angelic realm. He is also known as Satan, which means "the adversary." Diablo has to do with the accuser or liar. He is also called Apollyon, "the destroyer," and Beelzebub, which means "the restless lord." Some have described him as "the lord of the flies."

In Job, we have him walking up and down on the earth,[17] so I don't believe he is everywhere at the same time. But I do believe he has millions of beings who do his bidding, and there are undoubtedly hundreds of millions of so-called fallen angels that we know as demons. I do believe that he has what C. S. Lewis calls a "lowarchy," contrasted to our hierarchy, of relative power. They are demon princes. They are principalities and powers,"[18] said the apostle Paul.

When Lucifer left heaven, he took about one-third of the angels with him. These angels are present on earth in the form of demons. Some are more powerful than others; some rule over countries, some rule over cities, some rule over individual provinces, some rule over households. Some have various functions to accomplish under Satan's bidding.

Satan is not like God; he is not omnipresent. His power is limited, and he has to be in various places in different times. Nevertheless, he is real. He is a malevolent being. His days are numbered. He hates God and yet when it is over, he will be bound and placed in a lake of fire from whence he will not be able to escape.

---

15 Isaiah 14:12
16 Ezekiel 28:14
17 Job 1:7
18 Ephesians 6:12 (KJV)

WHAT ARE DEMONS?

What are demons, how do they "attach" to our lives, and what can be done about them?

DEMONS ARE FALLEN ANGELS. They are part of Satan's rebellion against God in heaven. According to the Bible, one-third of the angels followed Satan in this revolt against God and were cast to earth. Earth has become a spiritual battlefield between the forces of God—the good angels, if you will—and the forces of Satan, the demons.

These creatures have power depending on what privileges we human beings grant to them. I do not believe that a Spirit-filled Christian can be inhabited or possessed by a demon. But demons are liars; like Satan himself, they attempt to deceive. If we allow them, they attempt to play tricks with our mind. They can induce depression or even thoughts of suicide. They can torment us; they can introduce lustful thoughts to our minds and instigate lustful behavior. They can attack our bodies and bring on disease, and they can attack our minds and cause us to think irrationally. Demons can oppress and harass in many ways, and people who tolerate, welcome, or entertain them can easily become overwhelmed by them.

When demonic entities possess a person, they often cause that individual to do strange things. In the Bible, a demon-possessed man at Gadara, stripped off his clothes, lived among the tombs, ran naked throughout the hills, and cut himself with stones. That's how he lived! Day in and day out, he screamed with anguish, and when people attempted to subdue him with chains, he had such physical power that he snapped the chains as though they were pieces of string.

Jesus came to him and simply commanded the demons to leave. The demons were subject to the Word of God spoken by Jesus. They recognized who He was and that He had power over them. Their only request was, "Don't send us to the pit before the time." Jesus let them enter a nearby herd of swine, and when they did, the pigs went crazy, ran off a cliff, and killed themselves.[19] Like their leader, the ultimate goal of any demon is to rob, kill, or destroy. Demons are not to be trifled with or underestimated. They must be cast out in the name of Jesus.

The Christian should not allow any demonic influence in his or her life. As Martin Luther said, "It is one thing for birds to fly over your head, but it is something else to let them nest in your hair." We are aware that we will be tempted and seduced. The question is: Will we allow these creatures to come and take part in our

---

[19]   Mark 5:1–20

lives, and do we entertain them? I heard of one instance where a young girl went to a pornographic movie and afterward was possessed by a spirit of lust. When a person came to cast that demon out, the demon said, "But I have permission." Obviously, the young woman had opened herself to demonic oppression. We must guard against such incursions of the enemy.

How do we deal with demons? We command them in the name of Jesus to leave. We don't serenade them. We don't pray about them or to them. We don't carry on conversations with them. We remind them of our authority in Jesus' name, and we demand that they leave.

To do this safely, we need the power of God. We need prayer before we encounter demonic entities, and we need our own lives to be clean before the Lord. In Scripture we read of the seven sons of Sceva, Jewish sorcerers, who tried to cast a devil out of a man. They said, "In the name of Jesus, whom Paul preaches, come out of him." And the devils answered, "We know Jesus, and we know Paul, but who are you?" And the demon-possessed man jumped on them, stripped their clothes off, and beat them. The Jewish sorcerers fled away, defeated, because they neither possessed the power of the Holy Spirit nor were they authorized to speak in Jesus' name.[20]

You dare not oppose demonic power without being empowered by the Holy Spirit of God. Only then can the demons be cast out. Even the strongest demonic forces must submit to the name of Jesus; they must obey those who know the Lord and are filled with His Spirit. The Bible says, "I will put Satan under your foot, shortly."[21] There is no question that Christians have authority over demonic spirits. The spiritual power within the Christian is vastly stronger than any power of Satan and his demonic forces. The apostle John wrote, "Greater is He that is in us than he that is in the world."[22]

We recognize that demons are real, and we must be ready to confront them when and where we find them. But we shouldn't spend a lot of time chasing them. The Bible tells us that if we seek evil, evil will come to us.[23] Individuals and ministries that focus on demon possession risk grave danger; beyond that, they are making a mistake. Casting out demons is not our focus; telling others about Jesus is our priority. When we encounter demons, we take authority over them. When they come to harass us, we bind them and cast them forth. With our voices we command them to leave and to be bound, and they must obey the voice of the Lord. It's that simple.

---

20 See Acts 19:14–17
21 See Romans 16:20
22 1 John 4:4
23 See Proverbs 11:27

DEPRESSION AND DEMONIC OPPRESSION

Is depression caused by a demonic oppression?

Depression is a complex phenomenon that I discussed fully in chapters 1 "Love, Marriage, and Sex" (Depression and Divorce) and 7 "You are What You Eat" (Depression's Prevalence in Married Women). It may be caused by a number of things, but I've found that depression most often has physiological roots and origins. It can be caused by various chemical imbalances in the brain: for example, by the absence of serotonin in our brains, which happens when we don't get enough sunlight; by low blood sugar; by a tumor on the pancreas; or by a host of other physical causes. People who are drug addicts, for example, tend to stay in the dark; the longer they stay in the dark, the more depressed they become and the stronger their addiction becomes.

We need sunlight, we need exercise, a proper diet, and vitamins; otherwise, we can easily find ourselves in a depressed state. If we ingest too much caffeine, sugar, white bread, or alcohol or drugs, or if we fail to take in adequate B-complex vitamins, our bodies will show symptoms of depression.

Another kind of depression comes about when people know they have a duty to do something and they don't do it, or they are engaging in conduct they know to be wrong but refuse to stop. They feel ashamed of themselves, because there is something wrong in their lives, and they refuse to deal with it. Before long, this gets buried in their subconscious mind. Yet it continues to haunt them. This is not false guilt; they are guilty of something that they know is wrong, but continue on as though everything is fine. As a result, a morbid sense of gloom envelops them.

Certainly, other physiological manifestations of depression exist, but these are the ones I've seen most frequently. There can be prolonged periods of depression following the birth of a child, the loss of a loved one, or some other grief, tragedy, or failure. I don't minimize in any way the reality of depression. It is a serious disease, and it often requires professional help and medication to overcome it.

Moreover, demonic oppression can cause depression. Demonic influences can cause people to be fearful, and a spirit of fear can lead to depression. If someone is filled with real or imagined anxiety, his mind becomes a satanic playground. What starts as depression can become oppression, then possession.

I felt this once in India when I was getting ready for a major crusade. During the day before the evening meeting, I had feelings of unease and strange lassitude. I couldn't understand it, but I felt that something was seriously wrong in my life. I didn't know what it was, and I asked God, "What is it?"

The Lord said, "It is a spirit of fear."

I said, "Thank You, Lord." Then I said with great feeling, "You spirit of fear, I command you to leave!" It left immediately and I sensed a great feeling of peace and relief.

I later discovered that the part of India in which I was to minister was plagued by the spirit of fear. That night, I ministered to five hundred thousand people, at least 80 percent of whom acknowledged a spirit of fear. They had lived with that constant sense of foreboding for years! But they were set free that night! Looking back, I realized that God was showing me the resident demon that was trying to afflict me and what I had to do to set the people free. If I had not known how to communicate with the Lord, that situation could have been a nightmare!

Years before, I was in Seattle, Washington, with the goal of purchasing a VHF television station over which CBN could broadcast gospel programming. Seattle is a lovely area, but there seems to be a great deal of depression, darkness, and gloom due to climatic conditions, especially the fog that hovers over the area so much of the time. Unknown to me at the time, the suicide rate in that part of the country is higher than most other parts of the United States.

I spent the night in a motel near the Seattle–Tacoma airport. I awakened early, and before I was fully in control of my faculties and senses, I felt a flood of evil, negative thoughts bludgeoning my mind. I had a terrible feeling that something was wrong, that all my efforts and activities were going awry, and people were plotting against me—horrible thoughts. I struggled to break free from sleep and be fully awake. The moment I did, I realized that I was dealing with a demonic attack! It was a spirit of suicide. This was an emissary of the demon prince who presided over the city known as the "suicide capital of America." I spoke out loud, "You spirit of suicide, in the name of Jesus I bind you, and I command you to leave me. You shall have no part or lot over God's servant. Be gone!" The moment I identified the demonic entity and commanded it to leave me, it was gone! My mind cleared and the negative thoughts disappeared. I was completely free.

You can imagine how horrifying such an experience might be for someone who does not understand the spiritual realm or how we conduct spiritual warfare against demonic attacks. What sort of impact could that have had on his or her life? That type of attack could lead to possession, depression, and ultimately, suicide.

Every Christian needs to understand that the victory has already been won; Jesus defeated the devil on the cross. But the devil continues to mount a determined onslaught in, what even he knows, will ultimately be a losing cause. Consequently, our present responsibility is to appropriate the victory won by the blood of Jesus.

We are not unmindful of Satan's devices. We can stand against him and over-come!

HYPNOSIS AND VISUALIZATION FOR PERFORMANCE ATHLETES

I'm a college wrestling coach. I teach sports psychology to my athletes to help improve their performances. I use hypnosis and visualization in this process, based on the biblical truth that as a man thinks in his heart, so he is. Is this in line with biblical teaching?

HYPNOSIS IS INDUCED BY THE POWER OF SUGGESTION. The subject is instructed to focus on a specific object while a voice suggests repeatedly, "You're getting drowsy, you're getting very sleepy." When the subject slips into hypnotically induced sleep, his or her waking mind is shut out and circumvented. Suggestions can then be made directly to the person's subconscious mind. Sometimes these suggestions can be helpful or even humorous, but often the posthypnotic effects linger long after the hypnosis. Subjects who have been hypnotized once are often susceptible to further hypnotic activity, each incident becoming easier to impose.

I strongly counsel anyone against opening their subconscious gates to suggestions over which they have no control. In a hypnotic state, you put your mind into neutral, opening your spirit to all sorts of influences. Thoughts that are implanted under hypnosis may not always be wholesome. More importantly, when a person is hypnotized, he or she is putting their will in the hands of another person. This can be extremely dangerous. The only person to whom you should ever submit such absolute control of your will is the Holy Spirit.

Perhaps in some extreme cases of depression or emotional trauma, hypnosis may be appropriate if done by a trained psychologist or psychiatrist. But a college coach using hypnosis with his or her athletes is playing with fire.

On the other hand, visualization can be a helpful tool for a coach to use with athletes. A basketball player can be taught to visualize the arc, sight, and sound of his shot swishing through the net. A golfer can see his swing in his mind; he can hear the crack of the club against the ball, see the flight of the ball, and the landing spot's proximity to the pin. A baseball player can visualize the plane of his swing, seeing the ball sail out of the stadium. Many sports psychologists and coaches encourage athletes to see themselves performing correctly. The mind makes a connection with the body and actually seeks to fulfill the visions in the mind. These things are appropriate because they are training the body to respond in a positive fashion.

When Jesus was teaching His disciples how to experience miracles, He said, "When you stand praying, believe that you have already received and you shall have the things that you say."[24] This is visualizing by faith, seeing and believing the possible before seeing the reality come to pass.

One caution: Beware the mantras such as "visualize world peace" that encourage exercising your psychic power to tap into a vast cosmic subconscious. This type of visualization usually has occult overtones, and should never be engaged in.

---

[24]   Mark 11:24

CONTENTS

— CHAPTER 11 —

LIVING IN A POST-SEPTEMBER 11 WORLD

NONE OF US who witnessed the attacks on America will ever forget the horrific scenes of that day. I was just ready to begin a live broadcast as I watched the video of one airliner, then another, hitting the World Trade Center towers. I have been a pilot in the right seat of an airplane coming out of La Guardia Airport in New York, and I knew immediately that this was not, as some commentating were reporting, an accident. Before the FBI acknowledged it, I was reporting that this appeared to be an act of terrorism. I then showed on a map of the approach to National Airport the vulnerability of federal buildings to a plane diverted from final approach to National. Shortly after, another airliner made just such a maneuver and crashed into the Pentagon.

I realized that this attack was the first time since the War of 1812, 189 years before, that the mainland of the United States had been attacked by foreign militants. For all that time, the mainland of America, lying between two vast oceans, had been protected by Almighty God from attack by foreigners. It seemed obvious to me that God's supernatural hedge of protection had been broken and this great, free, rich land now lay terribly vulnerable before those who hated us. In a horrible moment, the symbol of our wealth had crashed to the ground, and shortly after the symbol of our military might lay mangled in smoke and ruin.

The cry of my heart was to rebuild the spiritual hedge that protected us. We announced "Fifty Days of Faith" and enlisted some ninety-six thousand people and thousands of churches to cry out to God during these fifty days after the tragedy to send a powerful spiritual revival throughout our land.

Since September 11, many people have expressed renewed interest in understanding Islam, the Middle East conflict, and why God would allow such a horrendous carnage. Others have sought answers for questions regarding future events and how the September 11 attacks might usher in the fulfillment of biblical prophecies. Still others have recognized that the only hope of the world is for people to find Jesus and allow His love to soften and change their hearts. They are asking, "How can we best reach nearly a fifth of the world's population who are openly sworn enemies of Christians and Jewish people?"

Against this backdrop, let's look at a representative sampling of questions on people's minds in a post-September 11 world.

WHAT IS ISLAM?

Just what is Islam, and why do those people hate Americans so much?

ON SEPTEMBER 11, 2001, America was jolted into reality regarding the dangers of militant Islam. The adherents of the Muslim religion, called Islam, number more than 1.2 billion people. Of that group, I estimate that as many as 30 percent hold extreme, fanatical anti-Jewish, anti-American beliefs. Obviously, many Muslims, just like many Protestants and Catholics, have little or no understanding of the teachings of their religion and are Muslims in name only. They like what sounds good and ignore that with which they disagree; or, as is the case with many American Muslim leaders, they deliberately deceive the American people about the core teachings of their faith.

Following September 11, in a statement intended, no doubt, to engender support of various religious groups, and to deflect the United States' anger from all Arab people to those who perpetrated such vicious acts, President George W. Bush assured America that Islam is a religion of peace. With due respect to the president, that statement was either meant to placate potential allies or it represented a grossly naive understanding of America's number one enemy in the world today. Islam is not now, nor has it ever been, a peace-loving religion. Its history is rife with violence and bloodshed.

The founder of Islam, a man named Muhammad, lived in Saudi Arabia approximately six hundred years after Jesus Christ. Muhammad claimed to have had a series of dreams and visions in which a being he called "Allah," who was the moon god among the deities in Mecca, a city in Saudi Arabia where Muhammad's father was the keeper of three hundred sixty sacred stones, including a black stone which was probably a piece of a meteor. The place of the black meteorite is still located at the center of Mecca and has become the holiest spot in Islam. It is called the Kaaba (which means "cube").

The moon god (the symbol of Islam is a crescent moon) supposedly appeared to Muhammad and revealed to him the tenets of Islam. The revelations eventually became the substance of the Koran, the Muslim holy book. The name means "recitations," possibly because it was meant to be read aloud, but more likely because it was delivered orally by Muhammad to his friends, who wrote it down.

Most scholars who have studied the religion consider Islam to be a Christian heresy, because the Koran borrows liberally from a warped understanding of the Old and New Testaments (estimated to be as much as 80 percent of its content). Yet for all its copying of content and ideas, the Koran is devoid of the consistency found in the Bible. The Christian Bible is a comprehensive and logical description of God's redemptive plan for man, as revealed through a series of prophets and holy men and women, and especially through Jesus Christ and His apostles. Although written over a period of nearly two thousand years, with contributions from forty separate writers, the Bible has a remarkable unity of theme. Throughout the Scripture, from the fall of the first man to the death and resurrection of Jesus Christ, there is a clear, logical outworking of God's purposes in history.

On the other hand, the Koran is not a logical, cohesive presentation and has little structure. It is a difficult book to read and even harder to comprehend. Therefore it is possible to deduce sentiments that are totally at variance with other sentiments taken from the same book. The only consistent theme is one of violence and viciousness toward those who chose not to acquiesce to the demands of Islam, and the often-repeated justification for the actions of Muhammad at various phases of his life.

Muhammad was a warrior who led at least twenty-seven military engagements in wars of conquest. Not surprisingly, the Koran endorses the militant conversion of people. The concepts of Islam require abject submission to the will of Allah but also demand that adherents do anything within their power to bring all other people into submission to Islam. The ultimate goal of Islam, as taught by Muhammad, is worldwide domination. The name *Islam* itself means "submission." The radical nature of this submission is clearly understood from Muhammad's comment: "If you find an infidel who will submit and pay alms to Allah, let him go in peace. If not, kill him." Muhammad never encouraged peaceful coexistence with other religions. In fact, he warned his followers, "If you find Christians and Jews, and you feel compassion toward them, remember that Allah sees you, and he will hold you accountable for such thoughts."

After the death of Muhammad, his followers conducted repeated *jihads*, "holy wars against the infidels," other religions, especially Christianity. They swept over the Christian civilization in large portions of North Africa and coerced the population to accept Islam or die. From there, the Muslims crossed over to Spain, forcibly converting people there, and entered Bordeaux in France. They were finally stopped and kept from overrunning more of Europe by Charles Martell and his battle-hardened knights at the Battle of Tours. The Muslims, or Moorish cavalry, retreated to Spain, where they occupied the country, and remained in control for centuries.

Subsequent waves of Muslims overran the Northern Mediterranean region now known as Turkey and founded the Ottoman Empire in their hopes to wipe out Christianity in Europe. The Muslims got as far as Vienna before they were defeated in battle. To this day, the struggle continues in the Balkans between successors to the Ottoman Empire and the old Austro-Hungarian Empire. The recent war in Serbia and Bosnia at its core was a Muslim-Christian struggle, although the chief Christian protagonist in that struggle in no way reflected the nature of Jesus Christ.

For the last five hundred years, Christian Europe has been in the ascendancy, and the Muslim world has been an impoverished backwash. Today, thanks to the enormous wealth flowing into Muslim coffers because of oil production, Muslim nations, especially Saudi Arabia, are able to spend billions of dollars in their efforts to supplant Christianity, Judaism, and other religions. Anyone who thinks that modern-day Muslims have reformed and have changed their goals because the sheiks travel in private jets and sleek limousines rather than foul-smelling camels of centuries past is either extremely naive or uninformed. The Muslims have not deviated from their desire for world domination. The Saudis, under the influence of the extreme Wahhabi sect, have funneled billions of dollars toward the expansion of Islam in Africa, the United Kingdom, the United States, and Asia. Schools in the United States funded by the Saudis pour out a steady stream of hatred and violence toward Israel and the United States.

The views of Islamic terrorists, such as Osama bin Laden and those who follow him, are very close to the radical views of Muhammad. Without question, the fanaticism that is seen in the Islamic jihad, the Egyptian Muslim brotherhood, the Hezbollah, the al-Qaeda, the Taliban in Afghanistan, the Iranian Muslim regime, the Abu Sayaf in the Philippines, the Lasker Jihad in Indonesia, and other radical Muslim groups around the world all take their inspiration directly from the writings in the Koran, which encourages martyrdom in fighting against the infidels.

The promises of the eternal rewards are bizarre, and the Islamic propagandists feed on the poverty, ignorance, and hopelessness of the masses, with offers of honor and grandeur, not to mention the promise of virgins in paradise for those who give their lives as martyrs. Each warrior who falls in battle is promised seventy-two virgins as his reward. Islam is a male-oriented religion. Women's rights are almost nonexistent. Therefore, the offer of "sensual delights" is not extended to women who die in battle.

Interestingly, of all the Muslim-controlled nations in the world today, not one (with the possible exception of Indonesia, which considers itself secular) is a true democracy. Instead, each Muslim nation is run in varying degrees by autocratic or dictatorial leadership. Many of the people in Muslim nations are living in squalor and fear. There seems to be little or no industry, innovation, or robust entrepreneurial capital markets in Arab Muslim lands. Other than oil, the total exports of all the Arab Muslim nations combined is only equal in dollar value to the exports of tiny Finland. These are warm, simple, gracious people struggling to eke out an existence, cursed by a fatalistic false religion, wondering why the United States continues to uphold corrupt dictatorships.

While the elite, aristocratic few in Islamic leadership positions are educated— many of them in American universities—the masses are for the most part illiterate and impoverished. This is due to another aspect of Islam that I find particularly pernicious, namely, the concept of kismet, the idea that human beings have no individual or personal freedom to make decisions, but rather that fate controls their destiny. In Islamic theocracies such as Iran or Afghanistan under the Taliban, the Christian concept of caring for the poor and needy scarcely exists. To a fanatic Muslim, a needy person is that way because of "kismet." If he's crippled, it's kismet. "It's the will of Allah." Compare that to Jesus' teaching about the good Samaritan and the consistent biblical message that we are our brother's keeper, that as we've shown compassion and concern to the least of the needy, we've done it unto Christ.

Unfortunately, the mullahs, the religious leaders, fan the flames of the street mobs in their desire to destroy Israel and achieve world domination in the name of Allah. For instance, when the news was broadcast that the World Trade Center and the Pentagon had been struck, cheers went up throughout the Arab world. There was no mourning among our so-called allies in Saudi Arabia, Kuwait, or Palestine.

Certainly, much of the Islamic animosity toward America stems from the intense Muslim hatred of Israel, and the U.S. support of that tiny Middle Eastern country. According to Muslim doctrine, once land has been possessed by Muslims, it becomes the property of Allah. Indeed, Muslims did occupy Israel during the time the Jewish people were in exile from their homeland. From A.D. 70, until May, 1948, the nation of Israel had been trampled on, occupied by foreign powers, and the Jewish people were dispersed around the world. The land was for a time controlled in the second millennium A.D. by the Ottoman Empire.

Today, the nation of Israel controls Jerusalem, a city once strongly influenced by Islam. Muslims live in the heart of Jerusalem and worship freely at the Dome of the Rock, where a myth exists that one night Muhammad rode a horse from there to heaven, despite the fact that his young wife said he never left her side that entire night. Jerusalem is now the capital of Israel, and the ruling authority in the city is the Israeli government.

Therefore, to the Muslim mind-set, it is appropriate to attempt to reclaim that land in the name of Allah. In fact, the Muslim nations have vowed that they will never rest until they have conquered Israel, "driven the Jews to the sea," as their leaders have repeatedly stated, and reasserted themselves in all of the land now known as Israel. According to Muhammad, the end of the world will not come until the Muslims kill all of the Jewish people in one great battle. From a biblical perspective, it is doubtful that this will ever happen, but the battle will rage until Jesus returns to earth in power and glory.

A few years ago, while I was visiting in Israel, I met with the famous Russian refusenik, Nathan Sharansky. He told me that since the fall of Soviet Communism, he regards militant Islam as the single greatest threat to world peace. I concur. Our CBN reporters have witnessed the persecution of Christian people in the Sudan, where as many as 2.5 million people have been tortured, imprisoned, or killed and thousands have been sold into slavery by Islamic oppressors. Christians in Saudi Arabia have been imprisoned, tortured, and treated as virtual slaves.

I spoke to a young man in Pakistan who had converted to Christianity and had been severely beaten as a result. I've also spoken personally with the intended son-in-law of Anwar Sadat, former president of Egypt. Besides being engaged to marry the president's daughter, this young man was an outstanding soccer player, much beloved by the population. Nevertheless, when the president's future son-in-law accepted Jesus Christ as his Savior, he was arrested, tortured, one of his arms was broken, and he was eventually expelled from the country.

Nobody will ever convince me that Islam is a peaceable religion. In fact, it is my considered opinion that the struggle between Islam and Christianity that has been going on since the seventh century will heat up even more intensely in the years ahead. The only way a full-fledged catastrophe can be averted is for God Almighty to intervene and put down the spirit of violence that has been let loose in our world.

As this is being written, suicide or terrorist bombings are taking place in Israel, India, Indonesia, Pakistan, and the Philippines. The hezbollah has ten thousand rockets in Lebanon aimed at Israel. The United States is preparing to overthrow the leader of Iraq. Iran is more dangerous than Iraq and is now working on nuclear weapons. Radical Muslims could gain control of Pakistan's nuclear arsenal and begin a nuclear war with India.

The September 11 tragedy served as a wake-up call to America that we were facing grave danger. Americans flocked to our churches. There was a flood of patriotism and faith. Our president gave a resolute call to action. Our armed forces prevailed in Afghanistan with skill and precision. Now the sense of urgency and faith seems to have ebbed from the people, despite the fact that the threats we now face are greater than those we faced prior to the tragedy.

Never forget, however, that the Muslim people are no more or less inherently evil than anyone else. Like any other person who doesn't know Jesus, many Muslims are confused, misguided by their leaders, and want assurance of salvation. The Lord recognizes that the Arab people are direct descendants of Abraham, through Abraham's son, Ishmael, born to an Egyptian woman named Hagar, Abraham's wife, Sarah's handmaiden. God clearly stated that His blessing would be upon Abraham's son, Isaac, from whom the Jewish people have descended. But God also promised Abraham that He would make a nation of Ishmael's offspring because they were Abraham's descendants.[1] Undoubtedly, there is a special place in God's heart for the Arab people, and He will ultimately bless them.

I have heard many reports of dreams and visions in which Jesus Christ has been revealed to Muslims. The number of Muslims who are finding hope in Jesus is growing rapidly. Love is always more powerful than hate. We know love will ultimately triumph.

ARE ALLAH AND JEHOVAH GOD THE SAME?

Is the Allah of Islam the same as the Bible's Jehovah God?

MANY PEOPLE ARE CONFUSED about who Allah is. Allah was one of the jinns in existence in Mecca during the time that Muhammad was having his

---

[1]   Genesis 21:8–13

purported dreams and revelations that inspired the Koran. Allah is the moon god, and the symbol of Islam is the crescent moon. Allah is *not* the God of the Old Testament. He certainly is not the God of love portrayed in the Bible. In fact, Muhammad indicated that Allah had three daughters who should be worshiped. Later he changed his mind and said that these verses in the Koran were given to him by Satan.

The one point on which Islam and Christianity agree is that God is one. Muslims say that Allah is one. Christians say the same thing about Jehovah God. He is one in three persons: Father, Son, and Holy Spirit; but nevertheless, one. So Islam and Christianity are often referred to as "monotheistic" religions as opposed to Hinduism, for example, which might have as many as a million deities.

While Islam and Christianity may indeed be monotheistic, that is where the similarity ends. Allah of the Koran is nowhere near the God of the Bible. There's no love, no compassion, no understanding, no encouragement—there's no course of salvation. How do you get saved under Islam? How do you know the way of salvation? The violence, the martyrdom, the mindless enforced conversions are not the commands of the God of the Bible. As Attorney General John Ashcroft said so aptly, "Allah asks his followers to give their sons to die for him. Our God gave His Son to die for us."

The most profound difference that the Jehovah God of Christianity has above all others is that our God died on the cross for us. He came, lived perfectly as a human being, was sacrificed for our sins, but three days later He arose from the dead. Because of His sacrifice and victory over death, we can be forgiven of sin, we can have intimate fellowship with God; we can know for sure that we will live eternally with our heavenly Father. You don't find that in Islam or in any other religion.

GOD'S PROTECTION LIFTED FROM AMERICA

Shortly after 9-11, I heard you say on television that God had lifted His hand from our nation. What did you mean by that?

THE FIRST ENGLISH SETTLERS to America landed on April 26, 1607, near the mouth of the Chesapeake Bay at what is now known as Cape Henry. Three days later, on April 29, 1607, the travel-weary settlers carried ashore a rough-hewn, seven-foot cross they had brought along with them across the Atlantic. They plunged that cross into the sandy shore and claimed the land for the Lord. Almost without exception, the founders of America were devout Christian men and women. Many of them felt they were planting a "new Israel," a nation that would exalt the name of the Lord. Similarly, the Massachusetts colony was settled as a city set on a hill, a bright-shining witness of God to the nations.

All of our nation's early institutions presupposed the existence of God. In early elections, pastors instructed their congregations concerning the political issues of the day and urged the people to vote according to biblical principles and mandates. People had a consensus concerning right and wrong, based on the Bible. In some states in the middle or late 1800s, citizens could not vote unless they were members of a Christian church.

All that changed, however, after World War I, when an even more deadly assault was launched against our nation by left-wing, radical groups who no longer wanted the United States to be one nation under God. By the 1920s, liberals had taken the mainline Protestant denominations and seminaries.

By 1930, humanism and cultural relativism were beginning their assault on the Christian values in our universities and our public schools. During the 1920s and 1930s, Marxist Communism began to take hold among a number of intellectuals and the cultural elite in academia, in the media, and in the world of art and entertainment. By World War II, our joint war effort with Russia against Nazi Germany brought a number of procommunists into the sphere of government.

After World War II, with most Americans preoccupied with rebuilding their personal lives, the assault on Christianity took on a new intensity. The strategy of the ACLU and the law school liberals was to accomplish in the courts what could never happen in the popular democratic processes. In 1948, the Supreme Court defied the Constitution and ruled that its decisions were "the supreme law of the land." In 1962, prayer was ruled out of schools. In 1963, Bible reading was struck down. In 1973, the Supreme Court made up a law to strike down all state laws opposed to abortion.

In 1972 and 1973, the radical feminists and the homosexuals assaulted state laws forbidding divorce except for adultery and cruelty. The snowball gained greater momentum as values clarification, amoral sex education, and situational ethics hit classrooms that had been stripped of their religious anchors.

Whether by accident of satanic design, the 1960s and 1970s saw our faltering nation sucked into a horrible war, which it lost, a president and two prominent leaders assassinated, an elected leader resigned to avoid impeachment, many of our youth in rebellion, and, under the leadership of charlatans like Timothy Leary, the drug culture destroying the lives of millions of young people.

By 2001, the Supreme Court had ruled God and His commandments out of our schools. Across the land, symbols of our Christian heritage were taken down for fear of lawsuits. Divorce is rampant, teenage pregnancy is rampant, there have been an estimated forty million abortions, and pornography seems pervasive. The American people profess to a belief in the fundamental teachings of Christianity, but in their lives and practice deny them.[2]

The Bible says that without a revelation of God the people are unrestrained and run amuck.[3] Certainly, this describes American society over the past fifty years. As the moral structure of our nation has been dismantled, we see increasingly blatant violations of common sense, right and wrong, and values based on the moral law of God. In the government, the church, the workplace, schools, and in our homes every person is left to do what is right or wrong in his or her own eyes. Coupled with ever more shocking corruption within the U.S., our nation exported our immorality through business, music, movies, and literature to other countries around the world.

It is logical to assume that any nation that has willingly slaughtered more than forty million innocent unborn babies, as we have done in the United States, would be subject to the wrath of God. Indeed, any nation that has embraced sodomy, adultery, fornication, and all manner of debauchery, as we in America have done should live in terror not from Islamic fanatics, but terror at what Almighty God will do when His patience is exhausted. At minimum, God is no longer bound to protect such a nation from its enemies. What right have we in America to expect God's blessing, much less to demand it?

WHY DID GOD ALLOW AMERICA TO BE ATTACKED?

Do you think God allowed America to be attacked as a result of our basic disregard for His Word and His ways?

WE HAVE ONLY TO LOOK at the kind of things that have been going on in America. The United States has the largest percentage of its population in prison of any nation on the face of the earth, and I'm told that includes Red China. We have the highest incidence of venereal disease and teenage pregnancies. We have the highest divorce rate in the world. We have every type of problem—murder, drug addiction, rape, incest, alcoholism, child molestation,

---

2   See Titus 1:16
3   See Leviticus 20:13

blue-collar crime, white-collar crime—you name it. America tops the list in nearly every area of pathology.

In 1962, the Supreme Court essentially ruled God and the Bible out of our public schools. Later, they forbade children to read His commandments on the walls of school buildings. The ACLU, People for the American Way, and others of their ilk, have worked ceaselessly to destroy the religious framework of this nation.

In addition to this, the Supreme Court allowed the killing of unborn babies in the 1973 decision *Roe vs. Wade.* Since that time, we have slaughtered an estimated forty million unborn babies. This is a shocking crime against God's moral order, but it is applauded in many segments of American society as a "woman's right to choose."

We have also begun to legitimize homosexuality, something that God clearly says is detestable.[4] Churches are ordaining homosexuals as clergy. Laws are being passed that make homosexuality not only a permitted activity, but a protected activity, as some sort of minority right.

All these things are blatantly offensive to God. Many people, myself included, feel that what happened on September 11 may be the prelude to even more violent shakings of our society, that God allowed that terrible tragedy as a wake-up call, and there will be much worse calamities coming if we don't repent and turn to Him. In the Old Testament, God's judgment intensified as His people continued to reject His corrective measures. Right now, God is reaching out a hand of love and compassion to say, *Listen to My voice before something worse happens to you.*

DID GOD CAUSE OR ALLOW THIS?

How could God allow an atrocity such as what happened to the World Trade Center and the other September 11 attacks? Did God allow or cause this?

SOME THEOLOGIANS SAY that everything that happens is either because God wills it or permits it. If that is true, we'd have to say that God allowed the events of September 11.

Shortly after the attacks, I said that God had lifted His hand of protection from America because of our sin, thus allowing the attacks to happen. Many people did not understand that statement. Many others disagreed. In a national poll, only 5 percent of Americans felt that the attacks on our country had any correlation to our sinfulness.

---

4   Psalm 76:10 (KJV)

In America in recent years, God has not been invited to our party. We have put Him on the shelf at our Supreme Court, in our public schools, in many of our civic functions, in our media, in a whole host of areas of our life. We bring God out when we have an emergency, and then we look to Him and glibly say, "God, bless America." While this is a wonderful sentiment, and I'm grateful for any expression of faith in God in our nation, why should God bless America when we willfully choose to disregard Him? We are a far cry from being "one nation under God," as our pledge of allegiance declares.

After the attacks on September 11, many people asked, "Where was God?" The question itself betrays our ignorance of Him. God was right where He has always been—ready and willing to respond to any people who genuinely call out to Him.

Interestingly, we hadn't asked that question in our country for some time. Nor had we seriously asked God to be our Protector in a long, long time. Prior to September 11, America had not been attacked on its mainland since the War of 1812. Although with modern weaponry, we knew an attack on America was possible, few of us actually believed that anyone would dare attack the U.S. on our own soil, in broad daylight. To receive such a horrific blow as September 11 shocked us deeply.

As I've said previously, I believe that the protection, the covering of God that has been on this great land of ours for so many years, had lifted on September 11, and allowed this thing to happen.

Did God cause it? Certainly not. It was caused by wicked, evil, fanatical terrorists who were bent on killing other human beings and destroying their own lives in the process. I do not think that we should attribute such actions to God. But did God allow it? He didn't stop it, so we'd have to say that He allowed it because He didn't intervene directly. I believe if America had been on its knees praying and crying out to God, and if we'd had a great spiritual revival in America, we would have had God's protection and the terrible events of September 11, 2001, may have been averted.

Nevertheless, God used this event as a wake-up call to America. The Bible says, "Surely the wrath of man shall praise thee; the remainder of wrath shalt thou restrain."[5] The tragedy triggered many people to pray who've never prayed before. A mighty wave of God's Spirit swept across the nation. Although several thousand lives were lost, a far greater good may unfold if we will embrace the blessing that God is bringing out of this evil.

---

5   Psalm 76:10

WHERE WAS GOD ON SEPTEMBER 11?

How do we respond to non-Christians when they say, "Where was God on September 11?"

GOD IS ALWAYS HERE WITH US. But if we reject Him, He will leave us.

If we seek Him, He will come to us. Scripture says, "'And you will seek Me and find Me, when you search for Me with all your heart. And I will be found by you,' declares the LORD."[6] It's not a question of where was God, but where were our hearts and our minds as individuals.

Similarly, the Bible tells us to call upon Him while you have the opportunity: "Seek the LORD while He may be found; call upon Him while He is near."[7] The obvious implication is that a time will come when He will not be so accessible. He is near to each one of us right now, and He answers prayers. Even in the midst of the carnage following the World Trade Center attack, there were dramatic, miraculous answers to prayer. There were also incredible acts of bravery and compassion. These emotions of love, compassion, and mercy come from God. When we honor firefighters and police who were willing to risk their lives to save other people, we're acknowledging God's activity reflected in human beings. Where was God on September 11? God was there. And He is there in the midst of every crisis that strikes your life.

Nevertheless, we must also remember that if we reject Him, His covering and His blessing can leave us. As a nation, we need to remember that in years gone by, our heavenly Father protected us. It behooves us as a people to remember our gracious Protector, our King, and our Lord, and ask Him to come and look after this nation again.

IS THIS THE BEGINNING OF THE END OF THE WORLD?

Is the 9-11 attack linked to end-times prophecy, and if so, what scripture do you believe supports this? Is this the beginning of the end of this world as we know it?

THE TIME CLOCK of God's prophetic Word centers on Israel, not the United States. Jesus talked about the fig tree budding, and the fig tree is a symbol of

---

6   Jeremiahs 29:13–14
7   Isaiah 55:6

Israel. Israel came into being in 1948. In 1967, the Jewish people took over East Jerusalem for the first time since 586 B.C. when Nebuchadnezzar of Babylon captured the city. Speaking of the last days, Jesus said that "Jerusalem will be trampled under foot by the Gentiles, until the times of the Gentiles be fulfilled."[8] To reverse that statement we might say, "When Jerusalem is no longer under Gentile domination, then the end of Gentile domination has ended. The apostle Paul put it another way when he said, "Blindness in part has happened to Israel, until the fullness of the Gentiles be come in."[9] These two conditions seem to be fulfilled in our time, and it is my feeling that we are in the generation at the end of the "times of the Gentiles." From a spiritual perspective, the great wave of worldwide evangelization among the non-Jewish nations may be coming to an end.

The revelation of God to the Gentiles has been going on ever since the Cross of Jesus and the resurrection. The preaching of the gospel went by the apostles, especially the apostle Paul, throughout the Gentile world, and through their spiritual defendants as far as the United States of America. But now, more and more of the Jewish people are beginning to come back to the Lord and to receive Him as their Messiah. I believe that what happened on September 11 put in motion some rather ironic and tragic circumstances.

Some of the nations that harbor hatred against Israel are now actually in our coalition against Osama bin Laden and the Taliban. To placate these people, the president of the United States endorsed a nation to be known as Palestine. To me, that is outrageous and wrong. We, the United States of America, are going to empower a nation governed by terrorists and give it crucial strategic territory next to Israel. Not only that, but with East Jerusalem as its capital, in contradiction to the express word given by Jesus Christ.

In Zechariah 12, we see a time when Israel will be surrounded by her enemies, fighting for her life, and the Lord Himself will come to defend her. I believe that the stage is now being set for this extreme crisis in the nation of Israel. I am convinced that when that takes place, it will trigger the coming of the Lord and the end of this age. Others differ in their interpretations of prophecy, but I believe we are much closer to seeing what the apostle Paul called "the blessed hope,"[10] the coming of the Lord Jesus Christ for His church. Jesus told us not to fear, or to be downtrodden or disheartened, but to be encouraged as we approach the cataclysmic end

---

8   Luke 21:24
9   Romans 11:25 (KJV)
10 Titus 2:13

of the age. He said, "But when these things begin to take place, straighten up and lift up your heads, because your redemption is drawing near."[11] The unfolding of events taking place right now could very well signal, after some two thousand years, the culmination of history as we know it.

AN EYE FOR AN EYE

Is the "eye for an eye" principle valid in the case of Osama bin Laden?

Jesus taught that we are to love our enemies, to do good to them that despitefully use us.[12] The apostle Paul said when our enemy hungers, we're supposed to feed him. If he thirsts, we should give him something to drink.[13] That is true on a personal level and, to a lesser degree, on a national level. Keep in mind, however, somebody must control malefactors. The apostle Paul said, "For rulers are not a cause of fear for good behavior, but for evil. Do you want to have no fear of authority? Do what is good, and you will have praise from the same; for he is a minister of God to you for good. But if you do what is evil, be afraid; for he does not bear the sword for nothing; for he is a minister of God, an avenger who brings wrath upon the one who practices evil."[14] Obviously a society cannot have chaos and anarchy where the wicked are allowed to kill innocent people. Some authority must exist to maintain law and order and to put down those who would war against the peace.

To root out and destroy terrorism and evildoers is not a matter of blood vengeance or "an eye for an eye." It is justice. People who draw blood and kill others will also find themselves being killed. Society has a right to protect itself, and God puts governments in place for that purpose.[15] When the United States leads the charge against terrorism, it is executing judgment against cold-blooded murderers. Terrorists and their followers must be taken out of circulation and prohibited from harming any nation and especially its civilian population.

The Bible makes it clear that God is on the side of established order. Throughout the Old Testament, particularly, you can read of kings who executed vengeance on those who did wrong, and God approved of it.

---

[11]   Luke 21:28
[12]   See Matthew 5:38–48
[13]   See Romans 12:17–21
[14]   Romans 13:3–4
[15]   See Romans 13:4

SALVATION FOR BIN LADEN TYPES

Would God save Osama bin Laden and other terrorists?

GOD CAN SAVE ANYBODY. It's His will that none should perish, but that all should come to the knowledge of the truth.[16] God doesn't delight in anyone's death, nor does He delight in anyone going to hell.[17] God wants everybody to repent and be saved. Even the worst murderer, rapist, or revolutionary could be forgiven of his or her sins, and welcomed into the kingdom of God. Take the apostle Paul, for instance. He violently persecuted early Christians, "breathing threats and murder against the disciples of the Lord," yet when he had a vision of Jesus, it completely turned him around.[18]

Even murderous terrorists could one day come to the Lord; but having said that, we must understand also that they would have to pay the price for the crimes they committed against society. The free grace of God and His offer of forgiveness for our sins does not necessarily negate the civil justice of the land.

HAS THIS CHANGED YOU?

How has the experience of the September 11 terrorist attacks changed you?

GOD SPOKE TO ME when I was in a time of prayer at the end of August 2001. He showed me that America was going to have a dramatic spiritual revival in 2001. He also showed me that as a result of what was happening in Israel and the West Bank, America was going to be attacked by terrorists. I had no idea of the magnitude of such an attack, nor did I have any specific details, but both of those revelations—terror and revival—were clear. I frankly expected the terrorism to take place in 2002, not 2001.

What I didn't know at the time was that the terrorist attack was going to be the trigger for revival. But at CBN, we were ready to begin a program of asking people to pray fifty days for revival. We were preparing letters to go out to churches and working on the various programs that we were going to implement that would encourage people to pray for spiritual revival in our nation. Then came the attacks of September 11, 2001.

---

16   See 2 Peter 3:9
17   See Ezekiel 33:11
18   See Acts 9:1–18

On October 1, we launched what was called "Fifty Days of Faith." We asked people across the nation to pray for revival every day for fifteen minutes. Close to a hundred thousand people said they would pray. We have twenty-five to thirty thousand churches praying for revival, and wonderful things are happening in people's lives.

So did September 11 change me? Strangely, the answer is, not really. God had already shown me to put our efforts toward supporting revival in the churches. September 11 added urgency to what we had already been instructed to do.

Yet in another way, September 11 did change me, drawing me nearer to God, seeing my own life in His perspective, and asking Him to bring about revival in the church in America.

Many Christians have gotten much more focused on what is eternally important. One of the great impacts of this terrible tragedy is that Americans are turning to godly values that matter. They're turning to faith in God, to prayer, they're turning to their churches. They're returning to their families and friends. And they are leaving behind, at least in some measure, the frantic pursuit of Wall Street and the materialism that has so identified this last couple of decades.

CHRISTIAN RESPONSE TO TERRORISM

What should a Christian's response be to terrorism?

First and foremost, we should not be afraid. The Bible says, "Fear thou not; for I am with thee."[19] It also says, "Perfect love casts out fear, because fear involves torment."[20] The word *terrorism* comes from the thought that certain acts done in a civilian population will bring about intense fear or terror, essentially disrupting people's lives because they're afraid. That's what terrorism is all about, so if you give in to fear, you are letting the terrorists win. Beyond that, you are not allowing yourself to trust in God's plan for your life.

Christians should never live in fear. Furthermore, as Christians, death is not a bad thing, but the beginning of our eternal homecoming. If some terrorist blows us up, we will go to be with the Lord. The apostle Paul said, "We . . . prefer rather to be absent from the body and to be at home with the Lord."[21] We should recognize that the best thing that could happen to a Christian is to be with Jesus.

---

19   Isaiah 41:10 (KJV)
20   1 John 4:18 (NKJV)
21   See 2 Corinthians 5:8

In the meantime, we don't have to fear. God is with us, no matter what. He will set His angels around us to protect us and to comfort us. In the Twenty-third Psalm the psalmist says, "Even though I walk through the valley of the shadow of death, I will fear no evil, for Thou art with me."[22] God is with us, so the psalmist's response to fear should be our response, as well.

Having said that, we should also encourage our government to take whatever steps are necessary to protect our civilian population, to keep us free from attacks. We should insist on better intelligence from the CIA and the FBI. They've been terribly weakened over the last twenty years or so, and these agencies that serve and protect us should be rebuilt. It is important that Christians demand that the government do the primary thing government is supposed to do: protect its citizens from foreign invasion.

As far as our personal lives go, however, we should do everything we can to help those who are afraid, to comfort those who are suffering, and to give praise and honor to God for His goodness to us.

CHRISTIANS' TREATMENT OF MUSLIMS

How should Christians treat those of Islamic faith, and how can we best attempt to witness to Muslims?

CHRISTIANS SHOULD TREAT THOSE OF ISLAMIC FAITH the same way we should treat anyone who does not know Jesus as Savior. These people need the Lord.

I heard a wonderful story of someone who was sent on business to Yemen. As he traveled there, he asked God how he should witness about his Christian faith in this Muslim country, where it is considered a capital offense to disparage Islam or to convert someone from Islam. God said to him, *Take a big black Bible, put it in your briefcase, and whenever you go into a business meeting, open your briefcase and put the Bible on the table.*

So the businessman was obedient to the voice of the Lord, and he did just that. At one meeting, he sat down, opened his briefcase, took out his big black Bible, and put it down on the table. When the meeting was over, one of the participants came to him and said, "I am to follow you. What am I to do?"

"What are you talking about?" the businessman asked.

---

[22]   Psalm 23:4

The man replied, "I had a vision that someone was going to be in a meeting with a big black book, and that that person would tell me the truth about life, and I was to follow him. So you're the one with the black book. Tell me what to do."

The Christian businessman told the Muslim about Jesus Christ, and he accepted the Lord! According to my information, the Christian businessman used this tactic on a number of occasions during that trip, often with the same amazing results.

To witness about Jesus to a Muslim, ask questions having to do with personal peace: "Do you have peace in your heart and mind? How do you know that you will achieve paradise? What assurance do you have that you are going to heaven? Do you have assurance that you have been accepted by Allah and that your life is worthy of paradise?"

Sadly, even the most devout Muslim cannot answer these questions truthfully, because he does not know. Even facing death, they still do not know where they will spend eternity. Are they going to heaven or hell? Is it "kismet" that they should go to paradise or that they should suffer eternally?

As a Christian, you can assure your Muslim friend that you *know* for certain where you will spend eternity. Jesus died for our sins; He rose again, defeating death. He is coming again to take us to be with Him forever. That confident assurance of eternal life is the Christian's best testimony to a Muslim who is seeking the truth.

How should we treat those of Islamic faith? We should treat them with the realization that they're not satisfied in their faith, that they cannot know peace in Islam, that they do not know that they are saved. They do not have absolute assurance that if they die they're going to heaven. They are often confused about what they believe. I'm told that Muslims believe that only those who read the Koran in Arabic have the true message; so if they read the Koran in another language, they supposedly don't have the true source.

There is a trend in the Muslim world toward seeking a genuine, vibrant relationship with the Lord. This is often a dangerous search for Muslims as well as those who would share the gospel with them. On the one hand, Islamic fanatics exert enormous influence, and we need to be careful, because they will do harm to us and to their own people. In Saudi Arabia, if a Muslim converts to Christianity, he or she will be arrested, beaten, and possibly executed.

On the other hand, millions of Arabs who have lived in spiritual bondage for years are tenuously reaching out, wanting to know the truth about Jesus. What a wonderful opportunity lies before Christians who will courageously take the gospel to the Muslim world!

Several years ago, CBN printed two million copies of the Gospel of Luke in Arabic and distributed them in the Persian Gulf region. People snapped up those books like hot cakes; they wanted so badly to learn about Jesus. The people of Islamic nations are desperately looking for hope; they are trying to please the only god they know, and they are open to the good news of the Lord. We need to present the life-changing gospel to them in love, rather than rebuke. The most effective weapon we have in our arsenal is love.

WAR: RIGHT OR WRONG?

When is it right to go to war?

THE CATHOLIC CHURCH has a concept of a "just war"—not a holy war, mind you, but a just war. I don't believe in so-called holy wars, that you're going into battle for a holy cause. Too often, such misguided jingoism leads to fanaticism.

But there are "just wars," when nations go to war to defend their people against aggression or to liberate the oppressed from wickedness. During World War II, for example, Adolf Hitler controlled most of Europe. He brought nation after nation under the domination of his wickedness, and in the process, he emptied Europe of a large part of its Jewish population. It was just and right for the United States of America to enter that war to prevent the annihilation of freedom and liberty and justice in those nations held hostage by Hitler.

Similarly, it was right for us to go to war after we were savagely attacked by the Japanese at Pearl Harbor. Franklin Roosevelt said that December 7, 1941, was a "day that would live in infamy."

We experienced a similar type of unwarranted, unprovoked attack on America on September 11, 2001. Consequently, it is appropriate for America to declare these attacks as acts of war, and the measured, calculated response of the U.S. has been within biblical grounds.[23] It is a just and right cause to do so.

IS GOD IN CONTROL OF WORLD EVENTS?

Is God really in control of current events?

---

[23]   See Romans 13:1–4

Gᴏᴅ ɪs ᴀʙsᴏʟᴜᴛᴇʟʏ ɪɴ ᴄᴏɴᴛʀᴏʟ of the events of this world. He knows the end from the beginning; He is not taken by surprise. He knows exactly what's going to happen, and He is bringing about His purposes on the face of the earth. Does that mean, then, that God is forcing people to do things, that He is manipulating their lives?

No, God has not created us as automatons, preprogrammed robots who have no choice but to do as He commands. Quite the contrary. Yet, as I have analyzed the theological implications of free will and predestination, I've discovered that both are valid New Testament concepts. The Bible says, "Work out your own salvation with fear and trembling. For it is God which worketh in you both to will and to do of his good pleasure."[24] Think of that, we are to work out our own salvation, yet it is God who is at the same time working out His sovereign will in us.

How can we reconcile these two seemingly contrary ideas? When I was writing about this in seminary years ago, I looked at it as if life were a basketball game. The visible players make the shots, or so they think, and the score they put up counts for them. Yet behind them, in every position, invisible players are somehow moving and directing the overall action. The visible players think they're doing it, but the invisible players are really in charge.

Now, I think this is true with God's plan for us. He's working with us. People are doing things, but God is working with us. The apostles met together, and James stood up and said, "It seemed good to the Holy Spirit, and to us, to lay upon you no greater burden that these necessary things."[25] You may ask yourself, *Well, if it seemed good to the Holy Spirit, who cares what the apostles thought?* But James is saying, "Look, we concurred with God, so we're partners with God." I think this is the way we should understand things: Human beings have free will, and they work together with God, yet God Himself brings about His purposes throughout the earth.

Jesus said, "In my Father's house are many mansions," or many dwelling places. He also said, "I [will] go and prepare a place for you."[26] Those dwelling places need to be filled up. God is preparing a new heaven and a new earth where righteousness dwells, and He wants to see the largest number of people possible in heaven. That's the greatest desire of God's heart, and He has entrusted the preaching of the gospel to human beings. He helps us, directs us, He supplies our needs, gives us wisdom, and He certainly gives us the anointing of His Holy Spirit.

---

24   Philippians 2:12–13 (ᴋᴊᴠ)
25   Acts 15:28
26   See John 14:2–3

But He will not send an angel to do what He has commanded us to do! We are to be out in the world, doing the work of God. God doesn't do the work Himself. He has ordained that spreading the news of the salvation of mankind should be accomplished by mankind.

He's in control of the nations, the stars, the skies. The entire universe dwells at His command, and it flows in brilliant harmony at the voice of God. Paul in Colossians said that "in Him all things hold together."[27] Jesus declared, "All authority has been given to Me in heaven and on earth."[28]

So is He in control? Of course He is. Do things sometimes happen that make it seem as if He's not? Certainly. But you can come to false conclusions if you don't have full knowledge of the facts. If we could see things from His point of view, we would understand exactly what's going on.

Nevertheless, you can be sure that God is still "on the job." The sun hasn't been late recently. He takes care to see the planets are kept in their orbits. Although nations rise and fall, God determines the bounds of their habitation. The apostle Paul said, "In him we live, and move, and have our being."[29]

FEAR FOR SAFETY OR TRUST IN GOD?

If we truly trust God, why do we still struggle with fear for our safety?

GOD HAS GIVEN US CERTAIN PRECAUTIONARY EMOTIONS for our own good. A man worked for one of my enterprises in the heart of Africa, in a place that was a known breeding ground for cobras. The cobras annually came to this place to lay their eggs and hatch their young. One day, our employee was walking on a trail, and all of a sudden, he sensed that he needed to stop cold. Instead of taking another step, he stopped and looked around. There, just a few feet away from him, was a huge king cobra about twelve feet long and about fifty pounds in weight. The snake had already coiled and was ready to strike. If my friend had gone one step farther, he would've been bitten by that serpent, and probably would have died. But something stopped him.

Certainly, we can say that God's Spirit warned him, but what emotion inside of him prompted him to stop? It was fear. Most of us respond in fear to danger. You don't just race down a highway at one hundred miles an hour. There's something

---

27 Colossians 1:17
28 Matthew 28:18
29 Acts 17:28 (KJV)

inside of you that says, *This is dangerous. Stop!* The Bible says, "A prudent man sees danger and takes refuge; but the simple keep going and suffer for it."[30]

Why do we struggle with fear? Fear is a good emotion if it's under control. Problems occur when we let fear get out of control, when we give in to it rather than giving it over to God. There exists a "spirit of fear." It is a pernicious thing that literally saps our energy. We don't feel like doing anything because we're afraid. This is what is meant by the Latin *phobia*. It's an irrational fear. Some people are afraid of heights, others are afraid of crowds, still others fear being near bodies of water. Instead of the normal emotion of fear, a phobia develops that controls a person's life and keeps that person from being joyful and productive. That sort of fear is not from God.

Why does this happen? Mostly because we let it happen. We entertain it. Instead, we should command unhealthy fear to leave us. We need to take control over it and treat it as if it were a demonic thing. "Perfect love casts out fear," the Bible says, "because fear involves torment."[31]

The other thing we need to do is to face our fears, to discuss the causes, both those on the surface and anything we may be holding onto inside. Furthermore, we need to inoculate ourselves against those things that seem to be causing the problem.

Fear causes us to seek to protect ourselves. Love causes us to think of the interests of others. Perfect love—the love that is the fruit of the Holy Spirit—casts out fear, because the focus is on Jesus Christ, on God, and on other people and their needs. We seek the glory of God and the good of others when we seek to walk in God's perfect love.

SCRIPTURES TO SHARE WITH THE FEARFUL

Which Bible passages do you recommend sharing with people who are afraid of another terrorist attack? What words can I say to comfort those who've lost loved ones in the terrorist attacks?

ONE OF THE MOST COMFORTING PASSAGES in the Bible is the Twenty-third Psalm: "The Lord is my shepherd; I shall not want. He maketh me to lie down in green pastures." Then it says, "Yea, though I walk through the valley of the shadow of death, I will fear no evil: for thou art with me; thy rod and thy staff

---

30   Proverbs 22:3 (NIV)
31   1 John 4:18 (NKJV)

they comfort me." This passage was quoted on September 11 by Todd Beamer and other passengers aboard the hijacked United Flight 93, just before he said to a few fellow passengers, "Are you ready? Okay, let's roll." They then launched a counterattack against the terrorists that resulted in the crash of the plane, but most likely saved America's Capitol and untold innocent lives.

Another scripture text that is so wonderfully encouraging is Psalm 91, sometimes known as the psalm of protection. "Thousands will fall at your side and ten thousand at your right hand, but it will not come nigh thee."[32] I heard of one company of soldiers in World War II that went into battle reciting that particular psalm. Amazingly, they repeatedly came out of battles without any casualties.

Psalm 91 tells us that those who "live in the shelter of the Most High will abide under the shadow of the Almighty." He will protect us from terror, from hostile weapons, from wasting disease.

Perhaps my favorite comforting passage in the whole Bible is in the eighth chapter of Romans: "Who shall separate us from the love of Christ? Shall tribulation, or distress, or persecution, or famine, or nakedness, or peril, or sword? . . . But in all these things we overwhelmingly conquer through Him who loved us. For I am convinced that neither death, nor life, nor angels, nor principalities, nor things present, nor things to come, nor powers, nor height, nor depth, nor any other created thing, shall be able to separate us from the love of God, which is in Christ Jesus our Lord."[33] What a message! We're more than conquerors through Him that loved us!

The Scripture is filled with similar encouragements for those who love the Lord. Jesus promised that He will "be with you always, even unto the end of the world."[34] Psalm 21 tells us that the Lord keeps us from all evil and preserves our lives; He keeps watch over his people as they come and go.[35] The Bible is like a love letter from God to His people telling us over and over not to fear for He will never leave us or forsake us.

What words can you say to comfort those who have lost loved ones? In times of loss, I often turn to 1 Corinthians 15, which gives hope of the resurrection of our bodies. We now have mortal bodies, but one day, we will be immortal. This life is simply a transition vehicle to the glorious, eternal existence that God shall provide for us.

---

32   See Psalm 91:7
33   Romans 8:35–39
34   See Matthew 28:20
35   See Psalm 121:7–8

SEEING GOD'S HAND IN THE ATTACKS

How have you seen God's hand through the terrorist attacks on America?

AMERICA CHANGED DRAMATICALLY in the weeks immediately following September 11. Unfortunately, in subsequent months, many people in our country quickly slipped back to their preattack attitudes and lifestyles.

For a while though, people all over this country were singing "God Bless America." Everywhere we looked, people were displaying the American flag with pride and passion. There was a great sense of patriotism; the nation was extremely united. We put aside some of the petty differences that have divided us, and we drew together as one people.

We also saw a tremendous hunger for God. Charles Stanley, a well-known pastor in Atlanta, offered one of his sermons dealing with comfort shortly after the attacks. He had more than five hundred thousand requests for copies.

At CBN, we've had 3.5 million requests for a book I wrote called *Steps to Revival.* People are buying Bibles at an extraordinary rate. They were praying. They were filling churches. They were seeking to know the Lord. A friend who pastors a large church in Brooklyn said that the Sunday after the attack, about six hundred people gave their hearts to Jesus Christ. Similar results were reported around the country. God has been moving in people's lives and stirring in them. Revival seemed to be coming in a mighty way to America.

Whether this is merely preparing us for something much worse or whether it will get us into a condition where we will be pleasing to the Lord, I do not know. I do know that God has touched the lives of countless millions of people in our land since this tragedy. Despite the pain and suffering of those who lost loved ones, this act of evil has been turned into something of great good for this nation.

PREPARING FOR BIO-TERRORISM

What practical things can we do to prepare for the eventuality of a bio-terrorism attack?

THE FORMER SOVIET UNION developed some diabolical biological weapons that could devastate a large population. Many of these weapons inflict suffering and death almost too horrible to imagine. Today, it is generally understood that

Iraq and other rogue nations have assembled some of the same biological pathogens and deadly chemical agents.

In recent years, the United States was targeted with several anthrax attacks in which a few spores of anthrax closed down entire government office buildings and nearly sent our nation into a panic. As serious as anthrax is, it can be overcome with simple inoculations even after exposure, if given promptly after the anthrax organisms are discovered. Similarly, a sarin gas attack in the Japanese subway system caused only mild sickness to a few people. More deadly is the threat of smallpox. In my generation, every child was inoculated against smallpox. Today such mass inoculations are not given to American children because the medical community declared that smallpox had been eradicated in our world. Worse yet, millions of doses of smallpox vaccine were destroyed because it was felt they were no longer necessary.

Now, government and medical officials are reluctant to vaccinate the population for fear of the perceived danger from the vaccine itself. Unquestionably, the disease is deadly. The death toll from a widespread infestation of smallpox would be incalculable.

Facing such horrendous, indiscriminate biological threats, the necessity of a strong immune system cannot be overestimated. No matter how virulent a strain of bacteria is, a healthy immune system has the potential of overcoming it in time.

Beyond that, we cannot even guess what chemical agents might be used against Western nations. The threat of nuclear radiation released by a small "dirty bomb" at a seaport or other public place has the potential to kill or horribly disfigure tens of thousands of people.

In Israel, since before the Gulf War, each citizen has possessed a gas mask, in the event of a chemical or biological attack. It would not be unreasonable for American citizens to purchase a high-quality gas mask and have it stored in an easily accessible location, ready for use in a bio-emergency.

In the final analysis, we simply do not have the means to protect the entire population against a widespread nuclear, chemical, or biological emergency. We must trust God to protect us and take wise precautions to avoid exposure.

PRACTICAL PREPARATIONS IN A "BRITTLE" SOCIETY

Living against the backdrop of impending terrorist actions, what should the prudent Christian do to prepare to maintain any sense of normalcy in our lives?

It's ALWAYS WISE to recognize that we live in "brittle" society, dependent on services being delivered by government agencies, by utility companies, by wholesale food distributors, by trucking companies, and airlines, and now, more than ever, computer links. If the supply routes of our nation were interrupted even temporarily, most Americans would find themselves in dire circumstances and extreme want.

Although a bunker mentality is unwise, it is nonetheless prudent to attempt to maintain some level of independence from the brittle system of sustenance which could easily break down as a result of terrorist attacks.

I once read a story about two couples who both went camping in the same woods at different locations. A freak snowstorm came up, trapping them deep in the forest. One couple died, while the other couple survived. The survivors had planned ahead, taken heavy clothing, a flashlight, a compass, matches, and crucial supplies. The couple who died were grossly unprepared for anything but a leisurely camping trip.

While we cannot prepare for every eventuality, we can maintain certain simple things such as the means of obtaining heat and cooking food, the tools necessary to do basic tasks, clothing and bedding that will keep your family from freezing in the winter. It would also be wise to safely store some extra gasoline. You should also maintain a reasonable supply of nonperishable foods such as dried beans and several gallons of drinkable water. In an emergency, these basic items may be the difference between life and death.

Following the September 11 attacks, Americans gave generously of their time, labor, and financial resources to help the survivors, and to care for those who were suffering and grieving. It took an enormous effort, but America bounced back. Such a mind-set is imperative for the church in these days. We must be ready to help those in need on a moment's notice, those within our church body, as well as those in the community.

Collectively, the skills possessed by people in the church and community can help us to survive almost any calamity or tragedy. But if we break down into selfish, isolationist units and fight to protect our own possessions at the expense of everyone else, the problems will be exacerbated beyond measure. Working together, we can alleviate the sufferings of those who are in danger, and survive relatively comfortably.

PREVENTING FUTURE ATTACKS

What steps should American Christians take to prevent another attack?

A FREE AND OPEN SOCIETY such as ours will always be vulnerable to certain acts of terrorism. Those willing to lay down their own lives to murder others can break through our best defenses and inflict severe pain on innocent people. Although it is unlikely that terrorists will ever have the power to subjugate a great nation, they can instill fear, confusion, and hold a nation under mental and emotional siege through ongoing acts of violence.

The greatest protection we can have is the spiritual covering of God Almighty over this nation. He puts a hedge of protection around us,[36] or, if you will, a heavenly covering over us. As a nation, we have had the protection of God upon our homeland since the War of 1812. For 189 years prior to September 11, 2001, we had never been attacked by a foreign power on our mainland soil; we have never had foreign troops overrunning our land.

God has led us, directed us, and certainly has prospered us. Abraham Lincoln once said we have grown intoxicated with our successes, and we have forgotten the gracious hand of the One who brought this nation into being. We have forgotten to thank Him and to be humble. God told King Solomon, "If My people who are called by My name humble themselves and pray, and seek My face and turn from their wicked ways, then I will hear from heaven, will forgive their sin, and will heal their land."[37]

Yet I am concerned that the vast majority of Americans will not acknowledge that our sins had anything to do with the attacks of September 11. Most Americans do not feel that they have done wrong or that America is guilty before God for its sin. From God's perspective, the only answer is a powerful revival in which we turn to Him and turn away from our sins, or there will be continuing acts of judgment with increasing intensity until our people fall to their knees and cry out to Him for mercy.

If we choose to follow the path to spiritual cleansing and revival, the first thing we need to do as a nation is to humble ourselves before God, to stop telling ourselves how great we are, to get on our faces before the Lord, and repent of our sins. We should cry out as Isaiah did, "I am a man of unclean lips, and I dwell in the midst of

---

[36] Job 1:10
[37] 2 Chronicles 7:14

a people of unclean lips."[38] As a people, as a nation, we should repent of our sins and acknowledge to God that we must have His protection or we cannot survive.

Shortly after the 9-11 attacks, the president of the United States called for a national day of remembrance. With all respect to the president, a day of remembrance is not the same as a national day of repentance, in which we admit that we have sinned, ask God for His forgiveness, and seek His power to live rightly.

The Bible also says that we should pray. We need to pray earnestly, to pray with fervor and cry out to God for His presence to be in our midst that we might see Him and behold Him and worship Him. It isn't enough to ask God for *things* in prayer. We need to concentrate on God Himself. We need to say, "God, we need You in our personal lives. We need You in our families, in our communities, in our churches, in the city councils, in the courts of justice. We need You in the halls of Congress and in the legislatures. We need You in the executive branch. We need You in the armed forces. We need You in our schools, our businesses, our factories, wherever we are." And we need to say, "We want You for You, not for what You can do. Please God, we want You to live and walk among us." This is what it means to truly seek His face.

Then the Bible says we should turn from our wicked ways. I believe that Christians need to repent. Until we as God's people willingly turn away from conduct and attitudes that are clearly wrong according to God's Word, we are ripe for judgment. September 11 will be a mere prelude to something far worse unless we turn back to God.

In my book *Steps to Revival* I suggest a helpful spiritual exercise. Sit or kneel down with a pencil and a pad and ask the Holy Spirit to show you the sin in your life. Then write down all that He reveals to you. Be specific. We don't sin generally, so we don't need to repent generally. We need to get honest with ourselves and get specific about our sin. We've slandered somebody; we've held hatred in our hearts; we've taken something that doesn't belong to us; we've been disruptive; we have maligned our leaders; we have committed adultery; we have indulged in pornography; whatever our sins have been, name them. Worst of all, we have not loved God with all of our hearts, souls, strength, and minds.

When you're through making your list, hold it up and say, "Satan, you tried to destroy me, but you lose!" Take a match to the paper and burn it up, as you say, "In the sea of God's forgetfulness, these sins are gone." Then begin to live as someone whose past sins are gone, as a prisoner who has been set free.

---

[38]   Isaiah 6:5 (KJV)

American should seek God earnestly for revival in our churches and in our society. If this happens, we will see the protective covering of God restored to our nation. When we do as God commands, He has promised that He will hear our prayers, that He will forgive our sins, and He will heal our land. I believe God can do that!

CONTENTS

— CHAPTER 12 —

END TIMES

SINCE THE DAY Jesus ascended into heaven, His followers have looked forward to His return. Jesus Himself told us that no person knows the day or the hour when He will return, and that we are to watch and be ready, because His coming will be at a time when we least expect it.

Recent events in our world have once again riveted our attention to biblical prophecies about the end times, the rise of evil in our world, and what is going to happen next on God's timetable.

- Is Jesus coming soon?
- Where and when will the Antichrist appear on the scene?
- How is all going to end?
- Has God's judgment already begun?

These and other questions are now topics of intense conversation where, just a few years ago, such considerations might have been mocked, denigrated, or written off as irrelevant. What an opportunity for Christians! We are the people with the truth; we know where we are going! We can point lost, confused, weary, worried travelers in the right direction by pointing them to Jesus. This can indeed be the greatest hour of evangelism the Christian church has ever known! We may not know all the specific details about what the future holds, but we know Who holds our future—the Lord Jesus Christ!

USE OF CREDIT CARDS AND ATM CARDS

Should Christians use credit cards and ATM cards? I've heard that these may well be the means by which the Antichrist will control society and that we are just playing into the devil's hands by using these financial tools now.

A RECENT FEATURE ARTICLE in a leading business magazine quoted the head of the Visa card company saying that his goal was to completely replace the worldwide use of checks and cash. Computer activated "smart cards" would soon handle all commercial transactions . . . no cash, no checks, no hard records . . . only files stored and updated in giant computers.

It is, therefore, no flight of fancy to envision a day when credit cards will have chips imprinted to carry most of our personal credit histories. They will have our medical histories and our entire financial histories, and they will be updated daily in relation to how we use them. That could lead us to a situation in which you cannot buy or sell without the computer clearing the transaction. If we ever get to the point in our society where we are truly a cashless society, where we no longer use negotiable instruments—no more checks, no more cash—but buy and sell strictly on the basis of electronic means such as credit cards and debit cards, the opportunity for some malevolent dictator to take over all the money is very real. All that person would have to do is cancel everyone's credit and we'd have no more "money"; it would all be gone. That is the scene portrayed in the Book of Revelation, in which the mark on the hand or the forehead is the means of access to commerce. We are rapidly moving in that direction.

We now have the technology to place a computer chip under a person's skin, allowing the individual to carry on the person his or her lifetime records. The information can be "read" by scanners at a point of purchase. Such an option exists already, and can be implemented with relative ease. No doubt, bankers and retailers would applaud this procedure, since processing the massive amounts of paper in everyday personal and business transactions is extremely expensive. Obviously, no one wants to take the risk of losing his "smart card," so the implant has appeal. Besides alleviating the hauling of checks back and forth, it would also eliminate overdrafts. We'd have no more "floating checks," because every transaction could be tracked instantaneously. The minute the transaction took place, it would be deposited or withdrawn from the bank account and the bank would get credit for the transaction. It would make perfectly good financial sense. This is why, no doubt, the world will accept such an intrusive procedure, which will eventually lead to total loss of privacy, and soon thereafter, in response to some artificial "crisis," people's financial freedom would be taken from them. It's scary, but coming.

THE TEN-NATION CONFEDERACY AND THE ANTICHRIST

A Bible teacher I respect highly taught that the Antichrist will arise from a ten-nation confederacy in Western Europe. He identified this group as the European Union. But there are more than ten nations involved in that group. Will the Antichrist come from this area, and how will these nations be involved in end times prophecies?

THE TEN-NATION CONFEDERACY, as it is called, stems from the prophet Daniel's discussion of the ten horns, representing ten kings.[1] I am not certain where the Antichrist will come from. We do know that present-day Europe is becoming a very godless society. It is post-Christian, postmodern, and is struggling to get out from under a legacy of socialism. The political system lends itself to such a confederacy as described in Daniel but is on the way to having more than twenty members, not ten.

Certainly, the potential economic and political power of the European Union could rival the United States. At present, the Europeans haven't been able to get themselves together enough to make the EU really effective. But it could be a serious threat to freedom, a serious threat to the United States, and it could have prophetic significance, but nothing in present European political reality points to that conclusion.

I'm reluctant to be specific about such matters, because many Bible teachers have made mistakes, misinterpreted prophecy, ascribed fulfillments where there were none, and basically missed it! For instance, during World War II, many people thought Mussolini was the Antichrist, then they thought Hitler was the Antichrist, then Stalin. A few decades ago, some people thought that Henry Kissinger was the Antichrist, because of his efforts at negotiating peace in volatile areas of the world. Some people are obsessed with pinpointing somebody as the Antichrist!

The truth is, we just don't know who the Antichrist will be or where he will come from. And as for the ten-nation confederacy, it's unwise to be dogmatic about that, since the political makeup of Europe seems to change regularly. Besides

---

[1]   Daniel 7–8

changes within the European Union, another group may arise in the future that we cannot even imagine at present.

Much of the writings in Revelation and Daniel may well have pertained to events at the time they were written, or shortly thereafter, as opposed to being "predictive prophecy." People have always read Revelation as if it were a clear guidebook to the end of everything. It was written to a church living under the oppression of Rome. There were ten persecutions in the church under Rome and ten emperors that did horrible things to Christian people. Could these be the ten horns described in Daniel? We don't know. We do know that Revelation was intended primarily to give hope and comfort to the suffering, persecuted early church.

The message of Revelation is that the kingdom of God endures over all. Whatever you are suffering now, take heart, because God reigns over all, and His purposes and plans will always be fulfilled. The prophetic matters over which Bible students quibble often cause them to miss the central message of the triumph of God's kingdom over Satan and all of Satan's surrogates.

There is a message about the Antichrist found in the apostle Paul's second letter to the Thessalonians, where he speaks of a coming apostasy, then the revelation of the man of lawlessness, "The son of destruction, who opposes and exalts himself above every so-called God or object of worship, so that he takes his seat in the temple of God, displaying himself as being God."[2] Paul goes on to say that this "mystery of lawlessness" is being restrained until the one who restrains him "is taken out of the way." Then the lawless one (the Antichrist) will be revealed and shortly thereafter will be destroyed by the Lord Jesus at his second coming. The Antichrist spirit is at work today, and although we are presently experiencing the greatest ingathering of souls in the history of Christianity, in my opinion we are not far from the lifting of the presence of the Holy Spirit from our world, the beginning of vast apostasy, and the possible unveiling of a satanic super dictator.

Again, I caution against jumping to false conclusions when the Bible is either silent or not clearly understood. Dogmatic statements about the veiled prophetic references in Scripture lead to confusion among believers and ridicule from nonbelievers.

---

[2] 2 Thessalonians 2:3–4

SHOULD WE WITHDRAW FROM THE ONE-WORLD ECONOMY?

From the Bible, it seems clear that we will one day have a one-world economy, that the U. S. economy will possibly be destroyed. In light of this, should Christians continue investing in stocks, saving in banks, etc?

THE BIBLE SAYS, "Occupy till I come."[3] Until the Son of Man comes back, there will be springtime and harvest, and people are going to buy and sell. They are going to marry and be given in marriage, as it was in the days of Noah.[4] Jesus warned us, however, about being caught up in the things of this world. He taught that we should be careful that our hearts don't become overly concerned with the financial cares of this world and the deceitfulness of riches, and that we don't spend our time in feasting and partying, losing our focus on the Lord.

Rather than saying, "Let's withdraw from society," we simply need to keep a proper perspective, and make sure we are investing in the kingdom of God, "where the moths and rust cannot destroy, and thieves cannot break in and steal."[5]

Certainly, as we see some of the cataclysmic events unfolding in our world, it causes some of us to want to hunker down and withdraw from the outside world, but that is not a biblical view. As the world approached the year A.D. 1000, for example, many people withdrew from society and sat on mountains waiting for the Lord to come back. But He didn't come back. We waited for similar cataclysms as the year 2000 approached, and again, Jesus didn't come back.

The message of Jesus is, "Occupy, until I come." Fulfill My mission, feed My sheep, win people to the Lord, and take the gospel into all the nations, teach them to observe all things in whatsoever I have commanded you.[6] Be faithful in My calling. That is what God tells us to do.

We are not to withdraw from the world's system of commerce and business, fearing some cataclysm. Normal prudence should be the order of the day.

---

[3] Luke 19:13
[4] Matthew 24:37–39
[5] Matthew 6:20
[6] See Matthew 28:18–20

LESSONS FROM Y2K AND OTHER FALSE ALARMS

The Y2K scare evoked many uncomplimentary qualities in Christians as well as nonbelievers—greed, selfishness, hoarding, worrying, fear mongering, etc. What lessons are there to be learned from that experience?

MANY NOBLE THINGS WERE DONE, as well, in preparation for Y2K. Many churches prepared to help their neighbors. They built storehouses and stocked them with food, water, and clothing in the event of some catastrophe. With Joseph as a model, they were ready to feed their friends, families, and others in case of an emergency.

Unfortunately, others went into a bunker mentality, hoarding candles, gasoline, food, water, guns, and all sorts of things. Many people bought generators so they could produce their own electricity. Thankfully, the crisis never developed, and our computers did a surprisingly good job of making the transition to the new century. Had we not been warned of possible Y2K malfunctions, however, we may not have gotten the computers set up in advance. Because we heeded the warning, more major institutions realized what was happening and spent billions of dollars correcting the problem, rewriting codes, and setting up new equipment.

What are the lessons from this? Primarily, the Y2K scare exposed just how self-centered people can be and that when push comes to shove, they are going to look out for themselves and their families' needs first. This attitude is unworthy of Christ. Christians should have a desire not only to take care of their own, which is very scriptural, but also to help their neighbors and friends. And they should always be willing to help the poor and the less fortunate.

Interestingly, in affluent times, people are more selfish than they are in hard times. When confronted with desperate poverty, people are more generous, even with the small things, than they are in times of relative affluence. YK2 should show us that we need to seriously repent of the selfishness that is in our heart. Moreover, we should emulate those who wanted to help their neighbors by doing good things for them, while storing up against the bad day.

DUPED BY END-OF-THE-WORLD PREDICTIONS

The sky is falling, Y2K is coming, 88 reasons why Jesus will return in 1988, and Jesus is coming soon are all being viewed with the same

disdain and skepticism nowadays. How can we adequately warn our world to get ready for Christ's return when many people feel they have been duped so many times before?

THE BIBLE MAKES IT CLEAR that nobody knows the day or the hour when He is coming back. Jesus said that even He didn't know when He would return to earth. Only the heavenly Father knows.[7]

Are there signs of the times that we can look for? Certainly. According to Matthew 24; Luke 21; and Mark 13, we see signs that lead us to believe we are approaching the end. A rational approach to current events in light of prophecy is very interesting to people. Whether they will prepare for the Lord's return is another issue.

The big joke for many years was the man with the long, gray beard, white garb and sandals, who went along with a placard saying, "The end is near." One day, however, the joke won't be so funny. The Lord will come back. He said, "When He comes, shall He yet find faith on earth?"[8] Jesus told us that life will be going along normally at the time of His coming. "It will be as in the days of Noah," He said. "For as in the days before the flood, they were eating and drinking, marrying and giving in marriage, until the day that Noah entered the ark, and did not know until the flood came and took them all away, so also will the coming of the Son of Man be."[9] All of these are completely legitimate activities. Jesus also warned that life will be similar to the days prior to the destruction of Sodom. People were planting, building, buying, and selling when suddenly an awful tragedy took place. It will be similar to that when He comes back again. People will be blissfully unconcerned. In Noah's day, they were unconcerned about the fact that violence was everywhere. And in Sodom and Gomorrah, they were unconcerned that they were living with the most despicable types of sexual perversions. Yet, they were going on with their normal business, as if nothing was wrong.

That is the danger today in America. Filth and depravity are pervasive in our society, and yet we have courts that say, "You can't censor; that would violate the Constitution." That's nonsense! We have vile, filthy music, movies, and television programs. Debauchery dominates activities on the Internet—women being raped on videos, depictions of sex with animals, and all sorts of lewd sexual license.

---

[7]   See Mark 13:32
[8]   Luke 18:8
[9]   Matthew 24:38–39 (NKJV)

We have slaughtered more than forty million babies in America since 1973. Our death toll exceeds by a factor of 6.5 the murderous deeds of Adolph Hitler and the Holocaust. Yet, we seem blissfully unaware of or unconcerned about our sin. Instead, we parade the fact that the Supreme Court made abortion a constitutional right. We have clung to that and said, "A woman has a constitutional right to an abortion." She has no such thing! The Constitution provides no such right. Rather, the Supreme Court made such a right out of the penumbras of the Fourteenth Amendment.

Can we warn people that such sin will destroy our country and bring down the judgment of God? Will people still hear? I believe we must warn as many people as will listen. Regrettably, it seems that only a tiny minority is willing to heed the warning. We have seen punishing drought, unprecedented forest fires, hundred-year floods in Central Europe, a world torn apart by mindless terrorism, yet we do not take warning. Regrettably, something much worse is coming. Time is running out. No doubt, at some point God will say, "Enough!" The only question is, when?

U.S. IN END-TIME PROPHECY

What does it mean that the United States is not mentioned in "end of the world" prophetic scenarios?

IN EZEKIEL, there is a reference to the "young lions of Tarshish looking on" while there seems to be an invasion of Israel by Gog and Magog, the people to the north of Israel.[10] Tarshish was a seaport town along the Atlantic Ocean, not far from what is now Cadiz, Spain. Settlers from Tarshish went to England and to Ireland, and it is believed that some of them eventually made their way to the United States. As such, "the young lions of Tarshish" could apply to America.

During the final conflict when Israel is invaded by this hoard from the north, the young lions of Tarshish are standing by saying, "What are you doing?" They aren't necessarily in the war, but they are somehow monitoring the situation. That is the only real reference that may possibly apply to the United States.

Other than that, you might think of the United States as the last of the great, enduring, Gentile powers, as noted in Nebuchadnezzar's vision in the Book of Daniel.[11] We are the successors to the Roman Empire, the last of the Gentile powers that come down from Greece and Rome.

---

10   See Romans 13:1–8
11   See Daniel 2:36–44

Some Bible students theorize that when Revelation describes "the mystery of Babylon, mother of harlots, who made the nations of the world drunk with the wine of her fornication,"[12] it may be alluding to New York or Hollywood, or other powerful cities in the United States that have exported our immorality to the world.

Other than these very subjective conjectures, there are no explicit references to the United States in end-times events.

CAN JUDGMENT BE AVOIDED?

Can God's judgment on the world be avoided or changed by our prayers?

JESUS SAID, "But pray that your flight be not in the winter or on a Sabbath; for then there will be a great tribulation, such as has not occurred since the beginning of the world, nor ever shall."[13] The implication is that a believer's prayers can have some impact right up until the moment when God's judgment falls. Whether Jesus was talking about Titus the Roman general and his troops sacking the temple in Jerusalem in A.D. 70, or the actual end of the world, it is hard to say. The two events seem to meld on the pages of biblical prophecy. Jesus indicated that our prayers may in some measure delay this final blow; but they will not put it off forever. God has a plan and a timetable, and while our prayers of repentance might forestall His judgment for a while, judgment will come.

Similar to when Abraham negotiated with God for the sake of the few righteous people in Sodom, we can pray right to the last that God will be merciful. Don't be discouraged if the masses do not respond positively. Keep in mind, however, God told Ezekiel that once He had pronounced judgment on a nation, even the intercession of great men of faith (Noah, Job, and Daniel) would not stop His wrath from falling.

King Josiah brought about the most sweeping top-down religious revival that had ever occurred in the history of Judah and Israel. Nevertheless, God said it came too late to cleanse the land of the innocent blood that had been shed during the reign of Manasseh. After Josiah's death, the land was conquered, their treasures looted, the temple destroyed, the royal family either killed or enslaved, and the people were carried into captivity.

---

12   See Revelation 18:2–3
13   Matthew 24:20–21

Right now, our prayers are effective. Presently in the U.S., we see flickering signs of revival, but I frankly see no great sweeping revival among the church or the general population. When that point of no return comes, the judgment of God will fall. Until it does, we can hope for His mercy. To His people God says, "Seek righteousness. Seek humility. You may be hid in the day of the Lord's wrath."[14]

---

[14]   See Matthew 6:33

CONTENTS

— CHAPTER 13 —

HELL AND HEAVEN

---

*T*HE BIBLE IS REPLETE with references vividly depicting a place of eternal punishment known as hell. The sheer volume of biblical data is overwhelming. Scripture has nearly three times as much to say about God's justice, judgment, wrath, and punishment of sin than it does the love and mercy of God.

The most frequently used word for hell in the New Testament is *gehenna*. Ten of the eleven times it is recorded, it comes from the mouth of Jesus Himself. (The other instance is in James 3:6 and refers to the destructive capabilities of a person's tongue.) *Gehenna* means "a final place of punishment for the ungodly."

Originally the word referred to the valley of Hinnom, located just outside Jerusalem. During the evil reigns of the kings Ahaz and Manasseh, the valley was notorious as the place where human sacrifices were offered to the heathen god Molech. By the time of Christ, it had become the garbage dump of Jerusalem. Because of the potential for disease and infestation from the refuse, the garbage was set ablaze. Still the maggots, worms, rodents, and other vermin were abundant. Keeping the health hazard under control was a constant battle. It seemed that the stench, squalor, fire, and smoke were a perpetual part of life in the valley of Hinnom.

When Jesus wanted to describe the horrors of hell in human terms, He used the word *gehenna*. He called it a place of everlasting punishment—a place of utter, absolute darkness. Seven times in the Gospels, He referred to hell as a place where people are weeping and gnashing their teeth.[1] He called it a furnace of fire, a place prepared for the devil and his angels, and perhaps with the garbage dump in mind, Jesus said it is a place where the worm never dies and the fire is not quenched. It is the garbage dump of human history.

This creates a problem for those who insist, "I believe in Jesus, but I don't believe in hell." What they fail to realize is that most of the information we have about hell comes not from fire-breathing prophets or apostles; it comes from the mouth of the Meek and Gentle One, Jesus Himself.

In the apostle John's futuristic view of the Revelation of Jesus Christ, hell remains just as horrible. John writes, "And death and Hades were thrown into the lake of fire. This is the second death, the lake of fire. And if anyone's name was not found written in the book of life, he was thrown into the lake of fire."[2]

Christ warned that hell is a place to be avoided at all costs! He said, "And if your right eye makes you stumble, tear it out, and throw it from you; for it is better for you that one of the parts of your body perish, than for your whole body to be thrown into hell."[3] Whether Jesus' words are to be interpreted literally or figuratively, there is no escaping the thrust of their content. Clearly, Jesus took the matter of hell quite seriously. Men and women who hope to walk with Him must do the same.

Similarly, the Bible mentions heaven frequently—fifty-two times in Revelation alone! Hundreds of other references to heaven can be found in Scripture, as well. Jesus used the term "kingdom of heaven" synonymously with His spiritual kingdom.[4] But the Bible also pictures a place known as heaven, which is the abode of God and the future home of the bride of Christ—our future home! He promised the thief on the cross that he would be with him in Paradise—which literally means a garden of delights.

Apart from a description of heaven found in Revelation 21 and 22, we don't know much about what we will do there, how the heavenly society will function, or where it will be located. But we do know that heaven is the eternal home of our Lord Jesus Christ. There we will see Him, alive and in person, King of kings and Lord of lords! What an astounding thought!

---

[1]　See Matthew 8:12; 13:42
[2]　Revelation 20:14–15
[3]　Matthew 5:29
[4]　Matthew 5:3; 10:7; 16:19

Jesus promised that where He is, we will be also.[5] So while we may not know everything we'd like to know about heaven, one thing is assured: Heaven will be a safe place, a glorious place, a place where all our fears, tears, and pains are gone. God Himself will dwell in our midst. We will be His people, and He will be our God forever![6]

IS HELL A PLACE OR STATE OF MIND?

Does hell really exist, or is it simply a state of mind, a fictional location that writers have created? What you are talking about sounds like an actual place.

AFTER DEATH, there is a complete, final, eternal divide between those who have known the Lord and served Him, and those who have rejected God's love and refused to serve Him. Those who have lived for God will be ushered into an eternal paradise that is so marvelous we lack the words to describe it. The other group will be condemned to an everlasting setting that is so horrible that the greatest fiction writers on earth have never been able to adequately describe it.

Jesus talked about Gehenna, which was the city dump outside of Jerusalem. He said the fire is never quenched and the worm never dies, which was a way of describing the pungent, putrid stench, and the constant enormity of the rubble. He talked about hell as a place of outer darkness, where there will be weeping and gnashing of teeth. Furthermore, in the Book of Revelation, Jesus mentions a lake of fire associated with hell.[7] Clearly, Jesus was aware of the awfulness of hell.

For the biblical writers to understand hell, they had to think of it as a place. Although hell may indeed be a place, a literal lake of fire, I see a far more dreadful future for those who refuse God's love. Consider this: We know that after death we are spirits. What pain or discomfort can a lake of fire physically inflict upon a spirit? Therefore, the lake of fire may describe the awfulness of hell, but that may not the worst horror of it.

I believe the most horrendous aspect of hell will be "the blazing fires of remorse." Imagine the unbearable remorse that will fill the hearts and consciences of those condemned for eternity. Imagine the heartrending despair as they recall

---

5   See John 14:2–3
6   See Revelation 21:3
7   See Revelation 19:20

that they could be experiencing joy and bliss forever with the Lord—but they turned down His offer of love and forgiveness—and there will be no exit, no escape, no way out.

Jean Paul Sarte, leader of an the existential school of thought in France right after World War II, wrote a play called *No Exit,* which portrayed hell as a group of people in a plush Empire-style drawing room. They couldn't stand each other, but they had no way of getting out; they were trapped there for all eternity with each others' pettiness, bickering, and caustic comments.

Magnify that feeling about a million times, and you still have not come close to describing what hell will be like. If you ignore God's offer of salvation, remorse will blaze in your heart and mind forever. You will think of all the spiritual opportunities you had in your life that you ignored or refused. You will think over and over again: *How could I have been so foolish?* There will be no way out, no possible rehabilitation and release, no chance of joy or happiness. That is what hell is to me. It doesn't have to be a literal location, it could be a state of being. But according to Jesus, wherever and whatever it is, it will be utter damnation and darkness.

Understand, God does not want anyone to go to hell. Scripture says that He is "not wishing for any to perish but for all to come to repentance."[8] The paramount issue for every human being today is: Have you received the forgiveness that is freely offered by the death of Jesus Christ? Have you placed your faith in Him and entrusted your life to Him? Or have you held on to your own self-will and sin? If you have trusted Christ as your Savior and are living for Him, you have no reason to fear hell. Heaven is your future home, and Jesus Christ, Lord of all, will be there to welcome you.

CAN A BORN-AGAIN PERSON GO TO HELL?

If someone has said the sinner's prayer and accepted Jesus Christ in his or her heart, is there any way that a born-again Christian can go to hell?

BIBLICAL SCHOLARS HAVE WRESTLED with this question for years, and it is one that has split some churches and spawned entirely new denominations. Clearly, many fine Christian people see this issue differently. Opinions generally land in one of two groups: One group says "Once you're saved, you're always saved." The

---

[8]   1 Peter 3:9

other group says: "If you sin and willfully continue in it, you can be lost." As one of my seminary professors used to put it: "I belonged to a denomination that believed in backsliding . . . and practiced it!"

I'm convinced that the Bible teaches that we should fear falling into sin. We should walk with humility and reverence toward God, rather than away from Him. No one should presume upon God's grace. Imagine saying, "I gave my heart to the Lord; therefore I can do whatever I please." That is ludicrous!

If you are truly a Christian, a person who has been born again by putting your faith in Jesus Christ, your life will reflect that change. The Bible says that you will be "a new creature, the old things passed away; behold, new things have come."[9] Now, when a child of God sins, the peace and joy of the Lord in your life is broken. You can almost feel it lift from you. But it can be restored when you sincerely repent and commit yourself to doing what God wants.

For instance, David, the great king of Israel, sinned despicably by committing adultery with Bathsheba and then having her husband, Uriah, killed on the battlefront. But a year later, when he finally confessed his sin, he prayed, "Create in me a clean heart, O God . . . take not Your Holy Spirit from me. . . . Restore unto me the joy of Your salvation."[10] The Holy Spirit was still with David, even after he had committed adultery and murder. But David recognized that something about his relationship with God had been fractured. The joy of his salvation, his sense of love and acceptance by God was gone. He needed a clean heart and a renewed right spirit. He was still God's child, but he was miserable because of what he had done.

When we sin, God's Spirit remains with us, convicting us of sin, righteousness, and judgment.[11] The Spirit reminds us of our sin, the need to be cleansed of it, and the potential consequences if we don't repent. When we turn away from our sin and turn back to God, He forgives, washes us clean, and gives us a fresh start.

It is dangerous and foolish to presume upon God's grace. Imagine saying to your spouse on your wedding day, "Yes, we are now married, but how many times can I commit adultery before you divorce me?" We just don't do that! Quite the contrary, we say things such as, "I love you, I want to spend the rest of my life with you, I am committed to you till death do us part."

Our relationship with the Lord is similar. We are committed to Him. We walk with Him day by day, drawing closer to Him, discovering more about Him the longer we live in His presence. The longer we live together with the Lord, the more

---

9   2 Corinthians 5:17
10   Psalm 51:10–12
11   John 16:8

assurance wells in our hearts. Frankly, I never even think in terms such as, "Am I saved or not? Am I going to heaven or not?" I have no fear of going to hell.

Why? Because I am living with God on a daily basis. I am His and He is mine. I counsel others and I advise myself to keep short accounts with God. "If we confess our sins, He is faithful and just to forgive us our sins and to cleanse us from all unrighteousness."[12] This attitude of heart is far different than saying, "I've made a deal with God, said a prayer, and now I can rely on that regardless of how I live."

WOULD GOD REALLY SEND ME TO HELL?

If God really loves me, how could He possibly send me to hell for being bad?

GOD DOESN'T SEND ANYONE TO HELL. Anyone who goes to hell will be there because of decisions they have made. In essence, you send yourself there. If you reject God's love, you are choosing hell. In the final judgment, when you stand before the Lord, your own conscience will accuse you or excuse you on that day. Speaking of how our own consciences will come into play, the apostle Paul wrote, "For when Gentiles who do not have the Law do instinctively the things of the Law, these, not having the Law , are a law to themselves, in that they show the work of the Law written in their hearts, their conscience bearing witness, and their thoughts alternately accusing or else defending them, on the day when, according to my gospel, God will judge the secrets of men through Christ Jesus."[13] You won't need anyone else to remind you of your sinfulness on Judgment Day. Your own conscience will remind you of the things that you have done.

God will say something like: "While you were alive on earth, I offered you the opportunity to live with Me, to be My child, to accept My salvation, and to receive My love, and you have chosen not to do that. Therefore, I will grant you your desire. You wish to be apart from Me, though it breaks my heart; because I love you, I grant you your desire to live apart from Me for all eternity." Hell is eternity apart from God, where there is no love, no happiness, no joy, only darkness. Heaven is eternity with God, where He will dwell among us. Today, you must make up your mind where you want to spend eternity. But desire is not enough. You must take definite

---

12   1 John 1:9
13   Romans 2:14–16

action; you must admit that you are a sinner and ask God to forgive you of your sins; you must believe that God raised Jesus Christ from the grave, and you must ask Jesus to take control of your life. It's a big decision . . . with eternity hanging in the balance. But it is your choice, not God's.

DOES HEAVEN EXIST?

Is there really a heaven or when we die, is that it?

THE APOSTLE PAUL SAID, "Eye has not seen, and ear has not heard, and which have not entered the heart of man all that God has prepared for those who love Him."[14] Heaven is so wonderful that we can't conceive of it, yet Paul went on to say that the Lord has revealed it to us by His Spirit. These things are spiritually discerned.

We read in the Book of Revelation of streets of gold that are like clear crystal. It needs no light because the light of God is in it.[15] It has a river flowing from the throne of God, with trees growing on either side of it that are for the healing of the nations.[16] You see people walking in bliss and the redeemed souls praising God. You have pictures in the Book of Revelation of the throne of God. Throughout the Bible there are scenes describing the seraphim, the "burning ones" that burn with their holiness, surrounding God's throne. We also read of the cherubim and the twenty-four elders that are throwing down their crowns before God.[17] God is sitting in the midst of this, the firmament beneath Him, and the brilliance of gemstones sparkling in His presence. Heaven will be blinding in its beauty!

The Bible says, "There shall no longer be any death; and there shall no longer be any mourning, or crying, or pain; the first things have passed away. And He who sits on the throne said, "Behold I am making all things new."[18] We will live eternally in a new heaven and a new earth. There will be no more fear, poverty, sickness, war, or suffering, because these things will have passed away.

Jesus believed in heaven, and He encouraged His disciples to look forward to their eternal home. He said, "'In My Father's house are many dwelling places; if it were not so, I would have told you; for I go to prepare a place for you. And if I go

---

14   1 Corinthians 2:9
15   See Revelation 22:5
16   See Revelation 22:2
17   See Revelation 4:8–11
18   Revelation 21:4–5

and prepare a place for you, I will come again, and receive you to Myself; that where I am, there you may be also.'"[19]

How do we know heaven exists? Not because of deathbed confessions or "life after life" reports from people who claim to have "died" while on the hospital operating table and then traveled down a long tunnel toward a bright light. No, we believe heaven exists, because Jesus Christ said so.

DO EARTHLY ACTIONS DENY OUR BELIEF IN HEAVEN?

If we really believe in heaven, why should we spend so much time, effort, and money trying to build a great kingdom on earth?

I THINK GOD HIMSELF asks that question quite frequently! No doubt, it grieves Him a great deal to see us so wrapped up in the things of this world, things that are passing away.

One thing is uppermost in God's heart: that people on this earth will receive Him, submit to His will, accept Jesus Christ as Savior, and be part of the heavenly kingdom. The family of God will spend eternity with Him, loving Him, worshiping Him, being in His presence and receiving His overwhelming love! What an incredible gift!

God desires a great company of people from every nation, language, every place throughout the world, to be among the ranks of the redeemed. Jesus commissioned us to go unto the nations and teach them to observe all the things that He has commanded. He promised to be with us always, even to the end of the age.[20] That is what is most important to God.

Why do we spend so much of our time, resources, and energy on things that are not paramount to God? Because we are far too easily diverted from that which is most important. We want to build things in this world, make a great name for ourselves, and create a comfortable living environment, yet so many of these things are intended to satisfy our own selfishness rather than to glorify God.

Certainly God blesses our efforts to build things that will facilitate our mission. Moses prayed for the favor of the Lord upon his work, and that the work of his hands would be confirmed by God.[21] We need to build churches, schools, roads, bridges, power plants, and factories; we need to grow food, mine metals from of the

---

19   John 14:2–2
20   See Matthew 28:18–20
21   Psalm 90:17

earth, and drill for oil out of the ground. All of these things advance society and make life better here on earth. God is pleased to see His people in productive labor, but our main focus should be on the fact that we are eternal beings. This world is not our final destination; we are going to live forever in heaven. Jesus said, "Do not lay up for yourselves treasures upon earth, where moth and rust destroy, and where thieves break in and steal. But lay up for yourselves treasures in heaven, where neither moth nor rust destroys, and where thieves do not break in or steal; for where your treasure is, there will your heart be also."[22]

RECOGNITION OF LOVED ONES IN HEAVEN

What sort of bodies will we have in heaven, and will we recognize loved ones and friends?

Look at a grain of wheat—a tiny, hard brown thing that a farmer drops into the ground, and a few months later, up comes a glorious stalk with beautiful heads of golden grain. So it is with the body we have now. We'll sow it as a mortal body, but it will be raised as a spiritual body.[23] Our spiritual bodies will be raised incorruptible and we will be like Him. We will see Jesus as He is.

We know that we will have spiritual bodies, but we don't yet know how they will appear, any more than if you had seen a grain of wheat before it was planted. You couldn't say for sure what a full-grown stalk of wheat might look like. Similarly, our bodies in heaven may be different than what we know now, but there will be some relationship to our bodies in this life.

Will we recognize people? I think we will. I am certain that we will have glorious reunions in heaven. We will have understanding of who people are, and we will recognize our loved ones. We will be together. I can't imagine that God in His great love and wisdom would want to separate people from one another.

Jesus told a parable of the rich man and the beggar in which the rich man died and went to hell and the beggar died and was carried by the angels to Abraham's bosom. The rich man looked up and saw Abraham and the beggar in Abraham's bosom, and he asked Abraham if he would send the beggar to just dip his finger in a little bit of water and put it on his tongue because he was tormented by the

---

22   Matthew 6:19–20
23   See 1 Corinthians 15:50–54

flames.[24] In that story, Jesus implies complete recognition. Not only did the rich man know the beggar Lazarus, but he was able to identify someone who was born centuries before him, namely Abraham.

Without question, we will be able to do the same in heaven.

HOW OLD WILL WE BE IN HEAVEN?

How old will we be in heaven? If a baby dies, what form will the child have in heaven? Will that child be an infant throughout eternity, or will the child grow up in heaven?

THIS IS AN OFTEN-ASKED QUESTION for which there is no clear biblical answer. It is my opinion, however, that a child will be allowed to attain to whatever is the ideal age in heaven. Jesus said that in the resurrection, we will be like the angels. I don't believe that there are "baby angels," "daddy angels," or "grandma angels." All angels are basically the same because they are spirits. Obviously, it is possible for angels to be distinguished in some regard. We know, for example, the names of at least two angels and one former angel, Gabriel, Michael, and Lucifer. No doubt, though we will all be spirits, there will be some way of distinguishing our loved ones and friends, but the Bible does not provide any specifics concerning this matter.

I believe the spirits of young children will mature (possibly instantaneously) to what they would have been ideally on earth. Similarly, people who die at an old age on earth may "regress" chronologically in eternity. In heaven, however, they will have their full vigor.

Jesus is our example, and He died when He was approximately thirty-three-and-a-half years of age. Perhaps that is the ideal age and we will all be similar to Him in that regard. Again, although it is intriguing to speculate about such matters, nobody can say for sure. One thing for sure, "There shall no longer be any death; there shall no longer be any mourning, or crying, or pain; the first things have passed away."[25]

---

[24] See Luke 16:23–24
[25] Revelation 21:4

WILL MY PETS BE IN HEAVEN?

I read in the Bible that the lion will one day lie down with the lamb. Will my pets be along with me in heaven?

I've often said that there must be horses in heaven, because the Bible talks about Jesus coming back to earth riding a white horse! John Wesley seemed certain that his horse would be in heaven, and that resonates with me. Of course, that may have more to do with my love of horses than it does with biblical hermeneutics!

On the other hand, no scripture states as fact that animals will be in heaven. Quite the contrary; the Bible talks about the soul of the beast going into the ground and the soul of man going up. The main argument against pets being in heaven is that we are going to be spirits; apparently dogs, cats, horses, cows, chickens, and other animals do not have a spirit, at least not in the same way humans do.

Isaiah speaks of the wolf and the lamb grazing together, yet they won't hurt or destroy each other on God's holy mountain.[26] But the prophet is not describing life in heaven. He is talking about the millennial kingdom on earth, when the reign of Jesus Christ will bring a thousand years of peace, justice, and righteousness on this earth before it all melts with fervent heat and God creates a new heaven and a new earth.

What's the bottom line on pets in heaven? I hope they will be there, but nothing in the Bible indicates one way or the other.

MARRIED ON EARTH, MARRIED IN HEAVEN?

Will married couples on earth be married in heaven?

The Sadducees, a group of Jewish leaders in Jesus' day, did not believe in the resurrection of the dead, nor in angels or spirits of any kind. One day, some Sadducees attempted to trap Jesus with a tricky question. Referring to an Old Testament law, they said, "Moses wrote that when a man dies without having children, his brother is to marry the widow and raise up offspring for the brother." Then they posed a dilemma for Jesus. "There were seven brothers, and the first one took a wife and died, leaving no offspring. She married his brother, who in turn died with no offspring. She married the next and still had

---

26   Isaiah 65:25

no children." Eventually, according to the Sadducees tale, she married all seven brothers and had no children to any of them. All seven died, and finally the woman did, too.[27] Then came the Sadducees' big question: "In the resurrection therefore whose wife of the seven shall she be? For they all had her."[28]

Jesus knew that the Sadducees didn't even believe in life after death! Yet they were cunningly attempting to trap Him in a conundrum from which there was no earthly logical answer. But Jesus saw through their deceitfulness.

Jesus replied, "You are mistaken, not understanding the Scriptures, or the power of God. For in the resurrection they neither marry, nor are given in marriage, but are like angels in heaven. But regarding the resurrection of the dead, have you not read that which was spoken to you by God, saying, 'I AM THE GOD OF ABRAHAM, AND THE GOD OF ISAAC, AND THE GOD OF JACOB'? God is not the God of the dead but of the living."[29]

Jesus clearly stated that in the resurrection, we will be similar to the angels, who do not marry, nor are they given in marriage; they are eternal beings. Consequently, marriage, sexual reproduction, and child rearing will no longer be necessary. Marriage will be superfluous, but that does not mean that we will not join our life partners in glorious spiritual reunions.

INTERMEDIATE PLACE FOR AFTERLIFE CLEANUP?

What happens when we die? Do we go to some in-between place to get cleaned up, ready for heaven?

I DO NOT BELIEVE in any intermediate state following death. Nor do I believe in some sort of "soul sleep," or reincarnation. Scripture says, "And inasmuch as it is appointed for men to die once, and after this comes judgment; so Christ also, having been offered once to bear the sins of many, shall appear a second time, not to bear sin, to those who eagerly await Him, for salvation."[30]

The apostle Paul wrote that he was in a strait between two choices. One was "to depart and be with the Lord." The other was to "remain in the flesh."[31] To Paul, there was no purgatory or intermediate place after death. It was "in the flesh" or "with the Lord." Jesus also said to the dying thief on the cross next to

---

28   Matthew 22:28
29   Matthew 22:29–32
30   Hebrews 9:27–28
31   See Philippians 1:23–24

Him, "This day you will be with me in paradise."[32] No purgatory, no cleaning-up period, no reincarnation. From death to paradise, or, in the case of the rich man and Lazarus, for the rich man it was death to Hades. There is absolutely no biblical basis for any intermediate place for the spirits of the dead after they leave their bodies.

At the point of death, our bodies immediately begin to decay, but our spirits live on forever. At the resurrection, God will give us new bodies, better than our present bodies. Our new bodies will be "spiritual bodies," similar to that of Jesus, and will be joined with our spirits. The Bible says, ". . . in a moment, in the twinkling of an eye, at the last trumpet; for the trumpet will sound, and the dead will be raised imperishable, and we shall be changed. For this perishable must put on the imperishable, and this mortal must put on immortality . . . then will come about the saying that is written, 'Death is swallowed up in victory.'"[33]

The enemy of death will have been beaten, and at the end of time as we know it, we will go to our final destination. Those who have accepted Jesus Christ as Lord will be with Him forever, and we shall be like Him. "Beloved, now we are children of God, and it has not appeared as yet what we shall be. We know that, when He appears, we shall be like Him, because we shall see Him just as He is."[34]

WHERE IS THE NEW HEAVEN LOCATED?

Where will the new heaven John mentions in Revelation be located?

John said, "I saw the new heaven and the new earth . . . And I saw the holy city, new Jerusalem, coming down out of heaven from God" and it seems to be almost suspended between earth and heaven.[35] He talked about the city foursquare, appearing as a cube, about fifteen hundred miles in each direction.[36] There will be no need for any sun, because the glory of Lord will light it.

Where is it? We don't know for sure. My best guess is that it will be in the middle of the universe, possibly suspended between heaven and the existing earth. Or, it could just as well be located someplace on the new earth. Again, the

---

32   See Luke 23:43
33   1 Corinthians 15:52–53
34   1 John 3:2
35   See Revelation 21:1–2
36   Revelation 21:16

references are too vague to say with specificity where heaven will be located. We know that God is going to dwell with His redeemed people. We know that we will have eternal fellowship with Him. We know that heaven is a glorious place that we don't want to miss. For now, that's all we need to know!

— APPENDIX 1—

PAT'S
AGE-DEFYING SHAKE

$\mathcal{B}$REAKFAST IS THE MOST IMPORTANT MEAL OF THE DAY. It is vitally important that your body have adequate supplies of protein and necessary minerals to get you started in a healthy, vibrant mode. Nothing is worse than to race your insulin production by the ingestion of doughnuts, sweet rolls, pancakes drenched in syrup, white toast with jelly, and coffee. This is the typical American breakfast that accounts for the fact that many people are drooping by ten or eleven o'clock in the morning, and they have, in the process, a number of ailments, not the least of which is adult onset diabetes because of a diet that is filled with sweets, simple carbohydrates derived from white flour and sugar, and caffeine. The shake I use is delicious, refreshing, and filled with energy-producing nutrients. Here's how to make it:

1. In a standard blender start with 6 or 8 ounces of orange or other fruit juice, water, low-fat or skim milk, according to your taste.

2. Add 5 tablespoons of soy protein isolate and 5 tablespoons of whey protein isolate. These 10 tablespoons of protein powder are easily digestible and have

approximately 32 grams of protein, or the equivalent of 5 ½ eggs, yet they have little or no fat, no sugar and no cholesterol. Soy protein has been shown to be a dramatic protector of the male and female body against breast cancer, uterine cancer, and prostate cancer because of a substance in soy known as genistein. Science has yet to uncover all of the wonderful health benefits of this remarkable plant food.

3.   Add in 2 tablespoons of natural apple cider vinegar. This is the vinegar that has the so-called "mother" in it...not the processed type you find in the average grocery store. This leads to the production of hydrochloric acid in your stomach, which fosters the absorption of calcium in your body and also leads to a number of health benefits. Raw apple cider vinegar and honey comprised a morning remedy for many families in the early days of this country and were popularized by Paul Bragg, who was considered the founder of the natural food movement. My secretary tells me that apple vinegar is a great fat burner, and I don't doubt her advice.

4.   Although we should avoid animal fat and what are called trans fatty acids, such as margarine and hydrogenated fats of all kinds, we need essential fatty acids that are found in natural oils called Omega 3 and Omega 6. Flaxseed oil or evening primrose oil are the best sources of Omega 3, and safflower oil is an exceptional source of Omega 6. Mix 1 cup of flaxseed oil with 1 cup of safflower oil, and then add 2 tablespoons of this mixture to the shake. The essential oils are able to reduce cholesterol, increase the HDL lipids in the body, lower the bad LDL lipids, and perhaps, in the process, lower high blood pressure, as well. If you suffer from prostate cancer, substitute fish oil for flaxseed oil.

5.   Add 2 tablespoons (or more if desired) of soy lecithin. Lecithin is also a great cholesterol fighter which produces the choline and inositol which is very dramatic in helping to open the flow of blood in the brain to facilitate a better memory.

6.   Add 1 teaspoon of MSM powder. MSM is a sulfur-based product which I learned about from Judy Lindberg McFarland who is an expert on vitamins and natural foods. According to Judy, sulfur is "necessary for healing and repair for most tissues in the body, especially our skin. It also protects us from internal injury of free-radical damage, aging, cross linkages and also helps with scar-tissue healing, and even recovery from burn and surgical incisions. Because of its

ability to protect against the harmful effects of radiation and pollution, sulfur slows down the aging process. It is found in hemoglobin and all tissues, it is called 'nature's beauty mineral' because sulfur keeps the hair glossy and smooth, the complexion clear and youthful, and the nails strong." MSM is also very effective in alleviating the effects of arthritis. It has a terrible taste which is one reason I recommend a sweetener in this shake.

7.   Add 1 teaspoon of glutamine powder. This is roughly 4.5 grams of glutamine, which is a tasteless white powder. Glutamine is essential for anyone who does physical exercise. In distance or marathon runners, glutamine has prevented the onset of any serious sickness in many of those who take it. One group of college athletes who took this quantity of glutamine before exercise raised their production of human growth hormone by 430 percent in a short period of time. Glutamine has been found to be effective in facilitating or speeding healing after surgery. Bill Phillips, the author of the best-selling book *Body For Life,* strongly recommends that weight lifters use glutamine powder after a strenuous session of weightlifting. I think so highly of glutamine that I take it more than once a day because it has very beneficial effects throughout my body.

8.   For taste, add 5 or 6 frozen strawberries or a peach or an apple or whatever type of fruit you like. If necessary, add 4 or 5 ice cubes to make the mix a little colder.

9.   Add some kind of noncaloric sweetener. I strongly advise against anything having aspartame as a sweetener because of the harmful effects. I use Sweet'N Low and have had no problem whatsoever. Perhaps there are some more noncaloric sweeteners on the market that may help.

10.   The mixture is then placed in a blender long enough to get it smooth and the ice cubes crushed. This makes an absolutely delicious drink and will get you off to a good start each day.

OPTIONS

SOMETIMES I ADD a couple of tablespoons of nonfat plain yogurt, which gives a little bit more body to the drink, or a banana which also does the same thing.

In my reading I have learned that almost all serious athletes are now ingesting a natural product that is found present in beefsteak that is called creatine. Creatine enhances athletic performance—enables people to run faster, jump higher, and lift more weight in a gym. It is one of those things that the famous slugger Mark McGwire uses as part of his nutritional regimen. Creatine can either be taken by itself or can be taken in what is called a creatine transport system, which includes high glycemic carbohydrates that enhance its effectiveness. Creatine can be added to the shake, or it can be taken before and after exercise. Creatine pumps water into the muscle cells and causes them to enlarge which, in turn, permits them to accomplish more work in an athletic situation. The muscles then become stronger, and in the process, the individual gains more lean muscle mass and loses more fat. With creatine it is necessary to drink quite a bit of water (at least eight ounces) in addition to what is in the shake. From all indications, it is accepted as safe and beneficial; however, the best practice is to cycle off items like creatine every month or so for maximum effectiveness.

Beyond this, I take quite a number of vitamins, but I think it is absolutely essential that we take one therapeutic vitamin with minerals per day. Of particular importance are vitamin E, vitamin C, the B-complex vitamins, and folic acid. Folic acid is important in reducing homocystine, which has been identified as a causative agent for heart attacks.

I hope that this formula for my Age-Defying Shake will prove of benefit to all from ages twenty to eighty or beyond!

Please remember that white flour, refined sugar, and products made from white flour and refined sugar are the equivalent of poison to your system. They will bring on any number of ailments and will weaken you in any kind of serious athletic performance. I strongly recommend fresh fruits and vegetables, whole wheat and wheat grain breads and pasta, the minimal amounts of beef and beef products, and a strong emphasis on low-fat, reduced-salt foods. This means reading the labels! In addition to this, it is necessary to supplement any kind of a food diet with additional vitamins and minerals and the protein powders I have mentioned in the recipe for the shake.

OPTIONAL INGREDIENTS YOU CAN TRY:

2 tablespoons nonfat plain yogurt or 1 banana (gives more body to the drink)

1 teaspoon creatine (5 grams). Creatine is intended to be used by those individuals who are engaged in strenuous physical activity and training. Individuals under

the age of 18 years should not use creatine. (If you add creatine, remember you need to drink at least 8 ounces of water in addition to your shake).

INGREDIENTS FOR PAT'S AGE-DEFYING SHAKE

6-8 ounces of orange juice (water, other fruit juices, low-fat or skim milk can be substituted)

5 tablespoons soy protein isolate

5 tablespoons whey protein isolate

2 tablespoons natural apple cider vinegar

1 tablespoon flaxseed oil

1 tablespoon safflower oil

2 tablespoons (or more) soy lecithin

1 teaspoon MSM powder

1 teaspoon glutamine powder

5-6 frozen strawberries (other fruits can be substituted)

Noncaloric sweetener to taste

4-5 ice cubes (optional, use for a colder shake)

PAT'S AGE-DEFYING ANTIOXIDANTS

In order to complete the picture needed to defy the ravages of age and promote radiant health, there are other vital substances that you need to consider. These are the essential age-defying antioxidant vitamins and minerals.

After the age of twenty, and more so after the age of forty, vital substances that protect our bodies begin to decline. In men, there is a decline in testosterone, which falls off dramatically after the age of forty or fifty. The same is true with the vital adrenal hormone DHEA that converts to testosterone. Around fifty, the presence of coenzyme Q10 falls off dramatically. At the same time, the pineal gland starts to shut down at an increasing rate and leaves the body open, especially the brain, and vulnerable to age-related degeneration and destruction.

As these hormonal processes are taking place, our bodies also experience destructive assaults from outside. There is pollution in the air from chemicals emitted by manufacturing and from tobacco smoke. There are pollutants and excess minerals in most of the water that we drink. Ultraviolet rays from sunlight damage and age our skin. Some chickens and beef are fed antibiotics and steroids to cause them to fatten quickly before they are marketed. When we ingest the flesh of these animals, we experience further assault. Fish, while otherwise having health benefits, may contain toxic mercury; plus, some mercury gets into the body from mercury-containing dental fillings. Fluoride from most drinking water and aluminum from various dietary sources also add to the body's burden.

In addition, during the complex processes of living, our bodies produce substances which attack our cells. These products of our own bodies are called *free radicals* that result when we breathe oxygen and burn food for energy. Free radicals are produced in large quantities by strenuous energy-producing work or exercise. The free radicals are called such because each free radical is missing an electron which makes it unstable and sends it on a course of destruction seeking another electron from otherwise healthy cells. I have read that even our DNA can be attacked by free radicals—up to one hundred thousand free radicals per day. The rate of the most serious DNA damage by free radicals increases tenfold from the age of twenty to the age of sixty-five.

Dr. Bruce Ames at the University of California, Berkeley, has shown that the lack of antioxidant nutrients like selenium, vitamin C, vitamin E, and others can result in DNA damage that mimics the same damage to DNA caused by exposure to atomic radiation. It is these free radicals from within or without that cause a weakening of our cells and bring about the many conditions associated with aging and such increasingly frequent ailments as cancer, heart condition, atherosclerotic disease, and very possibly all the neurodegenerative diseases such as Parkinson's, Alzheimer's, and ALS (Lou Gehrig's). People use the term "rust out" to describe some of the processes of aging and the term is not too far off, because it is oxidation that causes the rusting in metal and it is the oxidation brought about by free radicals that can cause gradual or very rapid aging in every human being. *Yet there is an answer!*

According to the book by Dr. Ronald Klatz and Dr. Robert Goldman, published by Keats Publishing, Inc., titled *Stopping the Clock,* "Over 100 studies have shown that people with a high level of beta-carotene in their diet and blood are only about half as likely to develop cancer in the lungs, mouth, throat, esophagus, larynx, stomach, breasts, or bladder. Harvard Research studying some 87,000 female nurses found that a high intake of vitamin C cut the risk of heart disease about 20 percent; high doses of vitamin E caused the risk to drop by 34 percent; and high levels of beta carotene cut heart disease risks by 22 percent. Moreover, high doses of all three vitamins slash the risk of heart disease by 50 percent. Coenzyme Q10 helps prevent arteriosclerosis, angina, and heart attacks." CoQ10 also helps prevent cancer and neurodegenerative diseases. To think that it is so simple and so inexpensive to prevent the ravages of aging! It is a mistake to think that aging is a disease or that the apparent effects of old age and senility are natural consequences of growing old.

The Bible says, "My people are destroyed for lack of knowledge."[1] I don't want to get into complicated scientific matters which you can read in two excellent books, *Stopping the Clock,* which I just mentioned, and Judy Lindberg McFarland's *Aging Without Growing Old,* published by Western Front, Ltd. However, with a few simple vitamins and minerals, you can clearly cut the risks of cancer, heart disease, hardening of the arteries, lesions of the skin, diabetes, and very possibly Alzheimer's by regularly taking the following age-defying substances which can be obtained at any health food store and as an added benefit, you can shed those unwanted pounds.

1. *Multivitamin.* Your age-defying vitamin schedule should include a therapeutic multivitamin with minerals. The so-called minimum daily requirements of vitamins published by the government are frankly nonsense. This may be adequate to prevent pellagra and scurvy, but it hardly gives you the protection you need to maintain the cells of your body at peak performance. Sometimes the therapeutic multivitamin and mineral preparation will include the necessary antioxidant vitamins and minerals without further supplementation. However, in addition, I supplement with larger quantities of some vitamins and minerals than even the high-potency multivitamins provide. A good multivitamin will contain the essential B-complex vitamins, plus many of the trace minerals like copper, zinc, magnesium, calcium, etc., necessary for good health. Most women, after menopause, and adult men should avoid vitamins containing iron. Iron accumulates with aging and is one of the most powerful free-radical generators known.

2. *Vitamin E.* I recommend supplementing the multivitamin with enough vitamin E to bring your daily intake up to between 400-800 IU per day. Vitamin E is considered the most effective biologic antioxidant. Vitamin E prevents the oxidation of cells and is a powerful antioxidant protecting against air pollution, damage against radiation, prevents clotting of blood vessels, prevents stroke, and strengthens the immune system. In addition, several studies have shown vitamin E's protective effect against the neurodegenerative diseases. It is particularly helpful for any type of endurance athletics. Some doctors have found that vitamin E returns an aging person's immunity to almost youthful levels. In one test with vitamin E, white blood cells that fight infection were up 10-15 percent within thirty days. Some other immune functions were up 80-90 percent.

---

[1]   Hosea 4:6

The free radicals in chemical air pollution attack the cells of our lungs. Vitamin E short-circuits the creation of lipid peroxide molecules according to Drs. Klatz and Goldman. Vitamin E reduces clotting of the blood and, therefore, reduces the risk of stroke. Most surgeons or dentists would recommend against taking vitamin E just prior to surgery because of their desire to minimize blood flow during those procedures. Additionally, the type of vitamin E you take makes a difference—I recommend D-alpha tocopherol succinate as the best variety, followed by E composed of mixed tocopherols. However, avoid synthetic vitamin E (acetate) because it is poorly absorbed (especially in the brain) and has no effect on cancer.

3. *Beta-carotene.* I recommend 10,000 IU per day. One doctor found, "Those physicians who took 50 milligrams (80,000 IU) of beta-carotene as a supplement every other day had not quite half as many heart attacks, strokes and deaths as those who did not."

Vitamin A not only protects against infection, but also seems to be one of the most important nutrients against cancer. Vitamin A is helpful in stimulating an immune function that is suppressed by extensive surgery and can correct age-related immune dysfunction, returning immunity to a more youthful condition. It is said to limit oxidation-type reactions that neutralize free radicals inside the cells. (Beta-carotene produces vitamin A in the body without some of the dangerous side effects of taking vitamin A directly. Vitamin A in very large doses has been found to be toxic, but usually that toxicity is in the 50,000 to 100,000 IU level of vitamin A per day, which is much higher than what is normally recommended.) Nevertheless, studies of beta-carotene, which converts to vitamin A in the liver, found no toxicity at any concentration in all age groups, including children. Beta-carotene is part of a class of nutrients called carotenoids—40 of which are in the human diet. Consider taking a supplement of mixed carotenoids that contains not only beta-carotene, but substances like lutein, lycopene, and zeaxanthin. None of these converts to vitamin A, and they are especially potent against cancer.

4. *Vitamin C.* The third in our trio of essential antioxidant vitamins is my favorite, vitamin C. I take 3,000 milligrams of vitamin C each day, and Nobel Prize winner Linus Pauling recommends dosages as high as 17,000 milligrams per day! For therapeutic benefit, I recommend at least 1,000 milligrams, which can be split into two 500-milligram doses daily. If I feel a cold or flu coming on, I boost my personal dosage to 5,000 milligrams twice a day.

Vitamin C is a potent antioxidant to protect against cellular damage. It helps with wound healing and burns. It provides for the proper functioning of the nervous system and plays a role in protecting against excitotoxicity. Excitotoxins are found in foods under names like aspartame (sweetener), monosodium glutamate (MSG), hydrolyzed protein, and yeast extract. Excitotoxins can stimulate brain cells to death and produce huge numbers of free radicals, according to nutritional neuroscientist Dr. Russell Blaylock, author of *Excitotoxins: The Taste that Kills.*

Vitamin C increases resistance to infections. It raises HDL (which is good cholesterol). It protects against industrial pollutants. It protects from cardiovascular disease and prevents the build-up of atherosclerotic plaque on the blood vessel walls. With the absence of vitamin C there can be excessive bleeding, bruising, muscle weakness and painful joints, and very slow healing of wounds. This vitamin also protects against the harmful nitrosamines produced by eating deli meats, sausage, and bacon.

With my vitamin C, I also make sure that it contains what is called a "citrus bioflavonoid complex," which is derived, as I understand, from the rind of citrus. The bioflavonoids are free-radical scavengers, help prevent bruising, and decrease the permeability and fragility of blood vessels (which lead to varicose veins and hemorrhoids). The bioflavonoids make vitamin C much more powerful. The tablets I get have 1,000 milligrams of vitamin C each, and 500 milligrams of bioflavonoids mixed together with the vitamin C. So if I take 3,000 milligrams of Vitamin C, I am getting 1,500 milligrams of the bioflavonoids. The bioflavonoids prolong the activity of the vitamin C in the bloodstream and help to control iron in the body. For some people, taking a buffered vitamin C may be preferable as this variety is easily absorbed and prevents stomach irritation.

Many studies have indicated that vitamin C reduces the risk of cancers of the colon, pancreas, esophagus, rectum, and especially the stomach. It reverses the biological clock by rejuvenating white blood cells in the elderly. According to one study cited by Klatz and Goldman and conducted by researchers at the University of California, Los Angeles in 1992, of 11,000 people, men who consumed the most vitamin C (about 150 milligrams a day) had a 35 percent lower mortality rate than men who consumed only 30 milligrams a day. According to them, some 120 studies show that "vitamin C is a virtual vaccination against cancer." The vitamin is also vital in protecting the brain, especially in conjunction with vitamin E. Alzheimer's patients have very low brain vitamin C levels.

Taken together, these principal antioxidant vitamins have a synergistic effect that clearly causes those who take them to have a much lower risk of debilitating disease, especially heart disease and cancer. Considering how cheap and plentiful these vitamins are, it would be folly not to take them in the quantities I recommend to maintain good health or reverse some of the effects of ill health.

If your therapeutic multivitamin tablet is deficient, I recommend supplemental beta-carotene (A), E, and C. I would recommend three other essential antioxidants which can help reverse the signs of aging and bring about more radiant health.

1. *Selenium.* I have found from extensive reading that the absence of a mineral called selenium can increase the risk of cancer and heart disease. Without selenium, neither vitamin E nor the glutamine I recommend for my shake are nearly as effective. Even those who keep horses notice that the absence of selenium in pastures can lead to a wasting and sickness in horses. Regional studies found a correlation between the so-called "stroke belt" (Georgia and the Carolinas, where the stroke rate is by far the highest in the U.S.) and low levels of selenium in the soil and water. It is my feeling that the absence of selenium can make me susceptible to viral infections that are so often prevalent when I travel on commercial airlines. A landmark study published in the *Journal of the American Medical Association* showed that a supplement of 200 micrograms of organically bound selenium (SelenoExcell) reduced the occurrence of virtually every form of cancer. I recommend 200 micrograms of selenium per day. There is some level of toxicity of selenium over 1,000 micrograms and, therefore, it is unwise to consider any more than 400 micrograms. Selenium is necessary for growth and protein synthesis, and it serves as an antioxidant for the cells to protect against oxygen exposure and exposure to toxic pollutants. According to Drs. Klatz and Goldman, "Selenium works with the antioxidant glutathione (derived from glutamine) to bind the toxic heavy metals mercury, lead, and cadmium in a process called chelation. Selenium also helps detoxify per oxidized fats, alcohol, tobacco smoke, and drugs."

2. *Alpha Lipoic Acid.* My Christian friend, fellow weightlifter, and personal physician, Dr. Charles Warne, told me about another substance that I had never heard of before called alpha lipoic acid, which Dr. Warne felt would enhance physical performance. In truth, alpha lipoic acid (which has only recently gained public attention) is described by Judy Lindberg McFarland as "an exciting antioxidant which is an important link in the vital antioxidant network and it is multifunctional." According to Judy in her excellent book *Aging Without Growing Old,* alpha lipoic acid "has been shown to energize metabolism, to be a key compound for producing muscles, and it is important for everything we do from physical activity to thinking. Alpha lipoic acid unlocks energy from food calories and directs these calories away from fat production to energy production. The excitement about this nutrient can be seen in the many recent studies focusing on how alpha lipoic acid improves the physique, combats free radicals, protects our genetic material, slows aging, helps protect against heart disease, cancer, cataracts, and diabetes, and many other diseases."

The body makes a small amount of lipoic acid, but you will need a supplement as you age. I recommend between 100 and 200 milligrams, depending on your weight. I personally take 250 milligrams per day. Alpha lipoic acid is available in health food stores. It is not recommended for pregnant women until further studies have been completed.

3. *Coenzyme Q10.* About three years ago, I learned of the substance that most people in the U.S. have never heard of, coenzyme Q10, which is described by Drs. Klatz and Goldman as "the miracle heart medicine." My good friend John Rea, who at age forty-nine came in third in the world in the 26-Hour Double Ironman Triathlon (just think 200 miles bicycling, 52 miles running, and 4 miles swimming— nonstop for 26 hours), said that one of his secrets was the continuous ingestion of the vitamins and minerals I have been recommending, plus large quantities of coenzyme Q10. CoQ10 is important to energy manufacturing in the human body and is found in the mitochondrial membranes where it manufactures adenosine triphosphate (ATP). ATP is the basic energy molecule of the entire human body. It is needed in great quantities in cardiac tissue cells and also in the organ that purifies waste (the liver). According to Drs. Klatz and Goldman, "CoQ10 declines rapidly beginning at age twenty, and drops almost 80 percent at the end of middle age. Some researchers believe that the loss of CoQ10 is related to degenerative heart disease at the age of fifty. Other possible reasons for the body's depletion of this enzyme could be attributed to free-radical damage to mitochondrial membranes or perhaps the process of lipid peroxidation—the same process that makes butter rancid, that damages other membranes in our cells." CoQ10 protects fat molecules from being oxidized by the free radicals that continually attack fat cells. It supports the activity of the mitochondria that burn oxygen to manufacture energy within cells. CoQ10 also dramatically boosts the immune function. CoQ10 has been recommended at between 60-90 milligrams a day. Some suggest 120-390 milligrams for those who wish to prevent signs of aging. Judy Lindberg McFarland indicates that there seems to be virtually no side effects to CoQ10. According to her, "It is one of the safest substances ever tested, even in high dosages." I personally take about 200 milligrams a day, but more if I am engaged in any kind of stressful athletic activity.

It takes about three months of use for the beneficial effects of CoQ10 to begin to be demonstrated. There is some thought that CoQ10 may be beneficial in such dreaded diseases as Lou Gehrig's, and Judy McFarland says that in addition to its ability to regenerate aging tissues and to alleviate the effects of many aging-related processes and age-associated diseases, CoQ10 is "effective in other areas such as periodontal disease (gum disease), hypertension or high blood pressure, muscular dystrophy, cancer, athletic performance, weight loss, antiaging, and thyroid and thymus gland function."

At CBN, we receive over two million calls per year, many of which involve some type of sickness or disease. I repeat what the Bible states, "My people are destroyed for lack of knowledge."[2] God wants us to be healthy, and so many of the illnesses that plague us today can be avoided or dramatically alleviated.

I also recommend moderate exercise (a 20-30-minute brisk walk three or four times a week with alternate workouts with light weights), adequate rest, and a diet which is free of sugar, white flour, margarine, and other so-called trans fatty acids, fried foods, large quantities of animal fat, and obviously tobacco and alcohol. Also, include in your diet the heavily colored fruits and vegetables which are loaded with beneficial phytonutrients. Eat sweet potatoes, broccoli, spinach, kale, beets, carrots, and similar vegetables, plus fruits like strawberries, raspberries, melons, apples, peaches, pears, plums, blueberries, unsalted raw or dry-roasted nuts of all kinds. Include oatmeal and oat bran and whole grain bread.

More than anything, rejoice in the Lord because the Bible says "a merry heart doeth good like medicine."

For information about Varsity Pack 2 multivitamins, contact Judy Lindberg McFarland's company, Lindberg Nutrition, 3804 Sepulveda Boulevard, Torrance, CA 90505, phone: 800-338-7979. For simplicity, this pack has everything I am recommending in the appropriate quantities, except CoQ10 and alpha lipoic acid.

Three books will give you a complete rundown on sports nutrition, vitamins, and minerals for maximum health. I strongly recommend that you purchase and read these books:

Bill Phillips of EAS, *Sports Supplement Review—Sports and Weight Lifting*, Mile High Publishers, Box 277, Golden, Colorado 80402.

Judy Lindberg McFarland, *Aging Without Growing Old*, Lindberg Nutrition, 3804 Sepulveda Blvd., Torrance, California 90505.

---

[2]   Hosea 4:6

Drs. Ronald Klatz and Robert Goldman, *Stopping the Clock,* Keats Publishing, 27 Pine Street, New Canaan, Connecticut 66840.

Any health food store or discount pharmacy should carry the vitamins and minerals I am suggesting, as well as one or more of the recommended books.

Disclaimer: Consult with your physician before starting this or any new health regimen or supplement program, especially if you have allergies to any of the listed or related products, or are under the care of a physician or other medical professional, or have any other health problems. No specific health benefit is implied or promised from the information contained herein.

This material has been previously published by CBN, 977 Centerville Turnpike, Virginia Beach, Virginia 23463 (telephone: 800-759-0700) by permission of the author.

— APPENDIX 2—

FOODS FROM BIBLICAL TIMES—ARE THEY STILL HEALTHY FOR OUR PATIENTS?

BY JAMES H. CARRAWAY, MD

**"One of the things we can do as cosmetic surgeons
is to teach our patients the value of nutrition. . . ."**

Why should we even think about what was eaten 2,000 or 3,000 years ago?

In this wonderful new and modern age, we have prepackaged, low-fat foods, vitamins added to milk and soft drinks, and pizzas available at the sound of a dial tone. We have so many good things to eat and most of the world has easy accessibility to foods of all sorts.

Why should we even consider thinking back in time to another pathway for nutrition? After all, the people who lived in biblical times did not have health clubs, microwave cooking, or vitamins in a bottle for quick consumption.

On the other hand, there was no significant incidence of heart disease, cancer, stroke, diabetes, or Alzheimer's disease.

Everyone walked to their destinations, and most stayed active as part of their survival routine. Although there was no guarantee of plenty of food for everyone, the diet at that time included adequate amounts of carbohydrates, proteins, and fats.

In the United States, where we spend the highest per capita on food of any country in the world, our life expectancy is ranked about 20th of all nations. One of three people will get cancer or heart disease, and Alzheimer's disease is prevalent.

The incidence of mature adult-onset diabetes at 20 million-plus is even rampant in teenagers.

One of the things we can do as cosmetic surgeons is to teach our patients the value of nutrition in terms of wellness and freedom from myriad degenerative diseases, which we suffer as humans.

By looking at the food choices, which are well documented in the Bible and in historical writings, we can see that they may have made better choices in food, some of which are still available today.

Relating nutrition to biblical times gives us some measure of reality in regard to these choices.

For example, all food was "organically" grown, all livestock was "range-grazed," and fruits and vegetables were in abundance. We are told that there were 2,600 plants in Israel then, and the Bible mentions at least 110 of these. The range-fed lamb was lean and not too plentiful, and the protein from this source was supplemented by plant-based protein.

There were certain rituals and beliefs about food that governed the way people actually ate.

For example, Ecclesiastes 37:30 states that "excess of meats bringeth sickness." And "The swine . . . is unclean to you, of their flesh you shall not eat." Additionally, Sirach 31:27 states that "wine is as good as life to a man, if it be drunk moderately. What is life to a man that is without wine?"

At the same time that the people of Israel and surrounding countries were experiencing good health from a rather ascetic diet, the upper class Romans, who had gathered the best of foods from their empire, were already experiencing degenerative diseases including obesity, gout, cardiac disease, and stroke.

The simple foods of the Israelis consisted of fruits and vegetables, nuts and beans, grains, fish, meat, fiber, and lots of olives and olive oil.

In Deuteronomy 8:7–8, on their way to the promised land, the Israelites saw "a land of brooks and water, of fountains and springs, flowing forth and valleys and hills, a land of wheat and barley, of vines and fig trees, and pomegranates, a land of olive trees and honey."

Another interesting "twist" in history, as chronicled by Bronowski in *The Ascent of Man,* is that something happened in the grain supply about 8,000 years ago which changed the total course of history and the population trends of mankind.

There was a spontaneous mutation enabling wild wheat of 14 chromosomes to cross with goat grass (14 chromosomes) resulting in Emmer wheat of 28 chromosomes. There was an additional mutation with another type of goat grass, resulting in the 42-chromosome bread wheat, which we eat today.

Because of the characteristics of the grain of bread wheat, it does not blow to the wind and has large nuts of grain on each stalk. It is possible to cultivate this wheat easily, to take the seeds and move them hundreds of miles to another location and cultivate other fields of wheat.

Animal husbandry was enhanced by the cultivation of grains, and for the first time it was possible to enjoy a stable food supply of both carbohydrates and protein, allowing the development of excess body fat from eating these foods. However, in biblical times, there was not an excess of foods for everyone, therefore, most people did not eat too much.

Before that time, the earth was only capable of sustaining a population of an estimated 1.5 million to 2 million people in the "hunter-gatherer" fashion, but after that time, the population increased geometrically and is still expanding at an incredibly rapid rate.

In the fertile sweet water plains around Jericho, the first established city of modern civilization, the combination of man, wheat, water, and an increasing population, sparked this population growth, which has never subsided.

When meat was not readily available, yogurt was the only animal-derived complete protein source frequently eaten.

It came from goats' milk curdled by bacteria, the pure strain of lactobacillus acidophilus, which is normally needed for digestion in the G.I. tract under ordinary circumstances.

However, the "good" bacteria in yogurt are able to convert the oils and fats to vitamins A and D, and B complex. It also produced a product that could be carried or stored for several days without spoilage. Interestingly, during the process of making yogurt or cheese, lactose in the milk product is metabolized. Most people in the Middle East and Asia are lactose intolerant and cannot drink whole milk. However, dairy products are an essential part of the diet.

Most people in the northern latitudes were lactose tolerant and drank milk, and vitamin D from sunshine is not as readily available due to climate and clothing requirements, therefore calcium was readily available by drinking milk products.

(The take-home message here is that in order to prevent osteoporosis in our patients, they need to be exposed to some sunshine—though not necessarily on their faces—when possible, or substitute with a high-calcium food product.)

Because meat from animals was not always readily available, the population in biblical times often had to gain "complete" protein from different sources. For example, grains alone did not furnish complete protein, but in combination with nuts, seeds, beans, and some select vegetables made a complete protein, which is adequate for growth and for maintaining the immune system. Beans plus brown rice, corn, nuts, or wheat also constitute a complete protein.

Fat was forbidden as a food for religious reasons, but olive oil was commonly used as a food source for cooking, and even as fuel for lanterns.

One of the problems in our culture today is that the "low-fat" craze has kept people from understanding that fat is an essential part of the diet. According to the American Heart Association, at least 30 percent of our caloric intake daily should be from fat sources, mostly from monounsaturated, polyunsaturated, and essential fatty acids rather than saturated or hydrogenated fats.

Seafood, such as oysters, shrimp, and fish were also part of the diet in some areas of the Middle East, according to availability and shipping possibilities. Some of the spices on hand were coriander, cinnamon, cumin, mustard, mint, and ginger. Although we supplement with antioxidants almost daily, it is interesting to realize that ginger has 400 known and chemically recognized antioxidants within it.

Among the plants consumed were garlic, bitter herbs for salad, leeks, lentils, English walnuts (originally Persian walnuts), pistachio nuts, olives, and pomegranates. The grains, other than bread wheat, included barley and rye. Barley was the "poor man's" grain, being leaner in carbohydrates, fats, and protein, but also being a very hearty plant, which was grown in most areas.

Bread wheat was the most common grain cereal and had seven "ears" for each stalk.

These could be roasted or ground, and when cooked yielded the highest level of nutrients.

There were no apples—as we know them—in the Middle East, even though legend says the forbidden fruit that Adam ate in the Garden of Eden was an apple. Most experts tell us the closest fruit to an apple at that time was the succulent apricot.

With their simple meals, the relative leanness of the diet, and the necessity to eat just the amount to sustain, people stayed lean and healthy as described in the "Red Tent" by Anita Diamant:

"Jacob arrived late in the afternoon in the week of a full moon, ate a simple meal of barley bread and olives, and fell into exhausted sleep," she wrote. Further on she wrote, "We rocked the narrow-necked jars, straining the water from the goat milk curd" in the process of making cheese. For festive occasions, "Rachel ate date honey and fine wheat flour cake, and drank sweet wine."

After eating the forbidden fruit in the Garden of Eden, man was directed to labor for his food by tilling the soil. In the book of Ezekiel 4:9: "Take thou wheat, barley, beans, peas, millet, and spelt, and make a bread of it. Eat this for 390 days with two cups of water each day." This was enough to sustain life because of the complete protein, carbohydrate, and fat sources available from the grains. This was similar to what the English called "staff of life" bread.

Today we have "white" carbohydrates consisting of bread, bagels, pasta, rice, potatoes, cakes, and excess sugar.

Part of the nutritional teaching in our practice includes instructing patients before surgery to keep away from the "white carbohydrates. This policy is largely responsible for allowing patients to have surgery minus swelling or pain.

Also, nutrition, supplements, stress management, and exercise are among topics on which we counsel patients.

We will not consider performing a cosmetic surgery procedure unless the patient has accepted part of the responsibility for his/her health and healing, and looking good after the completion of the procedure.

I inform my facelift patients prior to surgery that if they follow our nutritional regimen, they will have no swelling and no pain; that we will "turn the clock back" about eight or ten years; and that the incisions will not be visible at conversational distance. The important part of this assurance is lack of swelling or pain, which is really a function of the diet as well as technical considerations during the surgery.

The final thoughts in this discussion relate to the fact that we can change the life expectancy and incidence of disease in our patients because we can be a credible source of information.

It requires constant guidance, enthusiasm, and subsequent compliance on the part of the patients.

I can state for certain that this has been the most important part of my practice since I initiated this program more than five years ago. We have touched many lives with our nutrition and better aging programs.

Perhaps you can find a way to gain more compliance with your patients by letting them understand just how old, but valid, good nutrition information can be for them.

Carraway, James H. "Foods from Biblical Times—Are They Still Healthy for Our Patients?" *Cosmetic Surgery Times*, December 2001. Used by permission.

— SUBJECT INDEX —